T0374860

Advance praise for *Why?*

"This is an engaging, creative, and masterful exploration of human experience, stemming from the seemingly innocent question 'why?' Huneman expertly draws upon an exceptionally rich array of sources—from the philosophical to the everyday—brought to life through illuminating examples. Even if we never reach an ultimate answer to life's most pressing query, this lucidly written book not only evokes its necessity, but transforms the way we will forever approach the question."

—ANTHONY J. STEINBOCK, author of *Knowing by Heart*

"Ranging with ease and erudition across both contemporary Anglo-American analytic and so-called Continental philosophies of science and the history of Western philosophy, Huneman argues that the plurality of questions expressed by 'why?' nevertheless share an underlying unity. A stimulating text addressed to professional philosophers as well as readers seeking to deepen their understanding of philosophy's relevance to common concerns."

—HELEN LONGINO, author of *Studying Human Behavior*

"With wry humor, engaging examples, and indefatigable curiosity, Huneman takes the primeval question 'why?' as a launchpad to explore topics throughout the philosophy of science and beyond—evidence, cause, chance, natural selection, contingency and necessity, and in the end, love and the self."

—MICHAEL STREVENS, author of *The Knowledge Machine*

"This work offers a vast panorama that is both deeply researched and pleasant to read."

—SYLVAIN GUILBAUD, *La Recherche*

"This is a particularly well-crafted introduction to the philosophy of science, one that combines sharpness and quiet erudition."

—PASCAL ENGEL, *En attendant Nadeau*

WHY?

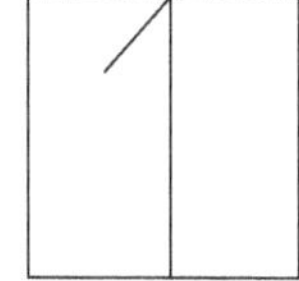

SQUARE ONE
First-Order Questions in the Humanities

Series Editor: **PAUL A. KOTTMAN**

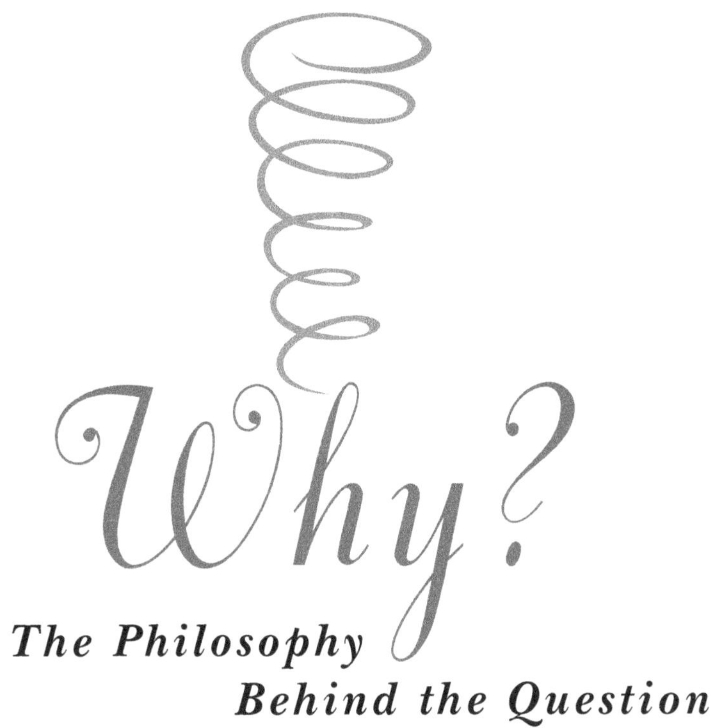

The Philosophy Behind the Question

PHILIPPE HUNEMAN

Translated by Adam Hocker

Stanford University Press
Stanford, California

Stanford University Press
Stanford, California

The first version of *Why? The Philosophy Behind the Question* was originally published in French in 2020 under the title *Pourquoi? Une question pour découvrir le monde* © Éditions Autrement, department of Flammarion, 2020.

Printed in the United States of America on acid-free, archival-quality paper

Library of Congress Cataloging-in-Publication Data
Names: Huneman, Philippe, author.
Title: Why? : the philosophy behind the question / Philippe Huneman ; translated by Adam Hocker
Other titles: Pourquoi? English | Square one (Series)
Description: Stanford, California : Stanford University Press, 2023. | Series: Square one | Originally published in French under the title: Pourquoi? | Includes bibliographical references.
Identifiers: LCCN 2022046040 (print) | LCCN 2022046041 (ebook) | ISBN 9781503628908 (cloth) | ISBN 9781503635715 (epub)
Subjects: LCSH: Questioning. | Metaphysics. | Knowledge, Theory of.
Classification: LCC BF463.Q47 H862 2023 (print) | LCC BF463.Q47 (ebook) | DDC 121—dc23/eng/20230222
LC record available at https://lccn.loc.gov/2022046040
LC ebook record available at https://lccn.loc.gov/2022046041

Cover design and art: David Drummond
Typeset by Elliott Beard in Adobe Caslon Pro 10.5/15.5

One does not see anything, but what it matters so little to see,
Nothing, and yet one shudders.
Why?

—HENRI MICHAUX, "*Je vous écris d'un pays lointain*"

I see these frightening spaces in the universe that lock me in, and I find myself tied to a corner of this wide extension, without knowing why I'm put in this place rather than in another, and why the little time given to me to live is ascribed to this point rather than to another one in all the eternity that came before me and the one that comes after me.

—PASCAL, *Pensées*, 427/194

Why are not all organic beings blended together in an inextricable chaos?

—CHARLES DARWIN, *The Origin of Species*

Contents

THREE
Limits

Series Foreword

PAUL A. KOTTMAN

AS ANYONE WHO HAS SPENT TIME AROUND YOUNG CHILdren knows, "why?" is a question that gets posed with dogged persistence. In this doggedness, says Philippe Huneman, children "learn [a] kind of grammar for why."

By grammar, Huneman does not just mean what those children will eventually learn to call "grammar" as they make their way through school. Huneman also means "a necessity . . . between logical necessity . . . and pure linguistic convention." In other words, when children formulate *why?* questions, the formulation of the sentence itself exposes and teaches a logical requirement, one that tells us something important about what we are doing when we ask *why*? Huneman puts the point this way: "Before even asking what the legitimate form of response to 'why?' could be, we presuppose that there is a response; and thus, that it is possible to ask why."

For instance, in learning how to ask *why?* questions, we simultaneously learn about different kinds of objects, different kinds of response possibilities, and various presuppositions that govern possible answers as well as possible misunderstandings. After all, a well-known issue for philosophers and children alike is how to make sense of what people do, and whether or how this might be distinct from explaining things that happen to us or that happen in our world. As Huneman sees it, following Kant, such different kinds of questions require distinct kinds of explanation. Huneman focuses in this book on three different kinds of *why?* questions. "When asking 'why?'," he says, "we can expect in response a cause, or a reason for believing something, or a motive and thus a reason for acting (a goal, in particular). These three types of 'because' are perhaps not independent but they are distinct."

By underlining this distinctness without independence, Huneman wants to note that events like a fire breaking out, on the one hand, and actions like remodeling a kitchen, on the other, can be said to have different logical forms. In the case of a fire, we might look for both a cause and a reason—not independently, but distinctly. Someone may have started the fire purposely such that they can give a reason for having done so, or the fire may have been caused accidentally by a faulty wire. In the case of the remodeled kitchen, we feel ourselves entitled to ask the renovator why a specific color scheme was chosen, and we can expect at least a minimally rational answer in return. The answer you get to *why?* questions can be a reason of some kind, or it might be a cause.

Of course, put like this, all sorts of complications are elided. "The deeper we delve in search of causes the more of them we find," wrote Leo Tolstoy in *War and Peace* (1812), "and each separate cause or whole series of causes appears to us equally valid and equally false by its insignificance compared to the magnitude of the events, and by its impotence—apart from the cooperation of all the other coincident causes—to occasion the event" (book 9, chapter 1).

How, then, to treat different questions, like "Why did Napoleon lose at Waterloo?" Huneman's book elegantly teases out the implications and stakes of these complications, through a series of examples like these, and through engagements with philosophical treatments of these issues.

In reading *Why?* I was struck by something about the grammar of *why?* questions as Huneman treats them.

As young children make vivid, we not only "presuppose that there is a response" when we ask "why?" We also presuppose that someone, or some others, can or will give this response. That is, we presuppose not only that an answer exists, or that an answer belongs to the realm of the known, or to an impersonal space of reasons—we also make a vocative appeal *for* an answer from someone who we expect to be somehow responsible for what they are saying. We make an appeal to others who, we suppose, are somehow accountable for what they claim, or know, or believe, or are motivated by. *Why?* questions not only presuppose a grammatical connection between the question and an answer; such questions and answers also evoke the presupposition of a dialogue between participants who uphold a space of reasons, and who can somehow be held to account for whatever answers they give.

In an age when young children can be witnessed addressing certain *why?* questions to the "artificial intelligence" at work in their devices, this presupposition might be hard to detect, and might invite all kinds of skepticism. Is there truly this kind of responsibility-taking dialogue that, I was just suggesting, we presuppose or evoke when we ask *why?*

To get the stakes of this question into view, one might ask further: Can we address, or even imagine addressing, all our *why?* questions to the collected wisdom of the archives, to the sedimented knowledge of the libraries, or to the artificial intelligence said to be at work on the internet—that is, to *no one* in particular? Can we collectively sustain the social practice of seeking answers for *why?* questions without supposing and expecting that others will comport themselves responsibly in light of whatever answers we might receive?

WHY?

Introduction

THE ROAD IS BLOCKED. A TREE LIES STRETCHED ACROSS it. The weather is fine with no trace of a storm, but the tree has just fallen, crushing a gray car in its path whose occupants are able to extract themselves, with difficulty but unharmed. The body of the car is completely wrecked, its windows shattered. Firefighters, rapidly on the scene, comfort the shaken victims, keeping the onlookers at bay while other workers, who also have arrived with remarkable haste, begin to cut the tree into pieces to remove it as quickly as possible. All around there is the ballet of tourist smartphones and wandering Parisians immortalizing the event, sharing it on multiple more or less well-known platforms, hoping to gather a maximum of *likes* and *retweets* and expressions of interest coming from other individuals who are amazed that their "friends" could have witnessed such an extraordinary event—as if they had accomplished something difficult like holding their breath for six minutes, climbing a particularly formidable peak, or writing a poem without vowels.

And I was driving just a few meters behind that car. Without thinking, I asked myself: "Why him? Why did the tree fall on his car rather than on mine or someone else's?"

Of course, there are responses: as a specialist in natural history who just happened to be there told me, the tree was completely eaten through. Rot could be clearly seen in the now visible interior of the trunk; and in the end, only a slight gust of wind would have been needed to topple it—or it could have toppled on its own once the parasites had finished their destructive work. Certainly, but why at this moment, while the gray Passat with the Dutch driver was passing beneath it?

In one sense, we know why. I can go through the chain of causes and inventory the circumstances: on the one hand, dryness, wind, internal infiltration of the tree; and on the other, the Dutchman's schedule—his plans which made it so that he happened to be on this avenue at this precise minute. The explanation is long and gets lost in countless fastidious details but it is available. Why then was I frustrated with this impression that my question—"Why him instead of me?"—did not have a response? Without a doubt, it is because there is no why for this precise question; or rather, the "why" that would satisfy me has no meaning here. Does that mean there are many whys, then? Or perhaps things without a why?

Starting from three or four years old, not long after the moment when they learn how to speak with clarity and coherence, it is well known that children never stop asking "why?" It is true that they gain precious knowledge about the world in this way. But by asking these kinds of questions, they also learn how the question "why?" works. When my five-year-old daughter asks "Why is it Sunday?", she learns that one does not or should not ask such a question. Perhaps the question "Why him?" regarding the tree accident and the unfortunate Dutchman is of the same order. But my daughter also learns through these questions that certain responses to the question "why?" only have a limited validity: "Why does water boil?" cannot be explained with "Because it wants to boil," while "Why do dogs drink water?" can potentially receive the response "Because they get thirsty"—or, said differently, "Because they want to drink." As she grows, my daughter will learn *science*, which will tell her why this and why that. In this way, the sciences develop a system of responses to a certain type of question "why?" But they do not include precisely those responses that would satisfy my desire to know why the tree fell on the Dutchman's car and not mine—hence my frustrating feeling that it was pure chance, a feeling that for others, on the contrary, could mean that it was the Dutchman's "destiny." But why in the end is it so frustrating to recognize that the tree fell on him by chance?

This small word "why" seems to weave strange links between the non-knowledge of children, the science of adults, and the idea of destiny. But what are these links then?

Asking Why

Language has interrogative words that spread out the sizable dimensions in which we can understand an event, a fact, an action, or a thing: What? Where? When? How many? How? and Why?

Let's imagine something like a gnu. A complete knowledge of the gnu clearly entails being able to respond to all these questions. In *Categories*, Aristotle explains that the first five questions determine the broad articulations of a living being or something that exists: a thing has a nature or an essence ("what is a gnu?"), encompasses temporal and spatial dimensions ("where is the gnu?" "when will we find this gnu?"), quantity ("how many gnus are there?"), and a certain mode of existence or appearance ("this gnu was fast, was shimmering, etc."). These dimensions are not always independent: the "how" will include measurements of acceleration, for example. For Aristotle, these "categories" are at the same time the major articulations of being *and* the sizable divisions within language—namely, that through which language has the capacity to really understand what is there. In the later philosophical tradition, one has sometimes questioned this homogeneity of language and being but—without entirely subscribing to it—we can already imagine that such a systematicity of language tells us something about being in how it is susceptible to being said or brought into language.

Among these large questions, "why" is perhaps the least understandable. Aristotle, moreover, does not include it in his *Categories* but evokes it in what we call *Physics*—his treatise on things in movement that he calls natural things ("physical" comes from the Greek *phusis*, nature). The *Categories* correspond to dimensions of being that one can easily name: substance (the response to "What?"), place (the response to "Where?"), time (the response to "When?"), and so on. The response to "Why?" is not, however, unequivocal.

An example will help us to see how "why" is so delicate. As an event, let's look at the victory of the French team at the 2018 World Cup. It is easy to respond to the five questions: *What?* It was the final of a global soccer competition. *Where?* In Moscow. *When?* July 15, 2018. *How many?* Some figures are pertinent: a 90-minute match between two teams of 11 players in front of 60,000 people. *How?* By a score of 4–2. And *Why?* "Because France scored four goals and Croatia two." Certainly; but is this not another more precise way of simply saying that France won? What we have now *allows for me to legitimately say* that France is the world champion, but not what *made it* so that France was world champion. Do we not rather want to know the reason why France won? It could be a question of identifying who were the scorers, who passed them the ball, etc. But we could also think beyond goals to distinct strategies in conflict with each other: France was more effective in defense, Croatia less effective in attack. Perhaps previous matches played a role in terms of the fatigue of the players, their motivation, etc. Croatia had one less rest day than France after their respective semifinals and had gone into extra time in each of its direct elimination matches. And outside of the World Cup itself, we could highlight the differences in soccer traditions between France and Croatia—their experiences in major competitions, the failure of the French in the Euro Final two years previously, etc. Barely broached, and even with such a simple subject, the question "why?" leads us into a tangle of explanations that are reminiscent of the scientific controversies of the genre: Is it the recent usage of pesticides that is responsible for the declining number of birds, or rather the expansion of agriculture that is destroying their habitats, or perhaps climate change that is disturbing their migratory and reproductive habits, or one of the many combinations thereof?

At the same time, this question "why?" traverses the expansive domains of speech and habit in which we all live together. In front of a certain animal, a child or even an adult may spontaneously ask: Why does a zebra have stripes? Why does a duck have webbed feet? "Why?" is also a question for historians: Why did war break out in 1940? Why did Christianity conquer Europe?

Of course, scientists make abundant usage of "why"—whether it is a question of simple things, like falling bodies; or of very sophisticated things, like the physicist who asks, "Why is the universe cooling?" But it is also a daily question: "Why do you say that?" we regularly exclaim when someone announces an unknown piece of information. This is what we say to a child who returns from school stating that "Marc is mean."

The varied scale of human feelings thus easily gives rise to such questions: "Why does Edith love Marcel?" we think, especially if Edith and Marcel seem badly suited for each other. But "why?" is also a doubtful question, that of an investigator. One thinks of television detective Columbo, who, after having questioned a business owner or a gallerist (always someone important) whom we know is the killer, puts on his beige raincoat as though to leave (assuming he ever took it off), and then turns around to ask the fatal question: "But Mr. So-and-So, why did you say that you were playing golf in Santa Monica when we know you were having dinner on Sunset Boulevard at the same time?" And these conspiracy theories that have been talked about so much recently suggest a generalized version of this detective-like doubt: "Why did the *Charlie Hebdo* killers forget their ID cards in the car?"

And last, the occurrences of this question "why?" go from the trivial to the vertiginous, like the "Why not me?" with which I opened this book; the "My God, why hast thou forsaken me?" that Jesus could not help but utter during the crucifixion in the Gospels; or in a still more metaphysical sense, "Why am I me instead of another?"

Conceived to unravel the complexities that envelop the usage of the question "why?", this book will consider in detail some of the questions that I have just mentioned. The book proposes a geography of thought, in the distant tradition of Kant—the philosopher whose university career was in great part devoted to teaching geography, and whose language is haunted by geographical metaphor (borders, territories, domains, maps, etc.).

A Single Word for Many Questions

Regarding this singular question—why?—metaphysical reflection wavers between two opposed positions. The first suggests that the question "why?" is so indispensable that it conditions the possibility of having experiences. Without the capacity to ask "why X?" and to respond "Because Y," experience would just be a web of disjointed events with no link between them. And from a practical point of view, the simplest action demands an identification of the means for the ends, of choosing, for example, a type of transport for a trip; yet this relationship involves an implicitly formulated question: "*Why* did I (or *why* must I) do something?", with its response, "*Because* I wanted something else." And, independent of us, events that occur only take on meaning in light of this question "why?" The small Pacific islands that will soon be submerged by the ocean owe their annihilation to the climate change generated by human industrial activity from the past two hundred years: I can thus respond to the question "Why will they vanish?" Starting from this rather dramatic point, my worldview acquires a certain meaning—one that I can also consider in light of my own goals and desires, while reflecting on what we could do to avoid the destruction of other islands.

A diametrically opposed position has been argued by philosophers according to which the question "why?" is merely the residue of a past prerationalist age, an antiscientific question that is thereby opposed to true rationality. Pierre Duhem—the physicist, historian of physics, and author of a major book about the philosophy of science in 1917 entitled *La Théorie physique: Son objet, sa structure (The Aim and Structure of Physical Theory)*—contested the idea that science had to ask why things are as they are. This question, as with the desire to explain in a more general sense, would later pertain more to metaphysics than to science, which tries to describe how phenomena occur and according to what regularities. And positivists like Auguste Comte pre-dated Duhem in relegating questions concerning "why" to the domain of what they called "metaphysics"—namely, wild speculation about the first principles—as if a newly ripened mind should be diverted more toward questions of the nature of "How does this work?"[1]

In this book, I will not align myself with this skeptical latter argument; the subsistence of the question "why?" as a crucial vector for the interpretation of our experience and the justification of our actions seems to me to be a fundamental fact that should be understood. I am not in bad company: Aristotle, as was mentioned above, dedicates a major work—*Physics*—to the explication of this question; Kant, in his *Critique of Pure Reason*, even proposes a justification of the possibility of asking "why?" about each event. Indeed, in his language, what he calls the "second analogy of experience" in the *Critique of Pure Reason* stipulates that "everything that happens presupposes something that it follows in accordance with a rule." This principle, which governs the use of the category of causality, is justified by Kant in this text—taking over in some way within the framework of his so-called transcendental philosophy from the more general idea that "everything has a reason," which Leibniz was among the first to formulate.[2]

About a century before Kant, Leibniz named this idea the "principle of sufficient reason" and saw it as a fundamental ontological and epistemological principle according to which "we hold that there can be no fact real or existing, no statement true, unless there be a sufficient reason, why it should be so and not otherwise, although these reasons usually cannot be known by us" (*Monadology*, §32). This principle legitimized our always asking why, even though in a well-known text Schopenhauer wondered why such an obvious idea waited for centuries to be explicitly stated by a philosopher.[3]

I will thus take the question "why?" seriously, because it plays a decisive role in the manner in which language can make sense of the human experience. And above all, it should be asked if the object of this "why" is unique, since this word is everywhere in our speech: it questions things and events—"Why do planets follow elliptical orbits?"—but also actions—"Why should I run away?"; it lastly concerns beliefs, as I can always ask "Why do you think that?" to someone expressing an opinion.[4] Thus, "why?" turns out to be a central question not only in science but also in logic (the justification of beliefs) and within what one could call the language of action.

This plurality of "why?" suggests that the types of legitimate contexts and of appropriate response formats are multiple. Such a plurality immediately raises a debate about its reducibility to a single, more elementary notion. Philosophers call this kind of debate "monism vs. pluralism": Is there an ultimate object that the question "why?" ("monism") aims toward? Or are all of its meanings, in different orders, fundamentally heterogeneous ("pluralism")? In other words, is the concept of "why"—to adopt Aristotle's words—"homonymous" (denoting that it bears only a nominal and arbitrary identity, like the verb "object" and the unrelated but similarly spelled noun "object") or "synonymous" (denoting that all meanings are truly connected and join together into one sole meaning)? This enigmatic multiplicity is one of the problems addressed in this book, which will propose that there exists a certain grammar behind "why?" according to which contexts and legitimate forms of response are organized.

When asking "why?" we can expect in response a cause, or a reason for believing something, or a motive and thus a reason for acting (a goal, in particular). These three types of "because" are perhaps not independent but they are distinct. Through their insistence on indiscriminately asking "why?", children between three and five years old learn precisely this kind of grammar for why. The particular responses to different "why?"s are perhaps less important for their cognitive development than the acquisition of a general sense of which "why?"s are pertinent and which are not. Children learn through this which kind of response is called for by which kind of why-question: for example, they ultimately accept that if ocean waves always destroy the sand castles that they obstinately rebuild, this is not out of ill will but because the wind or a sea swell gives the waves a rhythm and amplitude that results in them regularly coming to lap at and then dismantle the fragile structures.

The "grammar" that I am talking about is not exactly that of grammarians. It encompasses a necessity that we will call intermediary between logical necessity—namely, the certitude of deduction—and pure linguistic convention, which strangely assigns the masculine gender to the French word *véhicule* (vehicle) and the feminine to *voiture* (car). But like proper grammar, it separates what can and cannot legitimately be said. I borrow this use of the concept of "grammar" from Wittgenstein, although I don't accept all of Wittgenstein's views; it suffices that this term establishes a set of constraints that are not logical, but that still govern our way of speaking and thinking.

The Possibility of "Why?"

Many philosophical controversies concern precisely the use of such a grammar. When, echoing the Cartesians of his time, Molière in the caustic play *Le médecin malgré lui* (*The Doctor in Spite of Himself*) mocks how doctors turn to the "dormitive virtue" of opium, it is precisely a question of restricting the legitimate "because"s to a certain type of causes—in this case, antecedent mechanisms. Today, Molière appears to have been correct in mocking these ridiculous pedants, these doctors who are passionate about quoting Latin and incapable of examining a sick patient. Historically, however, this reflects a major moment in modern science that we somewhat unimaginatively call in traditional history "the Scientific Revolution," which runs from Galileo to Descartes—the moment where the very idea of what constitutes a legitimate response to the question "why?" was changed.[5] To the question "Why do stones fall when we let them go?" we could indeed respond, along with Aristotle: "Because they tend toward the ground, which is their natural place." After Galileo, Descartes, and Newton, this response is excluded: the Aristotelian tendency to fall appears to be made out of the same stuff as the Molièresque dormitive virtue—namely, a simple description of an effect, then portrayed as a trend or a power instead of a true explanation. Modern physics understands that the cosmos is inert, that nothing has any desire to go anywhere; this is even the first principle of Newton's *Principia Mathematica Scientia Naturalis* (1686), which named it the "principle of *inertia*." Galileo's inert stone simply follows the law of falling bodies, awaiting Newton to demonstrate that it is subject to Earth's gravity.

Debating the legitimate form of response to the question "why?"—as Galileo, Descartes, Newton, Leibniz, and their contemporaries did—forms a crucial philosophical challenge—crucial, in particular, in the sense that what can be accepted as a manner of making science depends on it. I do not intend to put forth a solution to these debates with this "grammar for why"; on the contrary, it is metaphorically more of a question of the space in which they can take place. In this sense, this book will examine what the question "why?" is actually asking so that a specific discussion about what response can be given to it is possible.

However, if "why?" is undeniably a proper question for raising a philosophically intense interrogation, this is also because before even asking what the legitimate form of response to "why?" could be, we presuppose that there is a response; and thus, that it is possible to ask why. This may seem trivial or far-fetched, but even the possibility of "why?" is undeniably problematic: why should there even be an answer? Is it necessary for the world to be of a certain nature in order for this question to be formulable and to receive responses? Or does every possible or conceivable world allow for us to rightly hope that we can respond "Because of this" to any question in the form of "Why is that?" In other words, if there are rules for the usage of "why?" or something that resembles them, we must understand their reason; what makes them this and not that; on what they are based; and, if they are indeed grounded on something, whether this foundation is more than a simple convention.

The Limits of "Why?"

The mastery of this grammar is never perfect. Saying why something will happen does not necessarily mean the reason why I believe it will happen; and the responses to these questions should not be of the same order as those of why I would act in such and such a way in regard to this thing. It does, though, occur that we unintentionally mistake one for the other, and the effects are far from insignificant. For a long time, identifying these *confusions* has been a part of the philosophical tradition.

Similar to how one makes ordinary grammatical errors when one wants to say something despite the rules, we likewise—according to the type of grammar considered here—want to ask why and respond where "why?" no longer makes sense. It is also these *limits* of "why?" that trace out its grammar. What does "limit" mean here? Good examples of this can be found in questions like "Why is a line a line?" or "Why does Tuesday come after Monday?", where we can only respond in a tautological way: a line is a line, Tuesday is the day after Monday, thus Tuesday. We often have the feeling here that "Yes, it's obvious." *Obviousness* is thus a limit of why. The other limit was already illustrated by the anecdote of the driving Dutchman: "Why him?" Technically, in philosophy we talk about *contingent* events to designate what could have or could not have been: the tree could also have fallen on a Nepalese tourist, a Sinhalese electrician, or myself. This is something akin to chance, yet chance is incompatible with "because"—unless "by chance" was a legitimate response to "why?", which would then quickly become the subject of metaphysical discussions. "Contingence," along with "obviousness" (or self-evidence), thus declares the "limits" of this territory that delineates the grammar of why.

There are then, in the end, two kinds of grammatical errors: mistaking one kind of "why?" for another (confusion of category) or asking "why?" where no "because" makes sense (transgression of limits). The equivalent is produced in ordinary grammar: a proposition like "Green numbers yearn for calm," which has no meaning because the involved terms pertain to heterogeneous ontological domains (colors/numbers), is different from a proposition like "The green is or" (a favorite among logicians), which does not even respect syntax and thus does not really *say* anything.[6] Asking why when no reason holds or is thinkable would be like stating "The green is or"; while mixing the types of "why?" produces something that has the appearance of meaning but ultimately has none, as is seen in the sentence "Green numbers yearn for calm."[7]

These grammatical errors allow for "idols" to emerge. This is a word used by Nietzsche in the title of his last work, *Twilight of the Idols*—a very short book conceived of as a handbook for his philosophy. God, the ultimate cause, values in themselves; for Nietzsche, these are idols that some kind of almost inevitable thought mechanism pushed Western humanity to forge and venerate—a mechanism that has a great deal to do with the question "why?" since it involves notions of cause and effect. The present book will also concern itself with what happens to thought when it mixes the different usages of "why?" and supposes that all "why?"s demand the same kind of response—or any response at all.

Likewise, in a great number of cultures there exist myths that are supposed to answer why-questions: Why must we die? Why are there men and women? Why is there good and evil? Without even leaving European culture, the biblical myth of the Garden of Eden responds to the first question, the myth of united souls transcribed by Plato (in the *Symposium*) to the second, the Greek legend of Pandora's Box to the third. It is clearly difficult to know exactly what our ancestors believed when they recounted these myths and very plausible that they did not believe in them the way that one believes the sun will rise tomorrow, as it has been forcefully argued by historian Paul Veyne.[8] However, it was through them that discussion about essential why-questions could take place.

Indeed, *myths* offer a response to "why?" where none is accessible; and where, I would add, it could be that the question "why?" makes no sense. The romanticized history of the birth of philosophy and science at the heart of occidental rationality speaks often of how *logos*—reason, as a giver of reasons (*logos* is the same word)—was substituted for *muthos*—the myth, a fiction transmitted with small variations from generation to generation.[9]

After having established the grammar of why, it will thus be necessary to very generally address those cases where we in some way fill the void left by an absence of why. Stated bluntly, the possibility of responding to why-questions establishes a coherent and compact universe of events and beliefs: "This because of that, because of that, etc." It is in this sense that David Hume called causality, which is a paradigmatical "because," the "cement of the universe."[10] When this possibility comes up short, we have something like a hole; and a certain number of discursive, mental, or ideational constructions are deployed to fill this hole.

Such holes are, however, crucial. In a famous text from 1950, Claude Lévi-Strauss tries to explain the word "*mana*," often associated with the practice of magic by sorcerers and shamans from Indigenous American tribes.[11] This word defies translation in how it is used in so many diverse contexts and seems to gather together totally heterogeneous usages. Actually, according to Lévi-Strauss, *mana* marks the gaps between language and knowledge. *Mana* objects, animals, or people doubtlessly have something special about them, but in a way that is not necessarily always the same and whose existence is precisely established without being formally identified in its nature. As this thing was not at all known, the founder of the myth attempted to grasp it with the resources of language, even if language could articulate nothing that is consistent beyond the fact of qualifying it as *mana*. The thing thus became *mana*.

This well-known analysis—which is contested and doubtlessly more suggestive than robust—sheds light on these "holes" and "idols." There where no why is needed, "pseudo-because"s appear and sometimes acquire a special, almost honorific status. The notion of destiny could illustrate it: as stories often show, it responds to questions like "Why was this person born?" The expression "to fulfill one's destiny" means that the agent accomplishes that for which she was put on Earth, while one can reasonably claim that asking "Why were you put on Earth?" is a meaningless question.

Now leaving religion, myths, and *mana* aside, the quest for "why?" manifests itself in other more contemporary auspices. Everyone is familiar with what are called "conspiracy theories." Believing, as certain conspiracy theorists do, that world history is directed by a malevolent secret society called the Illuminati—or in a less colorful and more serious fashion, groups such as the Jews and the Freemasons—often reflects a yearning for a unique theory that can give reason to important or tragic world events. Thus, certain psychologists have shown that the tendency to believe conspiracy theories—such as "the moon landing was faked" or "the CIA planned 9/11"—is broadly correlated to what they call a "need for cognitive closure"; or in other words, a loathing of these explanatory "holes" in the fabric of the world.[12]

Explaining or Narrating

When we say why, we are often explaining something. Today, science in all its forms represents the principal authority through which we gain access to explanations. Things that are explained can be very general (like planetary movement, vertebrate diversity, the transmission of biological traits) or singular (like the emergence of the universe, the extinction of Neanderthals, the current stagnation of life expectancy in the West). Explanations can exist in very different forms (equations and mathematical models, researching antecedent causes, subsumption under laws, etc.).

Besides science, there exists a more commonplace practice by which, without formal or scientific explanations, we respond to why-questions: storytelling. Indeed, narration—an historian's account, an article describing yesterday's protest in *USA Today*, novels, film scripts, or even me simply describing my childhood to someone I'm fond of—functions when it lays bare why agents act as they do and why events occur as they occur. Not in the sense where each line could be preceded with a "because" or a "why?", but simply that the multiplicity of events, words, and actions that are presented can only be understood on the condition that it is indicated why things happened as such rather than otherwise. And just how explanation is protean in the sciences, narrations are almost infinitely diverse—particularly in how they indicate in a direct, implicit, roundabout, or fragmentary way the reasons why what is narrated took place in the way that it did. Narrativity is thus a major subject for the philosopher interested in the grammar of why; and we will see how the "idols" I was talking about are formed in a strong connection to narrativity.

The Program, and the Big Picture

This book proposes a journey through what we will call, to adopt one of Kant's favorite metaphors, *the territory of why*. It will explain its "grammar," and then will focus on its limits. And it will, at each moment, remain attentive to the confusions, mix-ups, and blurrings between why's grammatical registers and categories. As such, I consider this book as quite Kantian in spirit; or, to use Kant's language, I see it as an exercise in critical philosophy. Indeed, the idea that there is a logic as well as a grammar of confusions governs what Kant called Transcendental Philosophy. He deemed the study of the norms and justifications of our ability to know and our faculties for action "analytic"; and the study of confusions that naturally result from the exercise of these faculties, and which result in a systematic and regular way, "dialectic."[13]

As a philosopher of science—of biology more precisely—I am decently acquainted with the issues related to why-questions in biology, and explanations more generally. Most of my academic activity focuses on precise aspects of the set of ontological and epistemological issues raised by these questions. However, it is also true that philosophy is not an archipelago made of many disconnected islands; and if this were the case, many bridges or walkable paths would connect them together. I mean here that the philosophical reflections one can develop with respect to the question "why the eyes?" (a question thoroughly confronted by Darwin in the *Origin of Species* as well as many others before him) and the science pertaining to it connect to issues related to other aspects of "why"—in other words, of the activity of asking and giving reasons. Thus, philosophy of science is part of an often unaddressed big picture—unaddressed because it doesn't belong to the current habits of philosophers as well as because of its complexities. In this book I want to trace the connections between those issues with which I'm more familiar (biology and the sciences) and some other aspects (for instance, language, reasons-for-action, and historical inquiries), and start portraying the big picture. It means that my arguments, although rooted in my practice as a philosopher of biology, will span a large spectrum that will include philosophy of science (of course), of language, of action, of history, and of metaphysics. This book is an attempt to reconstitute the big picture, or rather its articulations, in accordance with the views I defend as a philosopher of biology. Since I will be aiming at this big picture, the details of the accounts for which I am arguing will not be given; they will be referred to in the endnotes, if some readers are interested.

The "territory of why" that I am intending to explore will allow me to portray this big picture. To achieve this task, I propose a journey in three stages. The first part will present the three major meanings of why, starting from the analysis of daily language, judiciary activity, and scientific thought. Second, I will describe the articulations between these meanings, their confusions, and their legitimate or illegitimate shifts in content especially in biology and narrative activity. The third section will approach the above-mentioned "limits" of why—contingence, self-evidence—and the metaphysical idols that sometimes take their place. The book will conclude with the metaphysical question "why 'why?'" Therefore, the reader will successively journey through the philosophy of language, of science, of action, of history, and of metaphysics—not always in this order—but this gives a proper notion of the domains the book will explore.

Some Precisions, and a User's Manual

I would now like to talk briefly about a few books that a reader interested in my questions may have already seen. The sociologist Charles Tilly's *Why?* is a very important work, and also very different from mine.[14] It examines the types of discourses when we want to explain "why?" to specific people in particular contexts, and is a major exercise in the sociology of discourses and narrativity. Tilly uses 9/11 as a focal event, investigating the way several people—all differently situated within society and in relation to this event—talk about it and explain why they did what they did. He considers a fireman, a witness, etc. All their narratives are very different because they each obey different codes linked to their jobs, their habits of interrelations, etc.—which is also why they are so diverse, and why someone who is not in the same social space as the speaker may be unable to understand what is said. It is a sociology book and therefore does not ask the philosophical questions I am interested in here, although it can be very complementary to what I'm trying to do.

On the other hand, two philosophy books about "why?" focus on specific questions that I consider much more quickly as steps in the journey I am proposing. Bradford Skow's *Reasons Why* deals with explanations.[15] It equates "giving a reason why" to "giving an explanation," and explicitly does not address the reasons-for-action that occupy me in part here. It is a metaphysics book, arguing that explanations are about showing or telling the ground of something. Thus, it is a book about *ground*, and especially this precise case of grounds that are *causes*. As such, it may converge with some of my analyses on causation in the first chapters, as well as with my reflection on "reasons" (since reasons are grounds). I will write more explicitly about this convergence in the conclusion. But as it is much more centered on metaphysics, it ultimately differs from my own project.

There is also *The Book of Why* by Judea Pearl (and Dana McKenzie),[16] who elaborated an important theory of causal equations and structural modeling in his *Causation*[17] that has been strongly influential on philosophy (Woodward, Hitchcock, etc.[18]) while also providing computer scientists with a grip on what is causal when they model data. The book is largely about the connection between statistics and causation; it argues that under certain conditions statistical data indeed allows one to legitimately infer causes. Hence, statistics are not only descriptions; they also provide a "why" when they are correctly handled. This important work shares common themes with what I say about our access to causation through statistics; but as one sees, the project is different and focused on something other than my grammar of why.

In the present book, there will be a great deal of science and scientific explanations, as well as justifications for our beliefs and our actions. And beyond science and agency, I will approach this other mentioned domain: narrativity. Wherever fissures, oceans, or abysses appear in the territory through which we will be traveling, I will try to understand what fills them—sometimes bringing great benefits, and other times useless conflicts.

As we can imagine, the task (or the territory) is enormous. This book does not aim toward systematicity. To draw out the metaphor, it aims more toward something akin to a travel journal than a *Lonely Planet*. I will describe the landscape in a fragmentary manner—with the hope, however, that the accumulation of these fragments will allow the reader to form a fair idea of the territory.

"Fragmentary" is understood here in a very precise way. Each chapter will consider one kind of why-question. By demonstrating the logic of this question—its object, its response possibilities, its presuppositions—each chapter will try to present in a case-by-case fashion the grammar of "why?", its systematicity, and the type of logic that governs the possible misunderstandings that could arise around it.

Because of its overall conception, this book is intended for several kinds of readers. Academic philosophers and graduate students in philosophy can of course read it as a contribution to questions concerning explanation, causation, narration, and reasons; they may be well aware of everything within their own subfield (e.g., ethics or philosophy of history) but can still learn something about the other ones (e.g., philosophy of science or of language). In addition to traditional materials that can be of interest to students, the book also hopefully contains some original contributions to often discussed problems (among others: the conceptions of contingency, the causal structure of narrativity, definitional fragility, and a rethinking of the notions of chance and the "nature of something"); as well as some personal views on metametaphysics, interpretations of traditional themes such as the relation between causes and reasons as seen by classical rationalist thinkers, and a revised version of Nietzsche's critique of the "idols" of reason. Readers who are well versed in philosophy will have no difficulty in recognizing that this book continues a critical tradition mostly represented by Kant and Wittgenstein in the history of philosophy, even though there is nothing here from either of those thinker's doctrines.

But in the end, I conceived this book as something nonphilosophers could read if they are interested in the practice of giving reasons or in some of the questions usually labeled "metaphysical." By this, I mean, for instance, scholars in the humanities, scientists, lawyers, physicians, and anyone curious about why "why?" is such an important question. The endnotes are of interest to academic philosophers, providing details about literature on the topics I address as well as on my own views, indicating more technical questions, and answering certain objections an academic would be eager to raise; as such, one can entirely skip them. The reader who is not an academic philosopher can also skip more technical sections that engage some of the current debates among philosophers and develop some of my accounts in a more formal way. Not reading them will have no consequence on one's general understanding of the message.

ONE

Grammar

1

Why Is Oscar Pistorius Guilty of Murder?

YOU ALMOST CERTAINLY REMEMBER THIS SOUTH AFRICAN athletic star—a young runner who, although both of his legs had been amputated below the knees due to congenital anomalies, went on to set records for track events at different distances. With his prostheses, Oscar Pistorius ran as fast or even faster than the fastest to the point where at the peak of his career he argued for the right to compete in the Olympic Games rather than the Paralympics. He was undoubtedly the most visible figure in parasports, and certainly one of the most striking ambassadors for the cause of disabled people. His career ended in 2013 when, on the morning of Valentine's Day, he killed his fiancée, Reeva Steenkamp, by firing multiple shots from a revolver through the door of his bathroom at home where she was hiding. In September 2014, the court had great difficulty in untangling whether this was a murder or a terrible accident: for his defense, Pistorius relentlessly claimed that he did not know where the young woman was at that moment; and that in this country renowned for its extreme violence, he thought that his house was being broken into and he was trying to defend himself. As a result of the judge being able to establish an accidental homicide but not a murder, his five-year sentence was appealed by the prosecution (by definition, let's remember, a murder includes the intention to kill). Pistorius was ultimately declared guilty of murder in December 2015 and condemned to thirteen years and five months in prison in 2018.

The South African judiciary system abolished citizen juries during apartheid; judicial decisions are thus left to a judge. For my demonstration, and to make things more similar to the trials that we know through movies from Hollywood, I will be talking about "jurors" hearing pleas and witness accounts just like in our criminal trials. Let's thus imagine a guilty-voting juror at this trial and let's imagine that we ask him: "Why is Pistorius guilty of murdering his fiancée?" He would probably respond with something like: "Because he knew that his fiancée had left the bedroom, that it was thus reasonable to think that she was in the bathroom, that he aimed at the bathroom rather than elsewhere, that he had visibly made no effort to see if his fiancée could be elsewhere, that there had additionally been other acts of violence toward previous partners . . ."

We often say that the question "why?" marks the search for an explanation or a cause; for example, there exist "why books" in France (*Dis Pourquoi?*) for children who are six to eight years old where it is explained why the sky is blue, why we breathe, why Bactrian camels have two bumps, etc., and correspond to the *Just Ask* book series. Yet here, none of the reasons mentioned by the juror represents a *cause* for the athlete's murder of his girlfriend, as all of them are compatible with a case of involuntary homicide. The response to this particular "why?" is in reality a *justification* of the juror's belief. Let's note that the subject does not need to know the causes of the fact in question to be justified in his belief. On the contrary, it often happens in this type of juridical case that the explanation regarding the reasons for the act in question are unknown or out of reach. Thus, even someone who thinks that the reasons for a crime are buried in the depths of a criminal's soul—opaque to both others and himself—would be satisfied by a justification similar to that which our imagined juror from the Pistorius trial declared. And conversely, if this justified belief is true, the search for causes can truly begin based on this verdict since we know that Pistorius actually killed his fiancée.

The "why" that seeks a justification (the *reason-for-belief*, in other words) is thus distinct from that which demands an explanation, which is often given in terms of a *cause*—as I will return to later. Nevertheless, by dissecting this example we see how the two things—the justification of a belief, and the explanation for an act—are intertwined. Knowing a potential reason for what Pistorius did—firing a gun into the wall of his bathroom—would immediately become part of the larger reason why one would believe that it was murder. Let's suppose that the notoriously jealous Pistorius knew about an affair his fiancée was having; or that he was the sole beneficiary of a life-insurance plan his wealthy wife had taken out: the detective from a crime novel would thus have reasons to consider the hypothesis of murder as plausible. The motive according to which an agent could have acted—which is connected thus to the *explanation* of the act itself—becomes a *reason to believe* or at least to consider it plausible that he committed the act.

This example, one could counter, is too complex since it involves the subtlety of law and the moral qualification of an action. "Guilty" is indeed a more complex concept than "table," "chair," or "fire." Let's then take a simple situation that is empty of all moral concepts. If I exclaim, "There is a fire in the forest!" and someone asks, "Why?" I could respond by saying, "I see smoke." Here, the *effect* of fire and not its cause responds to a why-question seeking the justification of my belief that the forest is on fire—in the same way that the imagined juror responds to the question "Why is Pistorius guilty?" with facts that justify their belief that the athlete killed his fiancée. However, if one asks the slightly more specific question, "Why is the Massif des Maures on fire?", one would rather answer, "Because a careless person flicked a lit cigarette there"; we see that here the most immediate *cause* responds to this why-question.

We thus see the first important ambiguity between the two "why?"s: that which looks toward the *cause of an event* and that which looks toward the *reason-for-belief* regarding the event, which can very well be an effect of the event in question. "Cause" and "reason-for-belief" (or justification) are two essential and distinct meanings of the object of the question "why?"

Nevertheless, if I see someone flick their cigarette into the forest and the forest bursts into flames almost immediately afterward, that could form my response to either question: this information would justify my belief that there is a fire in the forest, and at the same time it would include the *cause* of this fire.

Two Actually Independent Questions?

In fact, the terms "cause" and "reason" are often used in what would appear to be an unobjectionably synonymous way. The cause of planetary movement—that being the sun's gravitational pull—is indeed the reason why the planets turn in an elliptical orbit around the sun. To the extent that they respond to questions like "Why this or that phenomenon?", the causes are indeed the reasons. Reasons explain by nature; and appealing to causes generally constitutes a perfectly acceptable form of explanation—particularly in science. For the moment, the question about Pistorius lets us see that a response to a "why?" is generally what we call a *reason*; and that this can be as much the cause of a phenomenon as a reason for believing in its existence (a justification).

Descartes and the post-Cartesians—Spinoza, Malebranche, and Leibniz—took a major interest in this multiplicity of meanings for the word "reason." Thus, among the first to do so, Descartes distinguishes the *ratio cognoscendi* (the reason for our knowledge of a thing) from the *ratio essendi* (the reason why a thing comes to be). What we call in the words of Leibniz "the principle of reason"—which stipulates that everything must have a sufficient reason or cause[1]—expresses the idea that any true proposition derives from other propositions as its consequence and is justified by them, while at the same time positing that the facts of the world (which are referred to in propositions) are not without reason; and, in other words, have a cause. Conforming with the distinction made above, this principle of reason is thus double: there is, as Leibniz says, a principle of reason for propositions, which demands that any true proposition must have a reason; and a principle of reason for things or facts, which claims that any thing or event must have a reason for why it exists.

In the two cases, the principle of reason thus seems to guarantee that a "why?" question has a response; conversely, asking "why?" implicitly presupposes a principle of reason in some way. The principle of reason for *propositions* seems like a rational demand, since believing a proposition means to hold it to be true; and a rational agent is supposed to have reasons for holding a proposition *p* to be true instead of a proposition *non-p*; therefore, those reasons should exist. (The principle of reason regarding facts and causes is actually less obvious, but we will extensively address it in the final chapters.)

Reading these first analyses, one could imagine that simple linguistic precautions could dispel the ambiguity of "why," making two totally distinct things out of "cause" and "reason-to-believe": in the first case, "Why is Pistorius a murderer?" would signify "Why *do you believe* that Pistorius is guilty?"; in the second, it would be "Why *did he become* a murderer?" It is thus a matter of two questions that are dependent on different logical analyses, and which are ultimately the object of a linguistic homonymy. This homonymy would thus be eliminated through well-formed language—exactly as, according to the German philosopher Gottlob Frege, a formal language would get rid of all the metaphysical problems stemming from our having only one word ("is") to say two distinct things (predication and existence judgments, e.g., "the cat is black" and "there is a cat").

An attractive argument such as this, however, loses sight of the fact that knowing the cause of an event is sometimes a reason—and even a very good reason—to believe that this event took place. Indeed, if I know that the cause of the fire has occurred, I know that the fire is happening; and doubtlessly know it better than if I had simply seen smoke, which only makes it plausible that my belief there is a fire is true but doesn't entail it (since it could be, for example, steam from a nuclear power plant, which does not come from fire). The epistemic superiority of knowing the cause rests on the fact that the cause, to adopt a word from Spinoza's *Ethics*, "envelops" the "necessity" of the effect. Where there is fire, there is smoke necessarily—and this necessity makes it so that this knowledge of smoke justified by my knowledge of fire is reliable.[2] As a result, it seems important to argue that "why?" always concerns one same question that includes many dimensions of one same thing that we could call "the space of reasons," to make use of a contemporary term introduced by Wilfrid Sellars.[3]

The misunderstandings between "reason as justification" and "reason as cause," which are sometimes potentially anecdotal as is seen in the preceding examples, can become major metaphysical problems. Nietzsche provided one of the strongest analyses of them; but before addressing them I will lay out some of the components of each of the two types of "why?" indicated here: *reasons to believe* and *causes.*

"Reason to . . ."

The word "reason" has a double meaning, referring to either the reason for something (a proposition, phenomenon, or act) or reason as a faculty. The rational agent is exemplarily human, but we can remain very general here; Kant spoke of "finite rational beings" as the designated subject of his *Critique of Pure Reason*, leaving the possibility open that there are others besides humans. Perhaps he was thinking of aliens endowed with a more refined body than ours, while modern biologists increasingly attribute rationality to other organisms—to other primates, for example, but also even to birds, animals, and insects.[4] The "reason" of the rational agent could be minimally defined as its capacity to give reason to its beliefs and its acts. In other words, to be rational means believing and doing things that are based on reasons.[5]

As we can see from the above, these reasons can be more or less good. Ever since Plato's *Meno*, we have known that the simple truth of a belief is different from knowledge. The visionary, someone who has what they believe to be a premonitory dream, or simply the winner of a lottery, believes what is true but believes it by chance in some way. In other words, there is no necessary—or in any case highly probable—link between what they believe and their way of believing it. If Stéphanie believes that the square of the hypotenuse of a right triangle is equal to the sum of the squares of its two sides because she saw the Pythagorean theorem in a dream, this is not a convincing justification because there exists no direct and highly probable link between dreaming a theorem and the truth of said theorem (many people surely dream up false theorems). On the other hand, there exists a necessary link between the mathematical demonstration of the Pythagorean theorem and the theorem itself, meaning that the belief in the theorem is justified in this case. What philosophers sometimes call the "problem of knowledge" includes the question of determining what turns a true belief into knowledge; and in a general manner, responses to this question since Plato have revolved around the idea that the knowledge of something is a justified true belief.[6] Divination or drawing lots are not good reasons-for-belief, since their link with the truth in question is debatable, aleatoric, and fragile. The question "Why X?" (in the sense of "Why do you believe there is X?")—for example, "Why do you think that Macron is going to win the 2022 French presidential elections?"—receives in response certain reasons for believing X, and these reasons can be more or less good. Thus: "Because the polls show him winning," "Because a president who has an approval rating of higher than 40 percent midterm is always reelected," "Because his opponents do not have a credible candidate," etc. For the agent, such reasons are *reasons to believe* that Macron is going to win; but it could be that there objectively exist better reasons to believe it (and even still better reasons to believe that Macron will not be reelected). The strength of the link between the reason-for-belief and the object of belief is a measure of this reason-for-belief's quality—and this strength can be evaluated in terms of probability: to what degree is it probable that there is this object of belief if there is this reason to believe it? For instance, in my example, can we compute the probability of someone winning an election when, at such a distance in time from the elections, he is currently scoring 40 percent in the polls? Probability, besides measuring the frequency of a class of events or the degree to which someone believes in a statement, also measures the weight that a stated fact X confers to a hypothesis A about another fact Y.[7]

Thus, the perception of any object in good visibility conditions is a relatively good reason to believe that this object exists; in other words, that the belief that "there is a visible object with such and such a form here" is true, because if an object is perceived in good conditions (clearness, light, good health of the subject, etc.) it is very probable that it exists. We can juxtapose this justification with "Why is there a Smurf here?" "Because I dreamed it."—which is ostensibly a much less good reason because, measured in terms of probabilities, the relationship between "dreaming up a Smurf" and "the Smurf exists" is very weak. If Jeanne knows that the earth's climate is changing because she saw it on Marlène's Facebook page, this is a much less good reason to believe it than if she had read it in *Le Monde*, because the probability that something seen on Facebook exists is much less high than that of a thing seen in *Le Monde* when one considers the different modes of information construction in *Le Monde* and Facebook. In this vein, philosophers talk about the "reliability" of knowledge, sometimes saying that a "good reason" often comes from a reliable source of knowledge.

I am passing over the countless discussions that could be had about, on the one hand, the justifying strength of perception, and, on the other, the sufficiency of the justification criteria for transforming a true belief into knowledge. I would simply like to highlight the role of "reason-to" in the very nature of what we call "rationality"; and to indicate that because of the nature of knowledge (as justified belief), the question "why?" is central in the activity of knowing.

Evaluating the strength of a reason to believe leads us to another fundamental activity of knowledge—one which was highly significant in scientific practice and illustrated most famously in philosophy by René Descartes: that of *doubt*. With all of my beliefs, I think of things based on reasons of varying strength: I believe that the Amazon is the longest river in the world because I was taught this (even though other sources say it's the Nile, because there are distinct and equally justified ways to measure their length); I believe that Brazil has won the World Cup five times; I believe that water boils at one hundred degrees Celsius. I also (pessimistically) believed that Donald Trump would be reelected in 2020, but I admit that my reasons for believing it were much weaker or less good than those of the other propositions; and in this sense, I am admitting that they could have been more easily doubted. We could tentatively believe that science constitutes a network of beliefs where the strength of justification that links the beliefs together is relatively high because they have been subjected to methodical doubt—meaning empirical tests that serve as attempts at refutation. A reason is *more or less good* than another if it is more or less strong, which could mean that the link between the reason and what it justifies includes a higher degree of probability. With this being the case, the question remains of determining what a "good" reason-for-belief is in an absolute sense since I have only given examples so far.

Thus, to the question "Why do you believe such and such a fact or generality?", the response "Because X or Y" can be more or less convincing; and *beyond a certain threshold* one can say that it is a "good reason." Below this threshold, one will say that the proposition should be doubted. But what is this threshold? Let's take another look at the Pistorius case; the juridical context of establishing facts will be full of information for our analysis of what a good reason to believe something actually is.

If our juror only knows that Pistorius fired four shots into the wall of his bathroom and in consequence assumes him to be a murderer, he has an insufficient reason to believe it; if I asked him, "Why do you think he is guilty?", I would indeed be unsatisfied with such a response; because it would be necessary for me to have a reason to believe that Pistorius *wanted* to shoot at his fiancée by aiming at the bathroom, and this fact is not induced by the reason that the juror has provided. Conversely, if with this same information he judged him to be not guilty, and if when responding to my asking why he said, "Pistorius said that he did not know his fiancée was there," I would also find that to be flimsy since Pistorius could very well have been lying. This is why the hearing seeks information other than that of the initial findings and statements from the suspect, information that will further influence whether the juror should believe Pistorius to be a murderer or not.

This judiciary case is interesting for us because it indicates other aspects of what is a (good) reason—namely, a (good) response to "Why (do you believe) such a proposition?"; or in other words, a response to "Why should I also believe this proposition?"

How to Assess a Good Reason

We can see that these two examples of weak reasons are not symmetrical: between the two options, which are based on the same (minimal) knowledge of the situation, the juror had to declare Pistorius not guilty because—in the justice systems of democratic countries—the accused must be given "the benefit of the doubt." With the opposing reasons having equal credibility, there is thus a reason for supporting one claim rather than the other when it comes to guilt. Beyond the relative strength of the reasons to believe, there is another supplementary principle to help decide between beliefs and determine why we must declare Pistorius not guilty on the basis of the information that I mentioned (in a scenario that resembles the first trial, which did not conclude in murder). But maybe we should ask where this judicial principle comes from? It seems to be ultimately invoking a moral asymmetry between two falsehoods: between declaring someone who is innocent to be guilty or declaring someone who is guilty to be innocent, the second option is rationally preferable. I will not go into the justifications that one can give for this principle, which is sometimes formulated in a more extreme form: "It is better that ten guilty persons escape than that one innocent suffer." This saying has the advantage of clearly demonstrating that there exists an asymmetry between two errors of judgment, and ultimately proclaims an ethical preference for one type of error. In reality, it is a question here of an ethical perspective on an extremely general consideration that is sometimes technically called "the asymmetry between false positives and false negatives."

Up until now, I have been talking about being right or wrong when I believe something or other. But there are always two ways of being wrong: believing in something that did not happen (the "false positive") or believing that something does not exist when in fact it does (the "false negative"). This seems very abstract but in fact covers a multitude of clearly important concrete cases: for example, it is very different to believe that I have COVID when I do not have it, and to not believe I have it when in fact I do; because in the second case, my behavior will easily transmit the virus, while in the first my behavior will change nothing regarding the transmission of the virus around me.

The imaginary Pistorius example above suggests that when there is not a strong enough reason to believe something (in the real case of Pistorius there was one) a supplementary consideration concerning the difference between the two types of error—the false negative and the false positive—will be able to form a reason for choosing one belief instead of another. This is especially the case in a trial where a juror is not allowed to be neutral because he is forced to give a verdict; in other situations, for instance in scientific practice, when one has two sets of evidence that equally support two different theses, one can wait for additional evidence and, in the meantime, refrain from believing.

But the judicial case provides us with a major lesson: until now, it has seemed that the reasons for believing a proposition were measured by the strength of the connection between the reasons and the proposition (particularly in terms of probability). And it is effectively here where we see an essential requisite for any reason to believe: it must first be founded on known facts and relate to them in an appropriate way—a way that generally includes a specific relationship of probabilities, with the believed thing being more probable than others on the basis of these facts. Yet the dissymmetry principle of the "condemned innocent party / freed guilty party" indicates in a very general manner that it is difficult to measure the strength of a reason to believe something without immediately also recognizing the *consequences* that the fact of believing this thing could bring. For example, believing that Pistorius is guilty would mean sending him to prison for a very long time. A reason that is strong enough to believe that it will rain and thus to take your umbrella (the cost of the error is weak: you just look foolish carrying your umbrella with you all day) is not strong enough to declare a man a murderer; because there, the cost of the error is much more dramatic. The "reason" for a statement or a belief is thus also evaluated in terms of the effects of the statement in the practical world; and this seems perfectly rational: it would be irrational to put the umbrella case and the life sentence case on equal footing.[8]

To continue with Pistorius, let's take another look at the jury during their deliberation: they have been provided with much information—witness testimonies, scientific police reports, an inquiry into the life and habits of the accused, etc.—and on this basis they have determined Pistorius to be guilty. The principle under which they were operating was that of "reasonable doubt"[9]: guilt must be pronounced "beyond any reasonable doubt," which is clearly derived from the fact that all doubt must be to the benefit of the accused.[10] This standard of juridical proof instantiates what I called earlier the criterion for a "good" reason-for-belief, namely, the threshold above which a reason becomes a "good reason." The asymmetry principle "condemned innocent party / freed guilty party" thus provides in some way a threshold for a "good" reason-for-belief during a trial. As such, this threshold is determined by the judiciary context, and thus by a regulated normative social practice. In particular, it is difficult for the weight of the consequences to remain separate from the evaluation of the threshold of this "reasonable doubt": when the life and freedom of an individual is at stake, this threshold is much higher than when it is a question of just one or two years in prison with the possibility of a suspended sentence. Thus, if we call "pragmatism" the set of conceptions that somehow connect the truth of a statement to the consequences that believing this statement has upon the believer of the others, it seems that pragmatism has a point here.[11]

A Minimal Pragmatism Indispensable Even Outside the Courts?

Although pragmatism may rule the norms of belief in courts—especially because the option of refraining to believe and to wait for more evidence is not open to jurors—it should be left out in science, theory, and journalism. Only evidence should count as the norm of belief. Or, at least, this is the classical position held by rationalists, and is often called evidentialism.[12] There are, however, caveats when one considers the practice of science, even if the scientist faces no deadline for deciding what she believes to be true.

In a landmark paper, Heather Douglas statistically showed that the asymmetry between false negatives and false positives is crucial in science as well.[13] Suppose you design a test for a specific infectious disease. As one knows, tests have false positives, which means their results cannot be reliably informative if they are not assessed against other information such as the frequency of the disease in the population. Yet it is often possible to perform several types of tests that are based on distinct models, thereby putting the scientist in the position of having to choose to minimize either false negatives or false positives. Ultimately, it is this decision that will result in the choice of the model and the final description of the diffusion of the disease within the population.

Analyses like this one can be applied to any branch of science where detection and measurements are practiced (ecology, meteorology, etc.). In each case, various considerations—which can be economical, political, ethical, etc.; and which can range from minimizing the number of undetected sick people likely to transmit a virus to minimizing the cost of delivering vaccines—will justify the choice of a particular model depending upon the way that asymmetric costs are assessed. Thus, once again, our beliefs must be grounded not only in collected evidence but also in other principled considerations that may be of various natures. As a result, it seems that even outside the court (and especially in the lab) the prospects for finding a simple, purely evidence-based determination of what is a "good justification" are weak. And if we take an even closer look at scientific practice, we find other additional grounds to hold this view.

Richard Levins was a major evolutionary biologist and ecologist; together with Richard Lewontin, Robert McArthur, and Edmund Wilson, he contributed to the rise of a model-centered, mathematized community ecology that was closer to population genetics than to natural history.[14] Unlike the others, he was also a political activist and worked for decades in Puerto Rico to improve crop yields as well as to provide education for farmers. As an ecologist, he developed reflections on the potential of ecological modeling, eventually writing an essay that became a classic among philosophers of science as well as ecologists entitled "The Strategy of Model Building in Population Biology" (1966).[15] In it, Levins shows that the model of a system can fulfill several epistemic goals—namely, that it can be realistic, general, precise (or predictive)—but that it can't reach these goals at the same time. As a result, modelers have to accept trade-offs among these goals (for example, being very general will often come at the cost of being realistic).

This argument constitutes another version of the question of having a "good reason" to believe something, but instead it concerns scientists. It may also lead to the same conclusions. Let's consider COVID-19. During the pandemic, we have been presented with a huge plurality of epidemiological models. Levins's idea of epistemic goals allows us to make sense of this diversity. Some of these models were very general—like SIR models, which stands for "susceptible, infectious, and recovered"—and considered the population based on these three criteria (those who have not been infected yet, those who have the virus, and those who are either recovered or dead and can no longer transmit it). The model deploys a dynamic of virus diffusion, with one key parameter being R_0 (rate of transmission of the virus)—which allows one to compute the amount of S, I, and R at each step along the way. When R_0 is above the threshold 1, any epidemiologist knows that the virus will spread and possibly invade the population.

But such a model is very general. In fact, the amount of infected people for a given sick person is not equal to R_0, which is only an average. In reality, some people may pass on the virus 10 times R_0, while others may not pass it on at all (for instance, if they never leave home, or never see other people). If one wants their model to be more realistic, they can partition the population into several classes defined by a specific level of social activity—which operates on the basis of assuming that the higher a person's social activity, the higher their chances of spreading the disease to many people.

This example of model duality is different from the case of the asymmetry between false positives and false negatives, but supports analogous conclusions. Indeed, which COVID-19 model should we use? The former (SIR) is simpler and more general; the latter is more realistic—but because it's too mathematically complex, it should be put aside. Thus, we have a scientific reason to choose between the two options. But let's think again about this second model: if I wanted to apply a criterion like "social class," how would I be able to know who is in which class? I would have to ask people; and more generally, I would have to integrate many sources of information that would likely violate personal privacy. Thus, there are additional reasons to prefer the SIR model, but they are ethical rather than epistemic.

As a consequence, the singularity of a situation found in a courtroom, which I considered ideal for explaining how a threshold for a "good" justification can be integrated within a practical context, fades away. To some extent, epidemiology, public health, and medicine are in a similar situation: practical determinants enter into the specification of a "good" reason to adopt a model, and thus into the choice to believe in something. Here, we see that even though a court seems singular because a juror must come to a decision before a given deadline, this same kind of deadline situation can exist for scientists in fields such as epidemiology or medicine. At certain moments, scientists must decide among various options in order to deliver reliable beliefs that politicians, physicians, public health experts, and other people will use to ground their own decisions; and as we have seen with COVID-19, these decisions must happen quickly.

Heather Douglas argues a similar view. The more a branch of science affects people (environmental science and medicine immediately come to mind), the more it is affected by the asymmetry in cost of errors—which means it should further include pragmatic reasons-for-belief. In addition, sciences that affect people are also those where one cannot dawdle in deciding, meaning that Douglas's conclusion concurs with ours.[16]

But what about other sciences? One could say that once a science has a minimal impact on our lives purely on its own (leaving aside technical applications), this question of nonepistemic reasons being involved in how one decides what to believe is out of place. In fields like paleontology or quantum physics, there may sometimes be reasons to believe some claim or to adopt some model or hypothesis, and then at other times no reason to believe or adopt them—forcing us to remain in a state of ignorance before our being provided additional evidence. The most fundamental sciences take place in the face of eternity, whereas jurors and environmental or health scientists have to act now or tomorrow at the latest.

Even though science is not the focus of this chapter, I will take the time to criticize this hypothesis apparently grounded in common sense. It would be true, indeed, if there were only one fundamental scientific problem to solve in the world; but unfortunately, there are many. Thus, in the real world, scientists have to decide—collectively and in general—how to allocate their cognitive and temporal resources in regard to these various problems. And the cognitive resources and efforts they put toward a problem will depend upon the nature of the other problems to solve, as well as how they assess their importance.

This makes science, once again, in a position similar to that of jurors. So, let's think again about the trial. After Pistorius is accused of homicide, how many testimonies should be required before a judgment is made? A priori, I would argue that if one questions many witnesses, the testimonies will either ultimately converge into one same narrative (wherein a verdict of "guilty" would be announced), or not converge at all (resulting in a verdict of "not guilty," for reasons we discussed above). So, when should we stop admitting witnesses and testimonies?

Similarly, if a scientist is researching a particular question, how do they know when they have enough data to form a judgment? As an example, let's consider pesticides and GMOs. Suppose, as is the case, that we have "longitudinal studies" of one product—namely, studies that look at farmers who are exposed to a given pesticide and then compare their medical histories to those of unexposed neighbors regarding various pathologies (leukemia, cancer, etc.). Suppose now that I have three such studies on three populations, whose result is that there is no significant difference in pathologies between those who were exposed and those who were not. Should the scientist conducting the studies then conclude that the product is safe? Or should they ask for additional longitudinal studies? And given that they will want to minimize biases in their statistics, how different should these new studies be?

Of course, this is environmental science, which has many impacts on human life. As a result, the fact that a sound justification depends upon the proper allocation of resources, which itself depends upon ethical or political values, is not surprising. However, this situation exemplifies the idea that allocating cognitive resources to gather data is always costly because resources are limited—since longitudinal studies done for this product cannot also be done for a different product, thereby weakening our capacity to assess this second product.

And yet this question of the finite allocation of cognitive resource also holds for the most foundational and nonimpacting sciences, even if it is far less intuitive. For example, let's consider fundamental physics. Imagine that there is a specific particle called the "kozon" that should exist according to our increasingly likely theory of fundamental forces and interactions but that we haven't detected it yet. We have many reasons (coherence, explanatory power, mathematical tractability, etc.) to believe in this theory, and so we design instruments to find this kozon.[17] Now let's suppose we don't find it; and that we prove that another more expensive and more complex instrument that collides particles is necessary to do so. Which choice should we make?

We'll be kind to ourselves: thanks to a large donation from a bored multibillionaire with too much money, there is funding for our new device;

but it fails again! And then again. And again. What then do we do if the experiment to find the kozon fails every time? Should we continue until we finally find it? Or should we weaken our confidence in the theory, since the predictions have not yet been proven true? This would, however, bear problematic consequences; because, given that this theory is fundamental, many other theories rely on it and would thus be weakened or disqualified without it. With infinite time and resources, we could of course keep making instruments until the kozon is found, never seriously giving up on the theory unless a better one were developed. But this is not a realistic prospect. In the real world, the decision to gather data and to ultimately assess whether we have sound reasons to support a theory depends upon whether we have a strong enough argument to mobilize resources for the inquiry (instruments, data gatherers, etc.). These reasons are of course primarily scientific, since they concern why priorities are given to certain scientific issues rather than others. In our kozon example, for instance, how should the gross amount of scientific resources be distributed between the kozon inquiry and other tests regarding physical theories in other fields? But there are other reasons for these priorities, including economic and political ones. In the end, this means that even in those sciences whose object has virtually no impact on our lives, it is difficult to define a threshold for a good reason to believe in theories or hypotheses without involving practical considerations.

Cause

Thus, to sum up this long development, it is not obvious that there is a clear universal criterion for what constitutes a "good reason" for believing a proposition, or a good response to the question "Why do you believe this proposition?"—whether it be it in court, in science, or elsewhere. Any threshold beneath which a reason-for-belief—a justification, in other words—is poor would seem arbitrary if the practical context is not taken into account.[18]

If we now examine "why?" as a question concerning the reason behind something coming into existence, we find that the concept of "cause" encompasses a good part of the possible responses to this question. The natural sciences often discover causes, and I will pause over this in the next chapter, but the concept of cause is much wider than its scientific usage: we must use it as much in our daily language as in juridical, political, and moral contexts. For example, it is rare for an argument to not have a sentence where one of the participants yells "*Because of you* the cat got out! / the bathroom is flooded! / our vacation is ruined!"; politicians jump over themselves to say that their policies are the cause of newfound prosperity, or that those of their opponents are the cause of higher unemployment; teachers during recess try to find out who caused a fight. And we have already seen how any trial presupposes being able to identify a cause.

But for one same thing, admissible causes can be multiple. For example, the cause of death for Pistorius's fiancée was four bullets from a fired gun; but it is just as correct to say that it was a successful attempted murder now that Pistorius has finally been declared guilty. To look at a less grisly example, the cause of the Maures fire was as much a lit cigarette as it was the thoughtlessness of the person who flicked it into the brush while out walking. The necessity for identifying causes in order to respond to the question of why things are as they are—which seems fundamental to the very existence of a rational subject—must apparently be ready to adapt itself to a plurality of different responses, which could in the long run create a problematic sense of relativism. Indeed, if there is a multitude of valid responses to one same question, and they depend on points of view, why for example are we making such a fuss about how climatologists are declaring that industrial activity is causing global warming?

What happens then when we respond to the question "Why did the fire happen?" by identifying a cause? The pine grove is on fire, the firefighters find a cigarette butt among the charred brush, it is very hot this summer, and so we say, "The forest caught fire because someone tossed their still lit cigarette." The cause is found, and the cause is understood. But if we look closer, we see that things are more complex.

Here again, the world of the courts can enlighten us: a major concern during a trial indeed consists in deciding who caused what, and the implicit usage of a concept of causality is drawn upon.[19] Let's then imagine that our negligent hiker was identified by video surveillance cameras or drones (with surveillance being so advanced, one can speculate that even wild nature will be subjected to it in the near future) and the police arrest him at the resort where he is staying. In front of the court, he is accused of arson. In a general manner, various questions arise during a trial that identify the committed acts (shooting at somebody, stealing an object, communicating secret information), qualify them (homicide, theft, accident, insider trading)—which involves determining whether the act was voluntary or not—and then decide on a penalty (but let's leave aside this last aspect of things). Let's say that nothing indicates that the action in my example was done intentionally. In response to the prosecutor accusing the hiker of having caused a major fire, the defense lawyer could perhaps claim: the forest was extremely dry, the wind was powerful, the brush was so abundant that the smallest flame could have spread far and wide. In other words, on that particular day, the forest did not need much at all to catch fire. The causal contribution of the casually flicked cigarette is thus not as great as it would be in a context where the forest is less flammable. In such conditions of extreme susceptibility to fire, can we be truly sure that there was not something else besides the cigarette that could have set the forest on fire?

Insurers are familiar with these kinds of disputes regarding the causal contributions of different factors. Imagine that your house gets robbed. You did not have a reinforced door, or your door was not locked; the burglars broke in and stole your jewels and your Dali engravings. Of course, they are the cause of the burglary; but after all, anyone could have opened your door with a kick or a credit card just like one sees in the movies. Your negligence toward locking up is thus a plausible enough cause for the robbery; or in any case, it largely contributed to this sad turn of events.

What is thus the *good* response to the question "why?" in all these cases? From a psychological point of view, it has recently been shown that attributions of causality are hard to separate from moral or ethical considerations. If Virginie leaves for vacation and her plant dies, one would say that it died because it did not have enough water; if, however, she had asked me to water the plant and I had not done so, people would say that I was mostly the cause of the plant's death—even though, in regard to the physical process leading to its dehydration, there is no difference whatsoever between the two situations. This now famous psychological test developed by the philosopher Joshua Knobe indicates that we include norms and values in our identification of causes.[20]

But psychology is not all. In general, the way in which we *attribute* causality (which is what psychologists investigate[21]) does not determine what *must be in itself* the causality (which is the concern of philosophers); just like the way in which we count—by usually favoring multiples of 10 and 5 (because of the number of fingers on our hands, probably)—does not determine the structure of arithmetic, for which prime numbers are the most important, and not 10s or 5s.[22]

Leaving psychology aside, a major lesson concerning the question "Why did such an event take place?" emerges from our reflections about burglars and fires: there is not an unequivocal response, but rather distinct responses that must be ordered in terms of their "causal weight." Thus, in terms of what started the fire, the cigarette would not have set the forest ablaze without the dryness, the wind, or the oxygen in the air: in other words, answering "why?" means indicating a specific factor that we call "the cause" among the whole group of causal factors that were necessary for or favorable toward the fire's occurrence. In any given context, there are always protocols for identifying this factor. For example, instead of the air's oxygen or the wood's flammability, we refer to the cigarette as the "cause" because the cigarette was *quasi-concurrent* with the start of the fire; and probably because it is also an element over which we, as humans, have control—whereas we do not have control over the existence of oxygen. At first glance, the cause that acts as a response to a "why?" question is thus an event or fact without which the focal event would not have taken place *and* which additionally fulfills the two conditions of *quasi-concurrence* and *human control* that I just mentioned.

In consequence, we can thus identify the difference between *causes* and *conditions*. The oxygen in the air and the absence of humidity in the brush where the cigarette fell are among the *conditions* of the "fire" event; the act of flicking the lit cigarette is the cause of it; and the requisites of *control* and *quasi-concurrence* indicated above allow us to draw a line between cause and condition. It follows that "why?" generally requires a response in terms of cause rather than conditions, as is indicated by the fact that in our example, no one says, "The forest caught fire because there was oxygen."

Further analysis could highlight the relative character of the "control" requisite. After all, whether a fact is controllable or not depends on the humans who consider it, on the state of society, etc. In the end, it is perhaps not so objective. This is the conclusion that Bertrand Russell draws in a 1911 article that finishes by arguing that the very concept of cause is nonsense.[23] In it, he claims that we privilege certain conditions among the infinite number of potential ones that exist for an event and call them "causes"; but that from the perspective of the nature of things, so to speak, this distinction is null and void. In its barest sense then, we have here a pragmatist conception of causality. Within this context, the disputes between insurers and policy holders about the cause of an event are in the end discussions that do not settle the pure facts of the matter; instead, they involve a debate between normative antagonistic criteria. Thus, when an insurance agent tells me that the cause of my window breaking is not hail falling but the fragility of the window's glass, they are devaluing the norm of "quasi-concurrence" mentioned above—since the fragility of the glass precedes its breaking—thereby favoring the criterion of control—as there is of course a human control over the fragility of the glass. But as for myself, being the victim in this case, I would do the opposite. (Let's note that this intervention of the normative is initially different from the "Knobe effect" cited above; even without this effect, the analysis concerning the consequences of the cause-condition difference still seem valid.)

Russell radically concludes that if science aims toward the understanding, explanation, or objective description of the world, the concept of cause thus has no place in it—as it is a residue of a bygone era, like the notion of monarchy in modern politics. But without going as far as Russell's extremism regarding causality, we can take note here of the pluralism of the concept: there are many possible and not necessarily compatible responses to the question "Why this event?" that are all legitimately formulable in terms of "cause."

Billy the Kid and Contrast Classes

Our usage of the category of causality seems so important in daily speech—for insurers, courts, newspapers, domestic disputes, etc.—that it may be good to quickly pause over it before focusing on science in the following chapter. To discuss Russell's extreme argument, let's bring a more focused attention to the very form of the question "why?" Since the 1970s, many philosophers of science have highlighted the fact that these types of questions often include implicit clauses of the genre "Why X *rather than Y*?" We call these "contrast classes," and they are crucial for understanding how different responses to "Why was there a fire?" can coexist.

Elliott Sober tells a joke to illustrate this that probably comes from Hillary Putnam: "Why did Billy the Kid rob banks?" "Because that's where the money was." The punchline works because it responds to a question in the form of "Why did he rob banks rather than stores?" instead of that which a judge would implicitly ask: "Why did he rob banks rather than working?" In the first case, the contrast class relates to banks vs. grocery stores, while in the second it relates to stealing vs. working. In the two cases, the given response is correct. Often, we give opposing answers to one same apparent question "why this thing?" because we understand different implicit contrast classes.

To go back to our example of the fire, we can now see that the opposition between the two possible responses to "Why did the Maures fire occur?" can be cleared up in the following way: the response "because someone flicked their lit cigarette" would respond to "Why was there a fire *that day rather than another day*?"; while the claim that "the forest was excessively flammable that month" would respond to the question "Why was there a fire *that month rather than no fire at all*?" (Indeed, in regard to the second case, we should highlight the fact that even if hikers often care-

Why Is Oscar Pistorius Guilty of Murder?

lessly toss their cigarettes, nothing happens in other seasons such as winter or autumn; while conversely, in that particular month of July, if another hiker had come one day earlier and had himself tossed a lit cigarette, the forest would have very probably caught fire. I'll come back to this idea in chapter 5, when I'll analyze the apparent inevitability of some events.)

These contrast classes are not just purely philosophical whims; they are often defined by dialogue contexts. For example, Billy the Kid could indeed respond to his accomplice—since he is already situated within a universe where one steals—that he robs banks because that's where the money is since the implied opposition between robbing banks and robbing grocery stores or hardware stores is contextually clear: in any case, we are here to rob someone. On the other hand, with a psychologist or a judge, the implicit opposition when discussing bank robbing becomes "to steal or to work hard?", which means that the contrast class becomes stealing vs. working in turn.

Thus, according to the definition of contrast classes—which are often relative to the social contexts of dialogue—one same "why?" can give rise to different but entirely legitimate responses.[24]

Nietzsche and the Confusion of Cause and Effect

This examination of the difficulties of the concept of cause shows to what degree the debates created by our question "why?" are based on confusions about how one understands its object—not only just between reason-for-belief and cause but also in regard to causality itself. However, when confusion envelops both cause and reason-for-belief, the consequences can be metaphysically important. According to Nietzsche, many of our most entrenched metaphysical beliefs arise from this confusion of justification—which is often an effect—with the cause itself. Entitled the "Four Great Errors," a chapter in *Twilight of the Idols* pithily demonstrates this in a paragraph about "the error of confusing cause and consequence." In fact, if one can mistake cause for effect, it is precisely because both of them can be reasons-for-belief and because this ambiguity is intrinsic to the question "why?" Nietzsche writes:

> There is no error more dangerous than confusing the effect with the cause: I call it the genuine corruption of reason. Nevertheless, this error is one of humanity's oldest and most contemporary customs: it has even been made sacred among us, it bears the name of "religion" and "morality." Every statement formulated by religion and morality contains it; priests and moral lawgivers are the ones who originated this corruption of reason.—Let me take an example. Everyone knows the book by the famous Cornaro where he promotes his skimpy diet as a prescription for a long, happy—and virtuous—life . . . The reason: confusing the effect with the cause. The honorable Italian saw in his diet the cause of his long life, whereas in fact, the prerequisites for his long life—extraordinary metabolic slowness, low expenditure of energy—were the cause of his skimpy diet. He was not at liberty to eat a little or a lot, his frugality was not "freely willed": he got sick if he ate more. But for anyone who's not a cold fish, it not only does good but also is necessary to eat properly.

The philosopher uses this argument against religion in general, which promotes believing in God as the source of a good life—when in fact, for its promoters, it is simply the effect of having a character that by nature wants to believe in God and which induces a certain form of contentment within these conditions. In regard to the text, the error targeted by Nietzsche can be formulated as an implicit misunderstanding of two responses to the same question: "Why is a radical diet good for a long life?" If asked, an ideologue might respond, "Because Cornaro lived for a very long time eating that way." Yet if this is a correct response to the question "Why *do you think* that a radical diet is good?", it provides us with no information about the *causes* behind Cornaro's long life; and in a more general manner, on the causes of having a long life for those who follow this diet. But the ideologue will still want to make this draconian diet into an irrefutable cause for longevity.

Why Is Oscar Pistorius Guilty of Murder?

Nietzsche's text exposes the magnitude of the confusions between cause and effect. One can certainly be surprised by how people can confuse the two, given that the category of causality is so important for how one makes sense of experience, and in particular for how one interacts with things—since, to be able to manipulate something, it is necessary to identify what is likely to have a causal effect on this thing and thus *distinguish* cause from effect. But the ambiguity of the question "why?", as has been analyzed in this chapter, may suggest an explanation for this confusion: cause and effect are *equally likely to form a response* to "why (do you believe) X?" In this measure, they may be interchangeable; and our speech may easily tend to take one for the other with sometimes harmless consequences—and sometimes massive ones when it is a question of religious or moral beliefs such as Nietzsche portrays them.

To Sum Up

This chapter showed the essential distinction between the reasons-for-belief in a proposition and the causes of the thing claimed by this proposition. These are the two first distinct responses to a why-question. Their relationships are complex: the effect of something can easily and legitimately be a justification for believing in this thing; but the knowledge of the cause of this thing is also a justification of this belief. In this sense, "why?" is ambiguous and one can easily and wrongly mistake the justification of some belief about a thing with the explanation of this thing. Often benign, this kind of confusion can, however, have major effects in moral and religious domains.

A preliminary characterization of the "reason-for-belief" and of "cause" has also been given. We have seen that defining a "good" reason to believe in a proposition is often very difficult in the absence of any consideration of the practical consequences of such a belief; and that the notion of the "cause of an event"—which is unavoidable in ordinary speech—poses grave philosophical problems if one wants to isolate "the" cause of an event or infallibly distinguish cause from conditions without taking pragmatic factors into account.

2

Why Do Things Fall When We Let Them Go?

"BECAUSE OF GRAVITY," AS ISAAC NEWTON SHOWED US. But "*la chute des graves*"—this lovely expression from the sixteenth century whose now obsolete terminology can still be seen in the nouns "gravity" and "gravitation" (*graves*, or "heavy bodies")—to this day still remains one of the defining images of physics. Who does not know the popular myth of Newton being struck by a free-falling apple? Thanks to this apple, he finally understood this most fundamental of phenomena, sharing his discovery of "universal attraction" to mankind in the formula $F=GMm/r^2$. With it, the force exerted by a body of mass M on a body of mass m from a distance of r can be calculated, with G representing the universal constant of gravitation—a fundamental value that is a defining feature of our universe.

Stones and the Four Causes

By all accounts, the will to know proceeds from astonishment; but unlike a total solar eclipse, a falling body is not a surprising mystery. On the contrary, it is entirely regular. Yet it is much more natural to be surprised by unusual phenomena like eclipses than ordinary phenomena like falling bodies or the succession of night into day and day into night. Many cultures invented divinities to explain these eclipses that shocked, frightened, or surprised them; but very few imagined a god of falling bodies—to which they were so accustomed that that they did not even notice them. But the reason for eclipses is ultimately the same as that of the succession of night and day: the movement of celestial bodies, which itself is based on the Newtonian law of attraction and how it explains why things fall when we let them go. For the physicist, understanding the ordinary, the habitual, and the frequent thus allows us to account for the frightening and the singular. As such, it was thus necessary to ask "Why do things fall?" and to have Newton's response to understand a broad range of much more bizarre phenomena occurring at every level of the universe.

Treatises about the history of science are full of analyses of the successive responses to this question. I find it interesting here because it is a good example of a *scientific explanation*—in other words, a response that science gives to a why-question. It was also a good example for Aristotle—to whom we owe one of the first "physics," meaning a systematic conceptual understanding of nature; and for whom physical science was in principle the science of movement, in the sense of spatial motion (like in modern physics) as well as growth or alteration. For Aristotle, unlike his teacher and best enemy Plato, the moving world is subject to science. Everything moves around us: whether in regard to space and its falling bodies; or just to its states—such as alteration, aging, and growth. Aristotle's physics asks why this all is, both in general and in regard to certain particular bodies; and his response consists in looking for causes. He goes on to argue that stones, and "heavy bodies" in general, have a natural tendency to fall. And in this sense, a natural movement—like that of a stone or an apple that falls from a tree—is different from a "violent" movement imposed by force (like me taking an apple and throwing it, for example).

The details of his theory do not interest us here except in highlighting that *modern* science begins with the principle of inertia famously put forth by Galileo, which can otherwise be described as the idea that bodies themselves have no intrinsic tendencies; if they move, it is because a force is being applied to them. However, in his theory, Aristotle introduced a reflection on the very idea of cause that is worth pausing over because it is one of the first analyses of the plurality of the question "why?" It will go on to form the framework for thought concerning causality in philosophy and, later, science.[1]

Aristotle distinguishes four types of major causes, which are moreover four complementary responses to "Why this thing?": the material, the formal, the efficient, and the final. Let's look at an example that clearly illustrates his idea. We are standing in front of a bronze statue that represents an athlete. The "cause" designates why this statue is what it is; and for Aristotle, this cause is quadruple: its "material" cause is the bronze of the statue that forms its matter; the "formal" cause, or its shape, is the figure of the athlete that it represents; the work of the sculptor, whose hands and chisel extracted this figure from bronze, is what later came to be labeled the "efficient" cause (in other words, the process through which the statue is concretely produced); and last, its goal: to glorify, for example, Olympic sport—with this goal being the reason why the sculptor began his work—is the "final cause." The total explanation of a phenomenon thus requires presenting these four causes. The material cause is often passed over in silence; it is also often difficult to distinguish the final cause from the formal one. But whatever the case, these four dimensions define how something like our statue came to be the thing that it is. Of course, in the history of scientific thought, material and formal causes are eclipsed by the tension between efficient cause—in other words, the mechanical process of the statue's production that temporally precedes the statue—and the final cause, which is achieved *after* this production but which ideally or conceptually exists *before* production (such as in the sculptor's plans for his project). For Aristotle, as is shown in statements like "Nature does nothing in vain" and "Nature abhors a vacuum," nature on the whole has goals and resembles something like a supreme agent. The art of the sculptor is just a pedagogical illustration of the four causes; but it's a perfectly legitimate illustration since, for Aristotle, art imitates nature.

Why Do Things Fall When We Let Them Go?

But modern science and its principle of inertia will ultimately rid nature of these goals, as we shall now see. It should be noted that Aristotelian analysis clearly distinguishes two aspects of "why?"—namely, that which precedes production and the final goal; or, in simpler terms, the "*pourquoi?*" (which explains *why* this thing is here) and the "*pour quoi?*" (which explains *for what* purpose this thing exists). For Aristotle, because artifice is an extension of nature, these two aspects are found everywhere and are always complementary; but for us since Galileo, such complementarity is not so obvious. However, awareness of this distinction remains an asset as it is fundamental to our language and adds to the ambiguities that I detailed in the previous chapter.

If we adopt this Aristotelian language, modern Galilean-Cartesian science thus banished final causes in order to work only with efficient ones. As such, there are no longer violent movements in opposition to natural ones because objects no longer have an inherent natural tendency to fall. In reality, a cause, namely gravitational attraction, provokes an apple to fall in the same way that my hurling it into the air is the cause for its temporary flight.

The Truth about "Why" and "How"

We often say that science deals with how and not why. If we associate why with the final cause, this is clearly true. There is no place in science to ask why, for example, God or nature made it so that objects do not remain suspended in the air; or what purpose it serves that they fall if we let them go. But it would be false to conclude from this that scientists do not ask why; on the contrary, if we can now say that "things fall because of universal gravitation," it is because someone asked *why* and not how they do so. Additionally, English-speaking philosophers of science often use the expression "why-question" to categorize a good deal of scientific questions (as is seen, for example, with Wesley Salmon and his *Four Decades of Scientific Explanation* [1999]).

Nevertheless, as the falling bodies example will illustrate, this distinction between how and why corresponds to a real distinction in science—namely, the difference between what we sometimes call a phenomenological model and a mechanistic model, and whose respective objects I will refer to here as *pattern* and *process*. The strength of Newtonian theory indeed consisted in offering an explanation for two phenomena that were perceived as being independent: falling bodies and planetary motion—with the first being rectilinear and forming a part of our daily world, which Aristotle called the sublunary; and the second being at the scale of the universe and cyclical. Of course, it was Galileo who launched modern science by abolishing the boundary that Aristotle had erected between our "sublunary" world—where movement is sometimes irregular or troubled by violence—and the astral world, which is cyclical and perfect. But it was Newton who showed that one same dynamic linked them together, governed by one same cause: gravitation.

But how do we know this? Before Newton, Galileo and Kepler had established mathematical laws for these two phenomena: falling bodies (whose law shows that the distance traveled by a body in free fall is calculated in relation to the square of its time); and planetary motion (whose law shows that the speed of all elliptical planetary orbits around the sun is such that in equal intervals of time the line joining the planet to the sun covers the same area (namely, Kepler's second law). These laws describe *how objects fall* and *how planets turn*, but do not say *why*. By afterwards showing that these two laws arise if one imagines a gravitational force operating between two bodies of mass M and m according to the equation for universal gravitation, Newton thus responded to the question "why?"

And so this one same cause (or one same *process*) of gravitation gives us a reason for these two laws that describe trajectories (or *patterns*). In the case of these two how-questions—"How do objects fall?" and "How do the planets turn?"—each response marked a major advance in the natural sciences, and they could be later joined under one same "why?"[2]

The strategy of first finding *patterns* in nature or the social world and then asking "why?" is characteristic of scientific activity in general. Evolutionary biology and ecology constantly give us examples of this way of thinking. When we examine the different species in a tropical forest or when we estimate the relationship between the surface area of an ecosystem and the number of species it houses, the *patterns* we see in these two cases will be somewhat constant globally and we will then seek out why it is this way instead of another. Community ecology is the discipline that studies biodiversity—the reasons why a community (namely, a set of species that live together in a territory) is made up of these particular species and what follows from this. Finding a pattern, such as the distribution of species abundances—or a ranking of these abundances—is thus the first crucial step in studying these communities. Many theories have been advanced to make sense of this pattern, which is often a so-called lognormal distribution, where most species are poorly or very poorly abundant and only a few are very, or extremely, abundant. Ecologists now often debate between the merits of a theory in which natural selection mostly accounts for diversity by fitting each species into their own proper niche, and the "neutral theory" proposed by Stephen Hubbell in 2001 in which biodiversity is mostly due to neutral processes, namely stochastic (randomly determined) ones in which natural selection plays no part (see chapter 7). Both accounts compete to make sense of particular species abundance distribution, and of the reason why these patterns are often lognormal. Other branches of ecology, such as biogeography, are also concerned with finding patterns in biodiversity at larger scales. For example, take the so-called "species-area law," according to which the amount of species in an ecosystem covaries with the size of this ecosystem; it gained much support among theorists and received a formal and groundbreaking treatment in the seminal book by Robert MacArthur and E. O. Wilson, *Principles of Island Biogeography* (1964). In this text, several simple models are presented in order to derive these laws from a small set of variables that describe an abstract situation where mainland species colonize several "islands" (an abstract term denoting, in addition to actual islands, any place that is separated from the mainland by any geographical entity that reduces gene flow: water, mountains, desert, etc.) that are distinctly remote from the mainland. Once again, we see that ecology is mostly about finding patterns, describing generalities concerning these patterns, and forging models that try to explain them.

But the explanation for falling bodies teaches us another fundamental lesson about the nature of modern science: it is all about *laws*, or universal regularities in a mathematical form. *Patterns* and *processes* alike follow laws: the law of areas or the law of falling bodies in regard to *patterns*, and the Newtonian formula for gravitation in regard to *processes*. Even ecologists deal with general patterns that they sometimes call "laws," even though these "laws" seem less nomothetic, as philosophers of science say (namely, lawlike), than the ones addressed by physicists (since they suffer more exceptions, don't always have a mathematical form, etc.).[3] We are now far away from the Aristotelian cosmos: for Aristotle, our sublunary world was not easily mathematizable because only celestial bodies had the necessary regularity to allow for mathematical abstraction. This is why he was always centrally concerned with identifying sets of causes, which are often linked to the nature of the things themselves—the tendency for things to fall, for example—rather than describing laws that govern these causes.

Galileo's famous phrase that "nature is a book written in the language of mathematics" symbolizes this turning point where nature became explainable through laws that can be stated in the form of equations, matrices, or probability distributions (among other mathematical formulas). This radical rupture affected how one could respond to the question "Why do things fall?": it was no longer a matter of determining a quadruple causality that explained both the nature of things and the purpose of nature itself, but rather of indicating the causes that could produce events and phenomena according to certain mathematical *laws*. And in classical Newtonian physics, a cause is always a *force*, since by definition a change in acceleration necessarily equals the consequences of a force (this is Newton's "Second Law of Motion" or the "fundamental principle of mechanics"): to ask "why?", then, means to determine what forces are responsible for an event or phenomenon and how they are interrelated. Physicists now list four fundamental forces—three of which operate at very close range, and whose effect is felt on the scale of elementary particles or atoms (electromagnetic force, weak nuclear force, and strong nuclear force); and one of which operates on a grand scale (gravity). The behavior of the entire universe could be ultimately explained through their interactions.

The essential notions at play here are metaphysically delicate. We know that the very idea of "law"—in terms of a formula that rules an entire aspect of the world—was doubtlessly forged in a theological context where laws were decrees from God that inextricably governed both the universe and mankind. This context would explain why the same word "law" concerns both the laws of nature (which are indifferent to men) and political and juridical laws (which are human conventions)—even if this origin of the concept has been lost; and even if post-Galilean, mathematical, universal, and ineluctable natural law no longer has much to do with the civil code or criminal law, which is always historically situated and often transgressed.

Whoever decides to try to explain the meaning of the notion of law, however, confronts sizable problems: how is a natural law distinguished from a simple generality, such as "all mountains are smaller than 10,000 meters" or "all Australians like to surf"? Everyone sees that the law that light always moves in a straight line bears greater depth than these two correct generalities; but what does "depth" mean here?[4]

And to make matters worse, even if we were to figure out what a law of nature actually is, David Hume—in his *Treatise on Human Nature (1739)*—brought to light a radical problem linked to how one checks hypotheses about the laws of nature, now known to all philosophy students as the "Problem of Induction": how can I validate a general claim along the lines of "all bread is nutritious" since I have not tested, and cannot test, all the particular elements that make up this generality (in this case, all bread in the past, present, and future)?

For the moment, let's put these problems aside and remember that the explanations for falling bodies in science are based within the framework of the very general idea that the universe is ruled by laws and has no room for final causes.

The Classical Theory of Scientific Explanation and Its Discontents

When the branch of philosophy that we now call the "philosophy of science" became a discipline in its own right, researchers largely devoted themselves to understanding the nature of scientific explanation. Carl Hempel, an Austrian philosopher who spent most of his life in exile in the United States, put forth a strong idea that made use of this solidarity between the idea of law and modern science that I just mentioned. For him, to explain an event meant showing that it *had* to take place; and this demonstration had a very simple form: that of *deduction from laws.*

To grasp the importance of this idea, let's remember that deduction is a simple and infallible logical operation: from a set of premises, one draws a conclusion that is already contained within these premises. Thus, from the statements "It rains every Monday" and "Today is Monday," I can comfortably *deduce* that "It's raining." The truth of the premises is maintained within the conclusion. After Hume, we always distinguish *induction* from *deduction*; because, as we have seen, induction does not possess this conservational property. Indeed, induction consists in jumping from the consideration of just a few cases to that of all the cases within one same genre. To use one of Hempel's examples, if I saw a large number of white swans, I would induce that swans are white. Yet even if "Swan A is white," "Swan B is white," "Swan C is white," etc., are true statements, "All swans are white" is not necessarily true because I have not seen them all—and, moreover, there do in fact exist black swans. And, should one invoke the existence of laws explaining why almost all swans are white, the difficulty still exists, since, if science indeed relies on induction, some inductions would have been necessary to establish these laws, and they would face the same objection.

Granted, it is plausible that induction plays a role in scientific discovery and imagination; however, philosophers are suspicious of induction when it comes to account for the veracious power of scientific explanation and its epistemological superiority over other forms of discourse—for example, myth or religion—and they thus prefer deduction. This is the case for Hempel.[5] For him, the scientific explanation for why things fall consists of a deduction that is based on the statement of a law (in this instance, universal gravitation) and of facts ("We have an apple with mass *m*, and the earth has a mass *M* . . ."). From this, called "the *explanans*," he deduces that the apple and the earth are attracted to each other in accordance with the Newtonian formula, and that the apple thus falls in in keeping with the Galilean law of falling bodies (which was the thing to be explained, or the *explanandum)*.

Our "why?" has thus found its scientific response: a deduction, which places objects under the jurisdiction of the law of attraction. Admittedly, the problem then reverts to questioning the nature of the law itself. But Hempel is quite liberal on this point: as soon as something has the shape of a law—in other words, has the form of a strongly corroborated general statement—a scientific explanation is possible that can respond to the question "why?" The laws that govern the *patterns* that we detect, as well as the laws reigning over the *processes* that produce these *patterns*, can therefore equally be used as grounds for scientific explanations. Hempel calls this the "Deductive-Nomological Model" of scientific explanation. Thus, by invoking his law of falling bodies, Galileo could explain why an apple touches the ground where and when it does. This of course leaves us hungry for more "why" but it remains an explanation; the Newtonian formula will itself provide a more profound explanation since it explains the mechanics behind this law. Science thus progresses by discovering more general and more fundamental laws that explain existing laws which are already used to explain the world—more fundamental precisely in the sense that a law like that of universal gravitation tells us why another one exists (in this case, the law of falling bodies; or for planets, Kepler's second law). As Hempel admits, many explanations are of course causal; but they are explanations by virtue of how they actualize the deductive-nomological outline "law; particular conditions => phenomenon to explain"—with the particularity that the law in question is a causal law like the Newtonian formula for universal gravitation.

Hempel's view of explanation is remarkably flexible. It accounts for the fact that explanations may be given for laws that are themselves explanatory as well as for the fact that explanations are often a search for cause; and in addition to those cases where one of the laws in the explanation is causal, it also accounts for something that some philosophers saw as an objection to the relevance of the notion of "explanation" in science—namely, the pervasive use of *models*. Ever since Auguste Comte and his *Cours de philosophie positive* (*A Course of Positive Philosophy*, 1856), positivists of various brands have indeed often been skeptical of causal explanations. The physicist and philosopher Pierre Duhem later explained how theories can be underdetermined and formulated the idea of what is now known as the "Duhem-Quine thesis"—according to which one cannot test only a single hypothesis, but must always consider a whole set of hypotheses that ontologically include general claims as well as physical theories involved in the conception of testing instruments. In his book *La théorie physique: Son objet, sa structure* (*The Aim and Structure of Physical Theory*, 1920) he also claimed that the common view that science *explains* the world is wrong. He instead argued that science mostly *describes* the world, and that advancing the best descriptions (some would now say: models) is the point of the various scientific theories.

By "explanation," however, Duhem was thinking of the ultimate causes of the world; namely, things pertaining to a deep metaphysical nature that for him was opaque or empty and which made the very idea of causal explanation irrelevant. While his viewpoint constitutes the core of an antirealist view of science (since our world's *explanantia*—such as genes, electrons, quarks, etc.—would then have to be interpreted as its best descriptors, as what optimally organizes our descriptions and unifies the various empirical laws we have identified rather than objects existing out there), it is not by itself a refutation of Hempel's view of explanations, as we shall see. Let's consider a more recent formulation of Duhem's antirealism, such as John von Neumann's claim that "science doesn't tell the truth, science doesn't explain the world, science mainly makes models." Von Neumann, a major contributor to mathematical set theory, quantum physics, and economics (he initiated game theory with his *Theory of Games and Economic Behavior*, co-authored with Oskar Morgenstern in 1953[6]), supported the popular pragmatist idea that scientists only build representations ("models") of the systems in which they are interested; and that these representations don't tell us why the systems function as they do, instead mirroring how they operate by capturing one or two interesting aspects of a particular system. This interest, of course, depends upon our projects and tastes; and thus models have to be judged according to various objectives, for instance the epistemic goals considered by Levins above—e.g., predicting the outcome of an epidemic, capturing a general dynamic that is likely to be followed by analogous systems, identifying targets of a specific action, etc.[7]

Models and Explanations

Indeed, most descriptions of what scientists actually do would agree with von Neumann's idea: scientists build models of various kinds that are tailored to a specific question and embedded in a particular project. This is why one same system and one same phenomenon may be studied by distinct models, without any of the latter being viewed as "the true model."

But a Hempelian philosopher could easily contend that these activities still represent forms of an explanation. For example, let's look at a classical model in evolutionary biology; namely, the Fisher-Wright model. It is drawn from the seminal papers by Ronald Fisher and Sewall Wright, who were two of the founders of population genetics—which describes the process of gene frequency change among biological populations. In it, a population of organisms of a species (imagine butterflies in a forest, or a field of strawberries) is a pool of genes. More precisely, it is modeled as a set of genotypes; and each genotype is understood as one or two loci—namely, a position on a chromosome that can be filled by several alleles, which are different versions of a gene. Each combination of alleles—each genotype—can correspond to one of two phenotypes. As Gregor Mendel famously demonstrated, one can study peas, consider the character "color," and hypothesize that two alleles at one locus condition the color green or yellow. Write these two alleles X and x. Now, the population has a given size N; each allele has an initial frequency p or 1-p. After the second generation, the distribution of the three genotypes XX, Xx, and xx is given by the Hardy-Weinberg formula, which states that if the frequency of allele X is p, there will be in the next generation p^2 XX, p (1–p) Xx, and $(1–p)^2$ xx. With each generation, the frequency will stay at equilibrium. But if the population size N is small, there is a high chance that the population will suffer a stochastic effect called "genetic drift," by which one allele will be lost by the population through a kind of sampling error. This sampling error comes from a principle of probability theory: the smaller the sample, the higher the chances that outcomes will not reflect what is the most probable; this is derived from the law of large numbers, which states that the frequencies of the outcome will be more likely to reflect their chances when the sample is large. Yet, if we assume instead that N is large and if natural selection plays a role—which means that the chances of reproduction of the organisms are different due to their having the genotype (XX, Xx, or xx) under focus—then the distribution will follow a transition law that will respect the probabilities of genotype reproduction defined by these reproductive chances (technically called "fitness" and noted W_{ij}).

Any Hempelian philosopher can see this model as an explanation: the *explanans* is constituted by facts such as the initial frequency of the alleles, the fitness of the genotypes, and the size of the population; the laws are the law of large numbers, which, as we know, explains the stochastic process of drift; and the principle of natural selection, according to which genotypes that have higher fitness reproduce more and therefore leave more descendants in the next generation. Our Hempelian will emphasize two things. First, the laws involved in the *explanans* are various; they include laws of statistics, which are a priori laws of mathematics.[8] Second, this explanation is not of a single fact: whatever the initial values of the variables N, p, and W_{ij}, one can forge a similar explanation by filling the "fact" category with these values in the *explanans*. Thus a model such as the Fisher-Wright model functions as an explanatory matrix—that is, as a matrix likely to provide explanations of a system for a wide range of initial facts that can characterize this system; and it can explain a large range of phenomena—namely, all the possible generic outcomes of the dynamics modeled by the Fisher-Wright model: loss of an allele, alleles reaching fixation, higher fitness alleles getting lost because of genetic drift or higher fitness alleles going to fixation in the population (which is the expected result of natural selection, when a genotype has the highest fitness and the population is large), and an equilibrium between heterozygous and homozygous genotypes when the heterozygote has the highest fitness but cannot be the only one in the population since heterozygotes always yield a quarter of each type of homozygote in reproduction.[9]

Critiques of the Classical Deductive-Nomological Model of Explanation: The Return of Causality in Science, and the Theory of Possible Worlds

Even if someone holds a model-based view of science used to support an opposition to scientific realism—namely, the claim that science tells or is oriented toward telling how the world really is—the deductive-nomological view of explanation conceived by Hempel can still account for this modeling practice. Yet, although seductive, the Hempelian model of explanation put forth several major problems whose formulation pushed a good number of philosophers of science away from Hempel's positivism, suggesting good old-fashioned causality in its place as the main response to a "why?" kind of question. Indeed, if scientific explanation is a deduction like Hempel thinks, then it is unfortunately going to appear as being *symmetrical.* In what way? Let's imagine a flag waving in the sun. The flagpole projects a shadow. What size is this shadow? If we follow Hempel's line of thought, I would explain this length (Argument A) by considering the length of the pole, the laws of optics, the position of the sun (the light source), and would then apply basic trigonometry formulas that would allow for me to deduce the length of the shadow from these premises.

However, as is seen in remarks by Wesley Salmon—one of the philosophers to have brought the notion of causality back to center stage—I can do this exact same process in reverse: that is, deducing the length of the pole by starting with the length of the pole's shadow and the laws of optics; and by applying the same trigonometric formulas in reverse (Argument B). Yet if Argument A *explains* the length of the shadow, this is not the case for Argument B; because no one would claim that the length of the shadow explains the length of the pole! Yet the Hempelian conception of explanation as being deductive and nomological would not know how to take note of this difference. Thus, true scientific explanation is asymmetrical, while the deductive arguments that, according to Hempel, make up an explanation are symmetrical.

We find here the same difficulty that the previous chapter showed us in detail: the confusion between two why-questions. In this case, we have "Why is the shadow two meters long at 9 a.m.?" and "Why do I know that the length of the flagpole at 9 a.m. is two meters?" In other words, a distinction between a "why?" that demands the reason for something and a justificatory "why?" The former "why?", focused as it is on the *ratio essendi*, is often a search for causes as we have seen. Understanding what a scientific explanation actually is thus involves highlighting the distinction between cause and reason-to-believe once again.

And likewise, the notion of causality allows for us to understand the asymmetry of explanation. If the length of the flagpole explains that of the shadow and not the opposite, it is because the pole *causes* its shadow; while the shadow causes neither the pole nor its length. It is indisputable that causality is intrinsically asymmetrical—meaning that scientific explanation's asymmetry can be very easily understood if the explanations are causal explanations.

As we can see, despite what Russell is cited as claiming in the previous chapter, it is very difficult to expel the notion of causality from modern science. It is necessary for us then to look back again at what "cause" actually means—and to look beyond its Aristotelian four-way division, which showed us different types of causes without, however, putting forth a determination of the concept of cause itself in its generality. This determination has kept modern philosophers busy enough to the point that the "philosophy of causation" has practically become a specialty in the profession—and then it has almost divided into subspecialties ("probabilistic causation," "manipulationist causation," etc.). We fortunately do not need to go into these subtleties. It is just a question here of clarifying what we actually mean when we respond to the question "Why X?" with "Y is the cause of X," and of determining how this constitutes a scientific explanation of X.

Wesley Salmon developed an alternative theory to the Hempelian theory of explanation in which he argues that the world is defined overall by what he calls "causal processes"—changes that move across space-time while respecting a law of conservation regarding an essential magnitude (quantity of movement, energy, or information, for example). "Causal interactions"—or encounters between causal processes—are added to this. Whereas most philosophers interested in causation used to propose analyses of "A causes B" that questioned what A and B should be (are they events? facts? properties? variables?), Salmon reversed the problem and started with causation itself as a primitive, calling it a "causal process." For him, these causal processes are somehow the elementary bricks of the world (instead of properties, facts, or events—which are usually seen as the basic bricks, while causation is a glue holding some of them together).[10]

Salmon's ideas rely heavily on quantum physics, for which he thinks that the classical Hempelian theory of explanation would not be able to account. A major reason for his rejection is the fact that quantum physics is supposedly indeterministic;[11] thus, knowing that a system—for example, a radioactive atom of uranium, has a 90 percent chance to disintegrate after a time T—is what we ultimately know about such disintegration. For Salmon, in this case, the explanation of the atom's behavior at T, whether it disintegrates or not, is wholly explained by uncovering this probability value. This contradicts two correlated assumptions usually made by philosophers who study explanations: high-probability values are more explanatory than low-probability values, and "an explanation of A cannot be an explanation of non-A." Here, establishing the probability of disintegration indeed explains at the same time A ("the atom has disintegrated") and non-A ("the atom has not disintegrated").

In these conditions, to explain a phenomenon is to locate it within the "causal structure of the world"; by such phrase Salmon means these processes and causal interactions—the foundational bricks of causality—whose defining characteristic is to satisfy the principles of conservation that I just mentioned. Placing phenomena within this structure made up of processes and interactions allows one to determine the probabilities they confer to various facts, which ultimately explains key events as well as their absence.

A Legacy of Salmon: The New Mechanists

Even though quantum physics inspired Salmon himself, his idea that to "explain" means to "place a system within the causal structure of the world" has been massively influential in philosophy through what is now called the "new mechanical philosophy," which is more oriented toward biology and the other nonphysical sciences than toward fundamental physics.[12] The precise ontological views that Salmon held—namely, those of causal processes and interactions, which are well suited for physics—are no longer as central to scholarly discussion as they once were. As such, I won't focus too much on this general account of explanation—which gained major traction in the 2000s after the paper "Thinking about Mechanisms" was published by Lindley Darden, Peter Machamer and Carl Craver in *Philosophy of Science* in 2000—but it is still worth mentioning for our purposes here. The core of the argument is that an explanation of a phenomenon puts forth a *mechanism*, which is made up of entities performing various activities that are organized in a precise way so that the output of this mechanism is the *explanandum*. This account very accurately captures how molecular biology operates. For instance, the explanation of gene regulation, as introduced by François Jacob, Jacques Monod and André Lwoff in 1961,[13] falls exactly in line with this idea, with the explanation consisting in showing a subtle mechanism made up of genes whose activities are either producing lactose or inhibiting other genes, which ultimately assembles an exact established pattern of outputs under specific conditions. Also, as Craver insisted in *Ex-*

plaining the Brain, mechanisms are *explanandum*-dependent and situated at a given level: the "entities" in a mechanism can become themselves the objects of an explanation that pinpoints a mechanism composed of lower-level entities, through which the activity of the focal entity is conducted. For example, in molecular biology one can propose a physical mechanism that would explain the inhibiting behavior of the genes involved in the lactose operon. In addition, as Stuart Glennan emphasizes, mechanisms are not exactly objects of study themselves.[14] Indeed, scientists reconstitute a *model-mechanism*, which means that identifying a mechanism consists in designing a satisfactory model which, by modeling the mechanisms, can give us a reason why the *explanandum* happens.[15]

Enter the Possible Worlds

With regard to his general idea of explanation, which downplays Hempel's insistence on the laws of nature in favor of an emphasis on causes inherited from the critique of the symmetry of Hempelian-like explanations, Salmon's particular ontology matters little here. It essentially represents a large family of different visions of causality in which "A causes B" is a relationship of "production" that satisfies physical conditions (which include contiguity, locality, etc.).[16] It constitutes a general way of understanding the statement "A causes B," and it stands in contrast with another family of theories of causality—whose most illustrious representative is without a doubt David Lewis, a major metaphysician from the second half of the twentieth century. His major work, *On the Plurality of Worlds*, is concerned with what Leibniz called "possible worlds." Lewis articulates a modern version of the Leibnizian theory of possible worlds that is based on an argument called "modal realism," according to which all possible worlds exist.[17] As such, in spite of the temporal distance, Lewis is very closely aligned with Leibniz; and so it is quite natural to consider his theories if we take a look at problems that preoccupied Leibniz: causes vs. reasons, "Why is there something instead of nothing?," or the relationships between the necessary and the contingent.

For us, Lewis's major contribution is an important theory about "counterfactual" statements. What he means by this are statements that—unlike "factual" ones—discuss what would have happened if an event in the world had been different. For example, "If the goalie had not dropped the ball, it would not have fallen at the feet of the striker for Real Madrid." Yet in an article with the austere title of "Causation," Lewis shows that "A causes B" precisely envelops affirmations like the one I just mentioned—namely, that "if A had not taken place, B would not have happened."

Following Leibniz's basic intuition about this notion, a world is a collection of facts, things, and events that are mutually compatible. We are in the "actual" world, but we can conceive of "possible" worlds—that is, worlds where we change certain events or things in regard to the actual world, making sure that these changes are compatible with everything else in place, and providing supplemental changes should this not be the case. Thus, we can think of a possible world where the continental plates of North America and Asia were never connected, and therefore where our early human ancestors never set foot in America; or we could imagine a world where Lenin lived to be 78 years old: Stalin probably never ruled the USSR, Trotsky had an important governmental role and was not assassinated, etc.

In our case, Lewis's argument is interesting because he proposes a semantic analysis of counterfactuals in terms of possible worlds, which forces an explanation of the concept of causality. "If there had not been a passage between America and Eurasia" indeed means: "Let's consider a world similar to our own, where the sea between America and Eurasia never closed and see what it's like." An assertion about what was caused by the proximity of America to Eurasia is thus an assertion about what would differ in the possible worlds where America and Eurasia never made contact.

The counterfactual conception of causality that Lewis is defending illustrates the second large family of theories of causality (besides the one put forth by Salmon and mentioned above) that are sometimes called "difference-making theories"—since they all try to construct the meaning of causality based on the idea that "A causes B" actually means that A makes a difference in regard to B.

Why Do Things Fall When We Let Them Go?

Thus, when I say that (p) "a mutation of the PAH[18] gene causes the disease phenylketonuria"—which is characterized by developmental problems affecting size (and which can be treated by following a specific diet)—I am apparently saying that if an individual does not have this genetic mutation, she does not have phenylketonuria. This particular analysis of a causal statement seems convincing. It also allows us to understand the main difficulty with the counterfactual conception of causality. Indeed, whoever has this mutation but follows a diet low in phenylananine will not develop phenylketonuria. It is thus not exactly because they have the mutation that persons suffering from phenylketonuria have the disease. To explain the causal assertion *p*, it is necessary then to understand that when we examine the possible worlds in which we imagine that the person in consideration does not have the genetic mutation in question, we are considering only those where the person's diet—as well as all other factors likely to impinge on phenylketonuria—is not different from what it is in our actual world. If we imagine a universe made up of all possible worlds, to say that "the mutation of the PAH gene causes phenylketonuria" means that we first consider only those worlds in which the individuals do not change their diet nor anything else except for their genetic mutation, and then see that in this group of worlds they do not have phenylketonuria. This set of possible worlds is closer to our own than those where the individual not only does not have the genetic mutation but also has a different diet, practices a different religion, and lives elsewhere. Our causal assertion concerns exactly such a set: what would happen in a world where the individual neither has the mutation nor adopts the same diet is not relevant for the meaning of the claim "Had he not suffered the PAH genetic mutation, he would not have had phenylketonuria," which constitutes the causal claim in question now.[19]

Lewis's counterfactual conception of causality thus demands for us to define how a possible world can be more or less close to our own—which we call a metric for possible worlds. What does this distance mean? A sort of measure of similarity: a world where Lenin only lived one more day is closer to our own than one where he lived for fifty more years. A world where America never touched Eurasia is farther from us than one where Lenin lived to be 70. And a world where the gravitational constant G is different from its current value is still farther away from our world than these two other possible worlds. In a general manner, it seems that the worlds in which we change laws of nature are more distinct from our world than those where only certain events are modified. But these few intuitive elements for understanding distances between possible worlds do not make up a rigorous and generalized definition of distance; and it is not clear that all possible worlds can be situated in regard to each other.

For instance, even though worlds where laws of nature differ from our world w are admittedly farther than worlds where mostly only the facts are different, it is still tricky to compare two worlds w' and w'' that have different laws of nature: would a world w'' where the law of gravitation changes because of the value of the gravitational constant G (supposedly an intrinsic property of our universe, like the speed of light) be more different from w than a world w' where this law changes because its formulation changes (e.g., $g = G\, mm' / r^8$)?

And even differences between worlds that differ only in facts are hard to evaluate. Intuitively we would say that the farther away a fact f occurs in the past, the higher the chances that modifying f into f'' would constitute a world w'' that is more different from our world w than the world w'—which is constituted by modifying a fact f', which occurred much more recently than f. *Why that?* Because *the* collected consequences from the older f'' were much more numerous than the consequences from f', and thus the world w'' diverged from w much more than w'. However, this intuition is not always correct: for instance, a change in the position of one lake during the time of the *Ediacara* fauna (in the late Cryogenian period 635 million years) would produce at the present time a possible world much less different than a world w'' defined by a small change in the trajectory of the Chixtulub asteroid, which wiped out reptilian dinosaurs at the end of the Cetacean (which was much more recent) and prepared the way for large mammals like us (see chapter 7).[20]

Therefore, constituting an overall metrics for possible worlds seems an almost impossible task. However, most often (as is the case in our example of phenylketonuria) one only needs to evaluate the distance between a small set of possible worlds and our own, and not that which exists between all possible worlds—which means that the plausible absence of a generalized metric for all possible worlds is not necessarily a problem when one is analyzing the notion of causality in counterfactual terms.[21]

Everything Else Being Equal?

This counterfactual notion is not alone in the family of those visions of causality that are understood through the notion of "difference making." A major variant of this counterfactual view, which is now quite popular among philosophers, is the view proposed by James Woodward in *Making Things Happen* that is often dubbed the "manipulationist view" of causation. Inspired by the formal treatment of causation by computer scientists such as Judea Pearl,[22] which formalizes statistics-based causal inference with diagrams likely to be implemented in algorithms, Woodward interprets "A causes B" as "intervening on variable A changes the value of variable B." This matches the practice of many scientists when they intend to discover causal relations, since they often use targeted interventions that change the value of a variable: for instance, eliminating a gene in a gene network can be seen as a change of the variable value "presence of the gene" from 1 to 0. Tweaking a variable's value in a model amounts to experimentally checking a counterfactual statement in the form of "what if the value of X were different?"

But another (and older) very important way of understanding causality as "difference making" consists of thinking in terms of *probabilities*. When I say that drought is a cause of forest fires, we can understand this sentence as an assertion that a forest fire is more probable in times of drought than in normal times. Phrased in a more general way, the cause is defined by that which increases the probability of the effect, *everything else being equal*. This preceding clause, *ceteris paribus* in Latin, is crucial: for example, if smoking were to be severely forbidden and punished during a period of drought, it is plausible that the probability of there being a fire would not increase—even if science indicates that droughts cause fires.[23]

Still, such an understanding of causality as "what makes a difference" poses a number of problems, starting with this reference to *ceteris paribus*. This reference prolongs the already-mentioned problem of how one can determine a metric for possible worlds, since the clause "everything else being equal" describes a group of things that stay fixed in our minds while imagining the modification of a specific thing so that we thus characterize a subset of the group of possible worlds, a subset in which this thing varies from world to world. Yet the notion of causality as an increase in probability is important because it fits in with a common way of detecting causality—namely, the use of statistics and thus of probabilities (probabilities are the flip side of statistics: if something is statistically dominant, it is more probable than another thing). However, it can still be asked if the increase of the probability of the effect *is* causality itself, or if it is simply an aspect of causality through which it is *recognized* and by which it can be measured or inferred.

We will also note that this understanding of causality in the form of "making a difference" is more general than that of causality as "production"—which I mentioned above in regard to Wesley Salmon, with its "causal processes" and "causal interactions." Indeed, if the world were such that there was no law of conservation, there would be no causal relation like production; and therefore, no causal processes along the lines of Salmon. We could still nevertheless make counterfactual claims, and thus respond to different "why?"s by appealing to counterfactual causes or, more generally, "difference makers."

Mathematical Reasons and the Mathematics of Reasons

The idea of causal explanation—whether interpreted in terms that are counterfactual or "difference making," or even those that fall in line with Salmon's process-based version—does not exhaust the different ways of responding to "why?" that we find in science.

Why Do Things Fall When We Let Them Go?

Up to now, we have only talked about the empirical sciences. The case of mathematics is something else, with "why?" being just as central a question as it is in the natural sciences. "Why do the perpendicular bisectors of a triangle intersect at the center of the circle that the triangle circumscribes?" we ask junior high school students. "Why is the square root of 2 an irrational number?" asked the ancient Greeks as they faced the "crisis of irrationality" that this discovery would ultimately cause. We respond to these questions through demonstrations (which state reasons why the "square root of 2 isn't rational" is true), hence we are in no way dealing with efficient or final causes, since nothing *produces* the fact that the root of 2 is an irrational number. Granted, there is a process that led to the *utterance* of the Pythagorean theorem by Pythagoras; but it is not this process that makes the Pythagorean theorem *true* (in the same way that Marie Curie discovered X-rays, but did not herself produce them).

But couldn't a mathematical fact such as the Pythagorean theorem have a cause in the sense of "counterfactual causation" rather than in the sense of production, since I distinguished these two meanings ? The answer is no, as we'll see easily.

When it comes to empirical facts, they happen in a range of possible worlds (a very large range, if they are fundamental laws of nature). This is why we can think of causation as a counterfactual relation: in some possible worlds these facts don't happen, and considering this allows us to understand why they actually happen. Now, about mathematical facts, they are always obtaining, in all possible worlds. So the reason why they happen is not of the same nature as the reasons why empirical facts happen—since it cannot be formulated in terms of counterfactual statements (namely, a statement ending with ". . . and they would not be the case"). No one could, for instance, claim that "if X was not the case, then the Pythagorean theorem would not be the case," since this latter proposition is true in no possible world.[24]

The response to "why?" in mathematics is thus not a cause. Could it belong to the order of justification? At first sight, it seems to be the case. Empirical facts have causes; and the reasons to believe that these empirical facts occur are often different from the causes of these facts (remember this: smoke is my reason for believing there is a fire out there . . .). Now, with a mathematical fact like "the square root of 2 is irrational," what makes it the case that this is true should also be my reason to believe that it is true, since nothing other than the reason why the square root of 2 is irrational constitutes a better reason to hold this statement as true. The possible distance between a reason of the fact, and a reason to believe in the fact, proper to empirical facts, does not apparently exist in the case of mathematics.

However, things are more complicated. A very good reason to believe a mathematical proposition such as "there is no x, y, and z such that $x^n + y^n = z^n$ (when $n > 5$)" is when a Field-medal mathematician tells me that it is the case. These mathematicians are reliable, and, by the way, this reliability of the knowledgeable is at the principle of education: it's rational to believe what teachers teach us. There is no chance that I can demonstrate this theorem (which was first formulated by Pierre de Fermat in the seventeenth century, but the demonstration proved to be horribly difficult and needed hundreds of pages involving computer-based computations, which was done by Andrew Wiles in the 1990s). Yet this is not the reason why this Fermat theorem is true. Hence, the answer to "Why the Fermat theorem?" or, more generally, "Why this mathematical fact?" is no more a justification than a cause. Thus, in mathematics, "why?" demands neither a cause nor what I have called a "reason-to-believe" (or justification). It instead concerns a "reason for truth," which is different from a reason why *I believe or must believe* in a true proposition.

We can, however, doubt that in mathematics the response to "Why *p*?" is an authentic explanation. After all, there is no recourse to a cause or to the laws of nature—two things which, according to the theories of explanation that we have put forth thus far, fundamentally characterize a scientific explanation. For this reason, until the last decade philosophers only used the word "explanation" when they talk about empirical sciences.[25] However, this case of the mathematical "why?" indicates another aspect of scientific explanation, which up until recently had been relatively unnoticed by the philosophy of science.

Why Do Things Fall When We Let Them Go?

I just argued that the "why?" in the mathematical disciplines always asks for a "reason for mathematical facts." But the opposite is not without meaning: there could sometimes exist a "mathematical reason for facts." Recognizing this would thus confer a new dimension to scientific explanation—one that is beyond the causality of Wesley Salmon and his many emulators, or Carl Hempel's argument for its subsumption under natural laws. This is what we are now going to try.

Let's imagine two ice cream vendors on the edge of a long beach. Where are they going to set themselves up? Let's also imagine that they are perfectly equal: they sell the same kind of ice cream, with the same flavors, the same cones, and the same toppings; and the beachgoers are all evenly distributed on the beach. Each one of course wants to attract as many customers as possible. Based on the fundamental presupposition that each of them is a rational agent, we can claim that they want to maximize their clientele. If from the outset they are both at opposite ends of the beach, and if we suppose that customers will go to whichever vendor is closest, they will each attract an equal number of them. But if one of them—let's imagine the one from the left—moves toward the middle, he will attract all the clients to his left (since he remains the one who is closest to them) as well as the remaining half between his competitor and himself, thereby seizing an advantage. But the competitor on the right may then follow suit and begin advancing toward the left. In the end, the two vendors will end up side by side along the middle of the beach.

This fable is often introduced in economics to present the "Nash equilibrium," named after the extraordinary mathematician played by Russell Crowe in the well-known film *A Beautiful Mind*. There are thus situations where if everyone changes their position general harm will result, forcing them to return to their original position. This explains why in Paris all of the furniture stores are concentrated in one street (le faubourg Saint-Antoine), why all of the music shops are in Pigalle, and why many Japanese restaurants are found on Rue Saint-Anne near the Louvre. But beyond economics, this also explains why the platforms of major political parties tend to draw closer together at election time; or why successful French variety, pop, or hip-hop songs sound similar to each other.

The important thing for us here regarding equilibrium is that the *reason* why the ice cream vendors find themselves at the middle of the beach is the fact that this position is the middle (because in the middle, neither of the two can increase his profits without harming the other and restarting the game of musical chairs in reverse, or perhaps even also harming himself). Up to a certain point, the explanation thus does not call for causes or movements that produce something. We could certainly explain the position of the vendors by saying, "This one went left, that one went right; the first said this, the second noticed that, etc." But in the end, other movements and the resulting set of new displacements would lead to the same result anyway. This is indeed part of the very definition of an equilibrium—in the sense that, following a classic example, if a marble rolls down a hill into a valley (in this case quite a large marble to prevent anything stopping it indefinitely in its tracks) it will have the tendency to keep heading toward that valley no matter how its course deviates; and that the trajectory by which it arrives is not important in understanding where it eventually ends up. Whatever its trajectory, the marble will ultimately land in the valley. A Nash equilibrium is an equilibrium, and thus behaves like this valley: the set of movements involved in arriving at it are not necessary to explain what is happening.

"Why is the marble in the valley? Why are piano stores all located on the same street? And why are all the ice cream vendors at the middle of the beach?" The response to these questions bypasses all mention of the set of movements that caused the exact position of the marble or the vendors. However, their movements could have taken different shapes—assuming that the vendors are rational, which is the basic assumption of economics—the marbles and vendors would have ended up exactly where they are.

Such a response provides some sort of mathematical reason for a fact. The property of being an equilibrium is indeed mathematically defined, just like how the middle of the beach is the endpoint for the ice cream vendors because it has the mathematical property of cutting the beach into two equal parts. This response is thus relatively indifferent to the fluctuations and vagaries of the causes that make it so that the vendors and marbles end up where they do. The "why?" is thus no longer that of causes, at least in the sense of a sequence of events that produces something.[26] Scientific explanation is no longer causal here. Instead, we could call it *structural*, since mathematical structures come into play when it is a question of complex situations.

A Personal Take on Structural Explanations

In the last decade, several philosophers (such as Alan Baker, Robert Batterman, and Marc Lange[27]) have advanced views of explanations that center on those explanations that apparently do not rely on causality, using distinct labels to characterize these explanations, and differing in the range of cases which they consider to be noncausal. Others have discussed *noncausal explanations.*[28] Lange, in *Because without a Cause,* proposed an extensive account of these explanations that is centered on the scope of their modal force, and which connects them to his argument that explanations also exist in mathematics (not just proofs or demonstrations). I proposed that "structural explanations" are such that mathematics play an *explanatory* and not a *representational* role in them. By this, I meant that whereas in many explanations the mathematics are there to describe a causal process (for instance, a mathematical function describes an input-output relationship) with the process itself accounting for the *explanandum*, in some cases the mathematical properties account for the *explanandum* and therefore are in themselves explanatory.[29] For example, in many of the cases of equilibrium, a mathematical property called the "theorem of the fixed point" is appealed to, and this theorem accounts for the existence of an equilibrium in such systems—giving us the reason for the existence of the equilibrium, so to speak. Indeed, John Nash's original paper that introduced

Nash equilibria in economics relied on Kobayashi's mathematical fixed point theorem, which states that for any function that is monotonous and maps an interval onto itself there is a point x_0 such as $f(x_0) = x_0$—namely, a fixed point.[30] Hence, supposing that the system has a transition function f (which fulfills the conditions of a fixed point theorem) such that the state x is always followed by the state $y = f(x)$, if the system reaches this point x_0 then f will indefinitely revolve around x_0 since it will constantly ascribe x_0 itself as its image to x_0. The causal processes (exchanges, consumption, and production in the case of economics) going on in the system can't explain why there is an equilibrium unless this fixed point theorem is taken into account.

This explanatory indifference to causal processes creates a remarkable property for such structural explanations—namely, the fact that they can apply to very different domains (as we have seen with Nash equilibria and how they can be applied to furniture stores and politicians). We often call this the *genericity* of explanations. Some phenomena instantiate behavioral or functional patterns that are indeed generic in that they belong to different ontological regions, which can range from social groups to brains, or from ecosystems to the internet. Standing ovations, like the kind witnessed after a performance when the crowd harmoniously stands up, occur in any domain where elementary entities spontaneously self-synchronize in regard to a specific behavior. Theoreticians of what has sometimes been called the "science of complexity" claim that complex systems are driven by very generic processes that may underpin a set of systems with very different natures. Scattered in various disciplines and nations, these people (including the ecologist Robert May, the meteorologist Edward Lorenz, the physicist David Ruelle, and the biologist Stuart Kauffmann among many others) provided tools and models to approach generic properties of complex systems, some of which we will now consider.[31]

Sadness in Social Media, Epidemics, and "Why?" without Causes

The genericity of structural explanations justifies the fact that I have allowed myself digressions ranging from ice cream vendors to Japanese restaurants in this chapter on falling bodies: in certain cases, structural—or "noncausal" as some others would say, notwithstanding theoretical differences—explanations respond to the question "why?" in an identical fashion for both natural facts such as falling bodies and social and economic ones like with the ice cream vendors. I am now going to give another detailed example of these structural explanations where one does not need to detect a cause or know a law of nature in order to be able to respond to a why-question, an example that illustrates an important part of scientific theorization today and pertains heavily to the science of generic complex systems. Focusing on it will make clear what "accounting for the *explanandum*" means when it comes to some mathematical properties, and therefore exemplify what "structural explanations" are.

We call a set of entities—genes, neurons, people, molecules, consumers, cells, etc.—that are connected together a "network," with each connection representing a potential interaction. We call the mathematical object that represents a network a "graph"; entities there are "nodes" and relations are "edges." At a time when the notion of networks is omnipresent in science, especially with rise of big data science,[32] graph theory provides a good number of structural explanations like those we just discussed.

Here's a question we have been seeing recently: "Why does spending time on Facebook make us sad?" This has been shown by many studies: most users believe that others have more friends and that they are themselves as a result unpopular. However, the response to this question is very simple and is based on graph theory. In a network, if we randomly examine a node (let's say an individual named Kevin Bacon[33]) and if we consider everyone who is connected to him (his "friends" on Facebook), a simple mathematical theorem will tell you that the average number of connections for all of Kevin's friends will be higher than the number of Kevin's connections. Thus, the average number of friends-of-friends is higher than that of direct friends; this fact will of course leap out from the screen and will make most people feel somewhat depressed.

This simplistic approach in no way considers the nature of social interactions, the way in which people come to call each other friends, etc.; in other words, all the *causes* behind the construction of a Facebook network. It only draws consequences from a graph theory theorem. During some past vaccination campaigns, physicians vaccinated all the contacts of the contacts of a random person; and this strategy is justified exactly for the same reason: by proceeding in this way, we maximize the number of people that we can immunize.

Such a case presents what I introduced as "topological explanation"; by this concept, I mean that we are confronted with a structural explanation within which the involved mathematical properties are topological properties.[34] As topology is often defined as the science that studies invariance in continuously transforming abstract spaces, the structure of a network is legitimately called its topology, and many instances of topological explanations are found in those branches of science where people study networks. This makes these explanations very common in the sciences of complex systems, since these systems often require to be modeled as networks, given the large amount of entities and interactions they encompass.

Zooming In on Topological Explanations

Saying that one topologically explains facts and properties can be more precisely explained in the following way, with another example. Let's consider an ecosystem in the way that theoretical ecologists do (as was mentioned in the previous paragraphs). A long-standing question raised by these ecologists concerns the relationships between diversity and stability. Initially, they had the intuition that the more a community is diverse, the more it will be stable. However, sophisticated mathematical modeling done by Robert May in 1974 showed that diversity *per se* does not beget stability.[35] Mathematically speaking, the more species you add to an ecosystem, the less chance there is that it will continue to follow the same dynamics and conserve the same approximate species abundances. Thus, the question arose of the kinds of diversity that were likely to promote stability (and what kind of stability) since we still have many examples of a positive diversity-stability correlation—which suggests that some particular kinds of diversity yield stability, but not diversity as such. I know this sounds like a purely theoretical question, but it is not: reasons for the stability of ecosystems or communities are a key subject of investigation for ecosystem management and the preservation of natural environments in general; so if plain species diversity is not a vector of stability, we need to know what the alternative option is so that we can target those actions which are best for the environment.

Among the many theoretical approaches to this question, some involve topological explanations.[36] Suppose a community is such that its trophic network is scale-free—meaning that there are very few species preying on many species; a large amount of species that prey on one species; and, in between these two extremes, several species that prey on a few other species. Rigorously speaking, it means that the degree of the nodes—i.e., the number of connections that each node has—is approximately distributed along a power-law (a few nodes with degree 10^n, 10 times more nodes with degree 10^{n-1}, and so on until 10^n nodes at degree 1). In this example, suppose that one species randomly goes extinct. There are many more chances that this species would be poorly connected, given that the amount of species which are highly connected is thousands of times lower than the amount of species poorly connected. Thus, the probability that the functioning of the system will be disturbed by this extinction is very low and the ecological community is stable. This reasoning is focused on trophic networks; but as we know, we can abstract away from predation and talk about ecological networks in general, where each interaction is an edge in the network—be it predatory, competitive, or mutualistic.[37]

Of course, I skipped many details here and this is just a brief example. But it is interesting to examine the high genericity of the explanation. The internet, for instance, has an opaque topology but we know that there are major hubs (such as the websites of Facebook, YouTube, Wikipedia, and Google), significant hubs (such as newspapers, social networks, and dating websites), and a myriad of sites that are poorly connected to other sites. The same kind of topology can also be seen with airlines (where talking about hubs is common). Some researchers have argued that topological explanations valid for ecosystems also hold for financial economy.[38]

A topological explanation can hence be formally described in these terms. First, there is a relationship between the ecological system (ecosystem, community, etc.) and a mathematical object (the graph) through its associated ecological network. Second, the network has a specific topological property (here: scale-free). This property entails that the low probability of an extinction is not likely to have major consequences upon the network. Last, this latter property corresponds to the ecological property of stability, which means that the topological property accounts for the stability of the network. Thus, as I said, this mathematical property plays an explanatory and not merely a representational role in the explanation. In our example, if the ecological community's network were not scale-free, it would not have had this property of stability; thus, in addition to the component of "entailment" (namely, the derivation of the low probability of disturbances from scale-freeness of the network), such an explanation also includes a counterfactual component.

This exemplifies the logics of structural explanations in general (where a mathematical property can be of any sort—topological, algebraical, statistical, etc.) that we discussed in the previous paragraph. As we can see, the nature of the causal interactions occurring in the system is not explanatorily relevant; therefore, systems of very different ontological natures that are thereby undergoing very different causal processes (such as ecosystems and the internet or financial economy) will receive the same topological or, more generally, structural explanation of some of their properties or outputs.

Why Do Things Fall When We Let Them Go?

Structures and Optima

Thus, "why?" does not always receive an understanding of cause as a possible scientific response. In numerous cases similar to that of "Facebook depression," the response instead consists of a mathematical reason for the fact. And on such a basis, this explanation will turn out to be entirely generic, resolving a group of why-questions that seem at first glance to be heterogeneous because they concern things of a different nature: epidemics or Facebook friends, ecosystems or financial systems, economies or the human brain.

Let's extend these insights beyond the consideration of topological explanations. In addition to graph theory, another set of mathematical reasons indeed reveals something of what Leibniz glimpsed when crafting his theory of possible worlds: considerations of *optimality*. Mathematically speaking, an optimum is indeed an extremum, namely, an extreme value—whether maximal or minimal—attained by a function that describes the behavior of a system. For Leibniz, the *best* is defined by the greatest possible quantity of "reality," with reality being the only positive (like, for example, light or heat) and the negative being by definition the absence of the positive and thus something unreal (like darkness or cold). The world that exists is the best of all possible worlds—that is, the one that maximizes the quantity of reality—because God chooses it in the same way that economists describe how we choose our own actions by selecting those that maximize our "utility."

The fact of being an extremum is a mathematical property. But when I say that a ray of light arrives at a particular place because it moved in a straight line, I am also referring to the existence of a minimum: the light beam took the shortest path between two points. For Leibniz, a scientist can legitimately rely on these kinds of extrema considerations to explain natural phenomena since the ultimate reason for things is the principle that God always chooses what is best, which in itself involves a reference to an extremum. Modern scientists can no longer invoke divine justification, but references to extrema principles remain constant: the principle of least action—which we owe to Maupertuis, and from which the idea of the rectilinear propagation of light was derived—the "entropy maximization," and the "minimization of free energy" are all central principles of physics. In each instance, the existence of an extremum is explanatory: it is because a certain strategy or a certain trajectory is an extremum for a behavior described by a certain mathematical function that the system will adopt it.

For Leibniz, just like how one can explain the marble's ending up in the valley both by describing its particular trajectory and by indicating the fact that the valley exists (and that all future marbles will ultimately wind up there), explanations that follow the details of cause and effect coexist with explanations that highlight the principle of optimality, which guides the order of things. "I even find that several effects of nature can be demonstrated doubly, that is, by considering first the efficient cause and then by considering the final cause, making use, for example, of God's decree always to produce his effect by the easiest and most determinate ways, as I have shown elsewhere in accounting for the rules of catoptrics [reflection] and dioptrics [refraction]."[39]

Modern scientists could say that the optimum does not have an ultimate theological justification but that it allows us to more easily explain phenomena through mathematics. This is precisely the principle of the "economy of thought" that was so dear to the physicist and philosopher Ernst Mach: there is no need to scrutinize or to overdemonstrate in order to have a solution. Even if we ultimately know that that there are a multitude of true causes and effects acting together in the world, the idea of an optimum simply allows for us to predict phenomena more easily. When one holds an instrumentalist or pragmatist view of science—according to which science is not aiming to uncover reality but instead building useful models that may support efficient predictions or any of our other goals (as we saw in von Neumann's *dictum* above)—a Machian conception of optimality reasoning is plausible. But what about the scientific realist's view?

And here is an even more general question: if we can no longer run back to God as the ultimate cause of everything, are explanations governed by mathematical reasons such as optima guaranteed? Or are they just a sometimes lucky heuristic?

Why Do Things Fall When We Let Them Go?

In regard to Leibniz, we have been discussing optimum-type mathematical reasons. But there are others; for example, we had to invoke the idea of equilibriums to explain the story about the ice cream vendors. Yet in all possible worlds, the fact that a situation is an equilibrium implies that the system that has attained it will maintain it or will have a long-term tendency to attain it. Likewise, a good part of the models that scientists make—and not just those pertaining to economics—tend to find points of equilibrium in different systems. In this case, one could say that the invocation of an equilibrium, and thus a mathematical reason for certain facts, is itself a good explanation; and that in reality, it does not need a divine warrant to be considered as more than a heuristic—in other words, as a legitimate explanation. In this case, even the scientific realist would probably be okay with this answer.

A Pluralism of Explanations?

We can now see that within even the natural sciences, the question "why?" is responded to in terms of causes, which coexist with another range of responses formulated in terms of mathematical reasons (or "structures," in my wording). This could be an even more radical reading of the Galilean aphorism according to which nature is a book written in mathematical language: not only are the laws of nature formulable in mathematical language, but mathematical properties themselves on their own can be under certain conditions a good explanation—and can even provide a generic explanation by which phenomena of apparently very different ontological genres prove to be identical.

But throughout this section, we have seen the tension between "efficient causes" and "final causes" regularly reappear—leading up to this strange persistence of the Leibnizian principle of a God-like "choice of the best" within modern physics and its principles of maximum and minimum. We are thus far from having resolved the enigma of the question "why?" by simply declaring that only efficient causes are a worthy response to "why?" (like certain simplified versions of the Scientific Revolution tend to claim).[40] As Aristotle already knew, the linguistic universe of cause remains very heterogeneous, and the universe of explanation is even more so. It is thus time to focus more on action and choice—and on the way we can respond to the question "Why are you doing that?"

To Sum Up

This chapter, which was essentially devoted to the ways in which we can scientifically respond to "why?", showed that many scientific questions are why-questions. Those that ask "how?" can be extended into a "why?" question: "How do the planets turn?" (The pattern of Kepler's laws of motion) becomes "Why do they turn?" (The process of Newtonian gravitation). They can also be reformulated in terms of "why?": "How does water boil?" means "Why does water boil at 100 degrees Celsius?"—with this "why?" being of the order of efficient cause, and never that of final cause (goal).

Classical philosophy of science tried to define scientific explanation by avoiding all reference to causality, favoring deduction over induction as it is more logically satisfying. But here we are confronted with the problem that an explanation—if it is a deduction—is symmetrical (as is the justification), yet a true explanation is asymmetrical. Causality takes account of this asymmetry—cause causes effect, and not the other way around—which makes it so that the act of explaining could very well mean "finding the cause" if we conceive a clear notion of causality. Two families of conceptions of causality were then mentioned that provide an explication of what a causal utterance is: difference-making, mostly illustrated by counterfactuals, and causality conceived of as process.

But in reality, many scientific responses to "why?" are not causes; they are "structural explanations," which invoke instead mathematical reasons, as we saw in the economic theories of equilibrium or in the ecological or social models of certain networks relying on topology; or again under certain considerations of optimality, whose justification becomes problematic if, unlike Leibniz, we no longer accept in science a divine origin of the world.

Why Do Things Fall When We Let Them Go?

3

Why Did Mickey Mouse Open the Fridge?

"BECAUSE HE WAS THIRSTY AND KNEW THAT THERE WAS orange juice there." Even a young child understands this when watching the humanoid mouse as he walks toward the refrigerator. But how is this possible?

Beliefs and Desires

Other people interest us, there is no denying it. They intrigue us, attract us, annoy us, worry us, amaze us . . . the list of verbs is long. And very often, our interest revolves around this simple question: "Why are they doing that?"

Sometimes, we ask them; other times, we know why without even having to think about it. Other times still, we construct a response based on what we see in their behavior and their speech.

Providing a response to this basic question is crucial: if I know why my friend Luca goes to Porte de Saint-Cloud every other Saturday—in this instance, to watch Paris Saint-Germain soccer matches—I also know that he would be happy if I gave him a Kylian Mbappé (PSG's world-class striker) team shirt for his birthday. And knowing why tons of people drive off in their cars on the first Saturday in July to head south on the highway—as they leave for vacation—allows me to avoid traffic jams by choosing another date to travel. Knowing how to respond to the question "Why are they doing that?" helps us in general to predict the behavior of others, a decisive faculty in our social life.

This capacity both to ask "Why are they doing that?" and to be able to respond to it is surprising—especially since it is practiced at all times and is available to us at a very young age, as is illustrated by the young child watching Mickey open the refrigerator to help himself to a glass of orange juice. In our "why?" grammar, desire, will, need, and intention are always accessible responses. They are generally applied to humans; nevertheless, we attribute them sometimes to animals—the dog nibbles at my shoe because he wants to go out—and often see how children include everything that moves within this domain: the sun is going to set because it is tired, the sea got angry and threw waves at my sandcastle to destroy it. But let's set these examples aside and focus on fully developed humans.

This type of "because" precisely constitutes a "final cause" in the sense of Aristotle: the response to "Why did Mickey open the fridge?"—namely, to drink the juice—concludes Mickey's act. Unlike a "because" that indicates the causes of an event, here the cause seems to come after the action. Or rather, the cause exists first *before* the action in the *representation* that the agent makes of it, and then *in reality after* the action.[1]

In the case of human actions, we thus respond to "why?" with a word that contains a goal: desire, will, intention, etc.; these terms always designate attitudes in which I relate to something that is *not* there, but in the mode of what *should* be (for me). To want a glass of orange juice means both not having orange juice and determining a course of action so that it comes into my possession. This kind of idea about orange juice makes up the reason for Mickey's action, his *reason for* opening the fridge.

Mickey Mouse is certainly a trivial example. But the same type of structure for questions like "Why are they doing that?" "For what purpose?" allows for us to understand the actions of people in a more general manner. In June 1940, General de Gaulle exiled himself in London. Without a response to this question, such a departure could appear as him fleeing. If we would like to argue that General de Gaulle was not running away, it is thus necessary to say *why* he left—namely, because his goal was to continue the struggle against the Nazis, and because he believed (rightly) that this was no longer possible on French territory. De Gaulle's case is much more interesting than Mickey's because without knowing de Gaulle's goal and his reason for going to London, we would wrongly describe his action. A correct description of an action is thus difficult to separate from a knowledge of the why of this action.

Historians often seek to determine such whys from the perspective of the agent themselves, since—to continue our example—it is a question of reconstructing de Gaulle's motivations even if one does not share them. To understand why de Gaulle acted as he did, the historian transports himself in some way into the general's person and says: "If I were de Gaulle, what beliefs and what goals would I need to have to act as de Gaulle actually acted?"

In a more general manner, a *narrative* makes its subject more understandable for us by indicating these reasons for action. And to these, we also join reasons for events—most often otherwise called causes—which make everything that is going on around us understandable. Of course, all events and all actions are not always explained in a given narration; just a few of them are enough so that the narrated thing is not completely opaque to us. Thus, a history book about the Resistance will say that Jean Moulin was captured by the Nazis even if we do not know exactly why; he was denounced, but we do not know by whom. These "why?"s without response are often like blanks in the text; and as long as the story is not entirely filled with them, it remains understandable. From this point of view, the narrative of a historian is hardly different from the narrative of a novelist. The texture of the narrative in both cases is based on the same thing: actions, and a set of reasons for those actions (the agent's beliefs and goals); events, and explanations of those events.[2]

The preceding chapter discussed "why?" in the context of scientific explanations; here, we will talk about "why?" and its vital role in narratives of all kinds—from Tolstoy novels to the peasant folklore of medieval Gévaudan to the narratives that we make about our own lives.

Folk Psychology, Suspicion, and Artifacts

"Why?" can thus receive in response not only (1) a *reason-for-belief* or (2) a *cause*—and more broadly, a scientific explanation that explains an objective reason which might not be causal—but also (3) a *reason-for-action*, a goal, a "what for." This is the third and last type of "because," concluding the list of categories defining what we have called the grammar of why. This reason-for is thus a state of the world that does not exist yet but that one wants to realize: orange juice in Mickey's stomach, France liberated from the Nazis, etc. It motivates the action in a similar way to that in which the reason-for-belief justifies a belief. It explains the actions of others but also our own actions, since we must explicate it when we want to provide reasons to ourselves or to others—even if they remain implicit most of the time. Through the action of the agent, this idea of a certain situation to realize produces (sometimes) the state of the world that we aim toward. When the realization demands very few favorable conditions—like Mickey's orange juice, for example—then the final cause that is the reason-for-action will explain the realized state of the world.

Thus, notice that reasons-for-action make sense of an action whether the goal is achieved or not, and that sets them aside from causes or other reasons for events. I could tell why someone rents a sailboat, crosses the Caribbean seas, and dives hundreds of times around a small desert island by saying that they hunt for a treasure in a forgotten sunk ship, even though they never come back with a treasure. Unlike causes, which explain things or events that follow them as effects, goals, ends, intentions, and all kinds of reasons-for-action make sense of actions even when the end does not actually follow from the means.

When it demands a great number of annex causes, the goal is not always achieved and it thus does not alone constitute a good explanation of the current state of the world: thus, the goal of Christopher Columbus—to find a short maritime passage to the Indies—is not a "final cause" for his presence in India since he precisely never went there. What explains Columbus being in America is the combination of his goal and the fact that his initial geographic beliefs were wrong—namely, that India was situated across from Europe. Sometimes, the goal is achieved so that it appears as the preferred explanation of the phenomenon; and when it is not, we have to consider the gap between the state of the world and the agent's beliefs. For instance, our treasure hunter falsely believed that there was a treasure, or that the treasure was reachable.

A reason-for-action—in other words, a response to "Why are they doing that?" or "Why must I do this?"—thus includes a goal as well as a belief that justifies choosing such means for such purpose. And this is how we understand other people: by attributing *beliefs* to them, and by supposing that they have *desires*. Psychologists call this spontaneous capacity to understand the actions of others and ourselves through the dual concept of belief/desire "folk psychology"; and there are some who even think that it already existed in the mental toolkit of the first *Homo sapiens* or of previous hominids. Sometimes, the possibility of this understanding is simple: I infer the beliefs of others because they are doubtlessly the same as mine since we live in the same environment. Of course, I am speaking here of basic beliefs: for example, if I were living in Mickey's house, I would believe that the orange juice is in the refrigerator because that is where cold drinks generally are, and I would thus imagine that Mickey—being an intelligent mouse—would put it there as well. At other times, I know the desires of others because they have expressed them, or because their behavior allows me to easily infer them: the act of drinking water implies a desire to drink; that one is thirsty, in other words. Sometimes, the context helps me to interpret these desires: someone raises their hand on Fifth Avenue right next to the road; I am "seeing" them hail a taxi because this gesture here is code for this kind of request. It is almost as if they are yelling out "I want a taxi!" But other times, the goal is difficult to infer: "What are they after?", "What do they want from me?", to bring up again those questions that the subject worries about regarding the Other, according to Lacan and psychoanalysis.

Intentions target something and always have consequences—with some of these being predictable, and others being less so. While it is rational to avoid ascribing the intention of launching a worldwide pandemic on the poor soul who (according to one of the narratives about the origins of COVID-19) ate a contaminated pangolin, since no rational worldview could have predicted this outcome, it is rational to say that someone wandering in the woods with a rifle and a hunting outfit intends to kill animals. This holds even if no animals are killed (because he's a terrible shot) or if a human is unintentionally killed (again because he's a terrible shot). There is an extended moral and legal lexicon for talking about states of affairs that are our goals versus states of affairs that are related to them and that are not unpredictable consequences (such as unintended but *tolerated* situations, situations for which we are unwillingly *responsible* and to which we contributed or that we *facilitated*, etc.). This very rich language allows us to express all the nuances between "my intention is X" and "I had no intention of causing or doing Y." Elizabeth Anscombe wrote an important book called *Intentions* (1946) about the reasonings that underlie our intentions and the way we can infer them—given that they stand in between the avowed goals of someone and the set of states of affairs that could be connected to them causally and more or less predictably. It is also something that is debated in courts, when the responsibility of someone is controversially involved in some form of harm experienced by someone else.[3]

But when it is a question of figures from the past, inferring goals and desires proves to be even far less simple. Much of the context for the action is composed of other agents and their implicit social norms. When we do not know them, as is the case when dealing with history, we are sometimes barely able to say why a certain person did a certain thing; this is why historians use documents, witness accounts, and all the archival data that they can gather to answer this question.

Could the structure of this response to action-based why-questions—as it is formulated by historians and ordinary people alike when confronted with the actions of others and themselves, and which is thus based on beliefs and desires—be a conventional construction allowing for people to discuss among themselves but ultimately covering something far more profound that is kept hidden? Such an idea of a hidden truth is tempting for our contemporaries, marked as they are by those thinkers whose focus was "suspicion." Grouped together under this label at the end of the nineteenth century, Nietzsche, Marx, and Freud indeed argued in extremely diverse ways that humans are relatively absent or foreign to themselves; and that in particular, we do not know what makes us act in the way that we do. For such thinkers, our reasons are always rationalizations that come after the fact, and we are blind to our actual motivations.[4]

However, the structure itself of "Why are they doing that?" is not affected by these philosophical suspicions. Let's look at the psychoanalytic explanations that Freud puts forth. The subject has forgotten their umbrella at the store: Freud would claim this is a parapraxis, that the act of forgetting manifests an unconscious desire to see again the attractive grocery clerk who seduced the subject without them being aware of it. But still in this case, when asked, "Why did they forget their umbrella?" we would respond by saying, "Because they had the unconscious desire to see the attractive clerk again." In other words, the explanation goes back once again to a desire—even if the subject isn't aware of it. Generally speaking, the masters of suspicion certainly did away with the naivete of believing that the desires that motivate individuals are always the desires that they are aware of having. For Marx, the social situation of subjects defines beliefs and interests that orient their actions toward the preservation of their social privileges, which forms the constant object of their desires; for Nietzsche, the individual is made up of more elementary wills that struggle against each other until one imposes its agenda—which the subject will attribute to themselves as their own and which will then be rationalized. But the very grammar of "Why are they doing that?" is still the same: it is a matter of identifying desires (whether known or unknown), and of indicating the beliefs within the framework in which these desires will be tentatively realized.

Why Did Mickey Mouse Open the Fridge?

We must also note that this goal or reason-for is attributed not only to people and their actions but also to the things they make. Aristotle already distinguished two different meanings of *making*: to make an action (*praxis* in Greek, which gave us "practice")—like running, where the action does not have any independence outside of the agent; and to make something in the sense of manufacturing it (*poiesis* in Greek, which gave us "poetry")—like a bridge, a cathedral, or a painting, where the manufactured object exists independently from its maker. The "why" behind the actions we make is, as we have seen, a reason-for-action, a goal that has been distilled to belief and desire. Let's now imagine that we are in the remains of a Neolithic campsite and that we find a pointed and slender metallic object that has obviously been crafted by someone. We would probably say that it is most likely an arrow, or a weapon of some kind, that was used for hunting or self-defense from enemies. The "why" of this object—"Why is it here?" "Why does it have this shape?"—would also receive a response in terms of goals and intentions. And certainly not those of the object itself, but those of its creator: to hunt, to make war. In spite of its apparent difference, "poetic" activity (or technical, we could say) is thus explained by the same reference to a goal as practical actions. The reason why these technical objects exist is this *"what for"*—their usefulness. It is helpful to remember here that Aristotle's favorite example for illustrating final cause is an artistic production: a statue.

Understanding or Explaining

We often correctly insist on the difference between first-person and third-person knowledge: we have direct access to our interior mental states, beliefs, and desires; and only indirect access to the mental states of others. I infer the latter on the basis of their behavior, their words, and my own past behavior. But from the point of view of the question "why?", whether in regard to ourselves or others, the structure of the response is the same, invoking goals—desires, wills, etc.—and beliefs.

This type of response, on the other hand, is very different from the explanations of an event by causes, which do not allow any reference to intentions, goals, or wills. At the end of the nineteenth century, when philosopher Wilhelm Dilthey wanted to understand the specificity of the nascent human sciences—sociology, linguistics, psychology—he developed the conceptual distinction of "Explaining/Understanding." Explaining, as we saw in the preceding chapter in regard to the natural sciences, consists of showing a cause or referring to a law of nature. Understanding pertains more to the approach of the human sciences and consists in reexamining reality from the point of view of those humans who we are studying in order to see things from their perspective and discern why they behave the way that they do. Explaining is in the third person, understanding in the first—in the sense that the interpreter positions himself in the same place as this first person. Understanding is precisely the comprehension of reasons-for-action. Max Weber, one of the founding fathers of modern sociology, conceived of the idea of an ideal-type, namely, a type of individual with typical beliefs, desires, and social habits, whom we can understand, and whose existence in turn allows us to explain the social facts of his time. Think of the Protestant capitalist entrepreneur, or the religious ascetic leader, two famous ideal-types that are supposed to allow us to make sense of capitalism or some moments of Christian expansion.[5]

The sense that the explaining/understanding framework envelops that of the natural sciences/human sciences, however, is much weaker now than it was a century ago—because in economics or sociology as much as cognitive science we have explanations in the apparent form of laws that hardly can be formally distinguished from explanations in mechanics or biology. For instance, Joshua Epstein in *Growing Artificial Societies* (1996) builds up simulations of social phenomena in the form of "agent-based models"; namely, computer simulations where individuals behave according to simple rules determining their actions on the basis of what the neighbors do. (Think of a standing ovation, in which me standing up or not depends upon how many people around me do it.) He intends to artificially simulate extant social patterns, which therefore would provide us with an idea of the individual-based mechanisms yielding these patterns.

Why Did Mickey Mouse Open the Fridge?

In the same vein, population biologist Peter Turchin launched several years ago the project of a Cliodynamics: a study of human history based on long-scale quantitative data, in order to extract from them recurrent historical patterns—for instance, concerning the growth and decline of civilizations, the fluctuating intensity of warfare, etc.—and model plausible mechanisms that account for them.[6] Clearly these novel approaches to social sciences don't share an ideal of understanding why people behave how they behave, but rather focus on explaining social dynamics and patterns.

But besides sociology this doubting of explanation vs. understanding as a mark of the difference between natural and human sciences is made even more serious since parts of sociology or psychology are now extensions of the natural sciences thanks to Darwinian biology and neurology; indeed, Darwin's books *The Descent of Man* (1871) and *The Expression of Emotions in Man and Animals* (1879) gave rise to research programs that aimed at explaining human beliefs, institutions, and behaviors from an evolutionary and often selectionist perspective.[7] But for the human sciences, this understanding/explaining distinction still indicates that the knowledge of "why" often risks being heterogeneous from what happens in the natural sciences.[8]

Even though we maintain that human sciences like psychology or sociology "understand," they still do not "justify" (although it is in fashion to think otherwise nowadays). They are certainly focused on discovering an agent's reasons for action; but determining that an agent had a specific reason-for-action doesn't mean that it was a *good* reason. Understood within this context, "justifying" still concerns a moral justification along the lines of "the agent was right to do that." But *having a reason* to do something does not make it *reasonable*, that one is *right* to do so—with right and wrong being understood here in relation to a certain, often moral, norm. Justifying, in the sense of the moral justification of actions, is a different practice from that of responding to the question "Why are you doing that?" Al-Qaeda practices mass terrorism because they want to liberate Middle Eastern land from the American military, but such a reason does not prove it is good to do so *ipso facto*.

Causes or Reasons?

Goals, when considered as reasons for action, and the efficient causes of natural science are thus two types of competing and incompatible explanations. The philosopher Fred Dretske subtitled his book *Explaining Behavior*—now a classic in the philosophy of mind—*Reasons in a World of Causes.*[9] This phrase encapsulates the metaphysical problem within questions like "Why did Mickey open the fridge?" Nature is a totality of events connected by causal relationships that are possibly subsumable under natural laws; like Spinoza said, since human beings are natural things, "Man is not an empire within an empire" (*Ethics*, III, *Preface*). From this angle, can the reasons for action that we express in terms of a goal (intention, desire, will, etc.) be the real explanations for actions? After all, if human is a natural being, and if nature is entirely governed by causes, why should we add a level of "why?" that is expressed in terms of beliefs and desires?

Within the framework of reflecting on the relationships between mind and body, the American philosopher Jaegwon Kim formulated the idea of a "causal closure of physics": any physical event (the door of the refrigerator opens while Mickey's hand is on the handle) has a physical cause (the movements of Mickey's muscles, the neuronal motion that initiated it, Mickey's brain state when he thinks "orange juice in the fridge, I'm thirsty"), and this physical cause is sufficient to produce such an effect.[10] From the existence of this closure, we deduce that the reasons for action cause nothing since all the causes are already given by different physical brain and bodily states. These reasons are certainly there, and are apparently causes, but the true causal explanation of the actions is not within their domain.

Certain philosophers take this to an extreme; they eliminate the level of reasons-for-action altogether and are called "eliminativists." Following their trailblazer Patricia Churchland (the author of *Neurophilosophy* [1986]), they think that the language of beliefs and desires is as unscientific as the sentence "the sun rises and sets": it certainly helps us understand each other but pertains to nothing real in itself. Here, the real explanation of our actions would thus be the causal relationships taking place between the neurons of our brains, and then those between these same neurons and the exterior environment. In the end, Mickey has the impression that he decided to drink orange juice and de Gaulle had the impression that he chose the Resistance; but these are in fact the consequences of small events that took place between their synapses, which were themselves consequences of events within their brains, of events existing outside of them, and in the outer world. Or rather: such choices are really just these small events.

Thus, if the world is indeed a compact universe whose cement is causality, is there space for "reasons-for-action" in this world of causes? Or are goals and beliefs only a useful fiction that allows us to communicate with each other while not having any real consistency?

I do not want to go into this gigantic philosophical question that ultimately involves the question of human freedom. There is a whole subdiscipline of philosophy concerned with "free will," in which "compatibilists" fiercely fight hardcore materialists, the former assuming that humans are free to choose even though the world is a material world, while the latter claim that science proves materialism, hence determinism, hence no free will exists. Modern-day freedom fighters repeat classical debates with which Spinoza and Leibniz were acquainted. Spinoza indeed famously compared the much-praised freedom of humans to a stone that, endowed with the faculty of thought, would say "I'm free to climb down the mountain," whereas it's only undergoing the force of gravity with no way to opt out. Freedom would only be the ignorance of the determinations that move us, a stance that has been constantly repeated from Spinoza to Bourdieu and other contemporary sociologists.

A Short Insight into Free Will

The issue of free will parallels here the question of the ontological consistency of mental states debated by Churchland, Kim, Dretske, and others. Causal closure of physics, as Kim says, entails the epiphenomenality of mental states as causes, and therefore, if one assumes that to be implies to have some effect upon other beings—a quite widely shared assumption about being—the inexistence of mental states. Similarly, the determination by exclusively physical causes prevents any self-determination of the agent, hence free will as it is usually defined.[11] With Kim, Spinoza wins. *Physicalism* is the current name of this materialism supported by the causal closure thesis, and justified by modern science, in which no "nonphysical" cause (nonefficient cause, as indicated in chapter 2) is accepted. However, I doubt that the a posteriori argument from physics or biology, about which many free will unbelievers (often coming from the exact sciences) think highly, is conclusive.

Such an argument would go something like this: Our best science shows that nature is made of matter and that nothing else exists; matter is inert, its motion is determined by other matter, and so on to infinity; thus, nothing moves unless some form of matter determines it; and thus free will is impossible. But, as it has been repeatedly argued by philosophers who have seriously investigated the foundations and conditions of the natural sciences, determinism is an a priori condition for science. As we saw, Kant formulated this principle in his Second Analogy of Experience: "Everything that happens presupposes something that it follows in accordance with a rule." (Transcendental Analytics, *Critique of Pure Reason*). Claude Bernard, a nineteenth-century French physiologist whose work on experimental physiology was groundbreaking and highly influential, reflected on scientific methodology in a widely read book called *An Introduction to the Study of Experimental Medicine* (1865). He explains that "determinism" should be the principle of science because it means that the same causes produce the same effects; and that no experiment is conclusive if one does not assume such a determinism—since in this case such an experiment can show that B has followed from some intervention on A, but cannot show that this intervention *causes* B as nothing prevents another identical experiment from displaying C as following A. Experimental physiology (and by extension experimental science) in general assumes, whether explicitly or not, determinism. Thus, no experimental scientist can *prove* without logical circularity that determinism is true, since they have already presupposed it.

Why Did Mickey Mouse Open the Fridge?

This circularity argument has been put forth several times in the past two centuries. It concludes that no one can scientifically prove that free will does not exist. But also that no science can prove the existence of free will, which is excluded *ab initio* by its methodology.

Thus, it may just be that the question of whether free will exists is poorly constructed—along the same lines as a child asking, "Do aliens exist?" A Wittgensteinian would say that given the a priori impossibility of justifying one or another answer within a scientific context, it is indeed a misleading question. Personally, I would stand with this skeptical stance here. But it does not prevent us from thinking about reasons and causes; and besides any ontological questions concerning freedom, from wondering how reasons-to-act can coexist with causes as legitimate answers to why-questions within a rational discursive framework.

A Plea for the Reality of Reasons-for-Action

From my viewpoint, in order to argue for the irreducibility of reasons-for-action, we should indicate that our reasons-for-action do not follow the same logic as causality—since a goal does not explain along the same lines as a cause, which means that the latter cannot immediately render the former illegitimate. A reason-for-action indeed does not entail that the action follows from this reason as the effect follows from a cause, since the reason often consists in the intended effect of the action, meaning that the action actually causes the realization of its reason. Serena Williams (a transcendent player who has her eye on retirement as I write this) practices day and night to regularly win Wimbledon tournaments; her training puts her in a position to win, and winning Wimbledon is her reason for doing it; but training day and night is not an effect of her winning Wimbledon, which is still her reason for training so intensively. And after all, even if she does not win Wimbledon, "winning Wimbledon" is still her reason for practicing day and night. However, in contrast, if the supposed neuron-level cause of her practicing day and night is absent (these causes that eliminativists think are the only real efficient reasons on Earth), she won't practice day and night. Therefore, a reason and a cause of the same event are not competing hypothesized causes where one would eliminate the other if it were proven to be true.

In addition, in the previous chapters, we saw that causality was one thing while the justification of beliefs was grammatically something else, even though it is also expressed with "because." Then, the reason-for-action is a third thing, and it should therefore be no more eliminable by the findings of natural causality than justification was by the latter. Just as there are relationships between facts that form the justification of a belief, there are relationships between facts that are described by the term "reasons-for-action," which are relationships of *motivation*: "If Mickey has the goal to drink orange juice, he will open the refrigerator" forms such a relationship of motivation. To understand that the relationship of motivation described here is real—and as real as a relationship of justification—there is thus no need to suggest that a goal is a special entity that ideally exists "next to" the world and has concrete effects in the natural world. Thus, the goal is not something that exists alongside the causes that are "in the brain" (neural states, etc.) and does not represent an alternative cause for the drinking of the orange juice.

I won't settle this century-long debate about reasons and causes here; but the heterogeneity among three types of "reasons" as answers to why-questions is a strong argument against seeing causes as alternatives to reasons in the explanation of behavior. Eliminativism, and even the supposedly obvious "causal closure of physics," deny the pluralism of reasons I have defended here by seeing the complex grammar of "why?" as a competition for the unique proper explanation of an action. In doing so, one commits a metaphysical confusion that runs parallel to the much more classical conflation of causes with intentions—which gives rise to theological worldviews.

Moreover, in the previous chapter, we also saw that causality is far from exhausting the grammar of scientific explanation. It follows that even if the expression "reasons in a world of causes" is striking and captures the singularity of human action, it forgets the very complexity of scientific explanation itself. Within nature, there are not only causes capable of explaining things: the world of science is not just a "world of causes"; it also includes reasons that are structural explanations of facts and even of generic patterns. And this insufficiency of cause as a response to a why-question suggests that reasons-for-action cannot be eliminated by causality when they offer another answer to the question "why?" Briefly: if some explanations in the natural sciences are not causal, then pointing to reasons as explanations of an action is not at all illegitimate. In fact, it can be a *bona fide* explanation even though it does not talk about any causes, such as the neural correlate of the relevant mental state of the agent. But notice that this does not commit us to any ontological stance that would contradict physicalism, nor that it corroborates physicalism. This parallels the case of structural explanations—about which it would be erroneous to infer from their existence a commitment to some Platonism about the existence of mathematical objects.

Economy as a Theory of Action

But why are we able to explain so well the actions of Mickey, General de Gaulle, characters from movies and novels, and our friends and loved ones? Because we suppose that they are *likely* to have beliefs and goals, unlike clouds or mountains. Economists have an interesting way of understanding this massive assumption because it introduces the notion of "rationality." Let's immediately note that "economist" does not mean here a researcher who deals with falling interest rates or calculating the impact of labor laws on the GNP—but rather what has been called since neoclassical economics a theory of individual choices, which is easily transformed into a theory of action, since acting is ultimately choosing to do one thing instead of another. This theory of rational choice lies at the foundation of economic models for the actions of agents (microeconomics) but is studied mainly by a small group of economists. (It is now also being developed quite differently by some authors who claim to be closer to psychology—we sometimes speak of behavioral economics or economic psychology.)[12] It is interesting to us here, first, because it offers a rigorous and detailed approach to reasons-for-action that answer certain why-questions; and second, because it allows for us to specify certain fine distinctions concerning rationality and reasons—particularly in how it distinguishes a minimal sense of the rational agent's human reason from a richer one.

To explain the choices of agents, microeconomists suggest two types of entities—*preferences* and *utilities*. Preferences are simply the way in which one ranks their action objects from best to less good; utilities are a somewhat quantitative measure of these preferences.[13] The utility of something often has the property of decreasing after a certain consumed quantity: if dark chocolate is my favorite food, the first square from a bar will bring a higher utility—in terms of satisfaction, well-being, etc.—than the rest of it; but the 63rd square will doubtlessly have an inferior utility to that of the first one. This utility brought by item *n+1* as compared to item *n* of the same kind is called marginal utility; and as a rule, marginal utility of a given object generally decreases.

We can then assume that agents always have to choose between different combinations of a particular set of goods (for example, "chocolate only"; or "67% chocolate, 15% caramel, and 18% strawberries"; and so on). Each of these "baskets of goods" has a utility for the agent that we can calculate. For the economist, the human subject will maximize this utility by always making the choice that will bring them the maximum utility.

We thus have here a strong explanatory principle for human behavior. Of course, it is not easily applicable: in a precise case, it supposes that we know the preferences of a subject; yet in general, we know them only by the choices they make (this is called the "revelation of preferences")—which raises a problem of obvious circularity. We should also note that "goods" are not necessarily material: one can talk about the utility of a symphony, or that of the resolution of a geometry problem (for certain subjects, this is very high). Such generality allows for the near-universal applicability of the theory.

Another point worth highlighting is that the monetary value of things does not directly intervene here; it is one of the aspects of utilities, but the determination of its weight depends precisely on the subject's preferences (for some, money is almost everything; for others, almost nothing; and variations thereof).

In this sense, economics is a very powerful means of modeling—if not explaining—behaviors and choices. If the subject chose to live somewhere close to three chocolate makers, this is because dark chocolate was their preference among all possible goods. Preferences can be reformulated in terms of goals and beliefs. For example, if Mickey's goal is to drink, and to drink orange juice in particular, his preferences are ordered at that moment in such a way that drinks are preferred things and orange juice the most preferred of all—at least among all the drinks he thinks are in the refrigerator. Conversely, given the preferences of an individual, their desires will be directed toward the choices that bring them the most utility, i.e., what they prefer. And in regard to folk psychology, the economist's formulation allows us in some way to model choices and actions more quantitatively, as well as to consider finer distinctions. In particular, it takes into account the fact that the satisfaction of a desire is exposed to fatigue—like in the example of the 63rd chocolate square.

Speaking in terms of preferences and utility thus allows for us to respond in a systematic way to "Why are they doing that?" while revealing several important aspects of what an action and an agent are. Indeed, given some beliefs about the world, for the preferences and utilities to lead to the determination of a choice, only one condition is required: that the individual systematically chooses the largest utility. This is what economists call *rationality*. Such rationality requires at least one condition so that a maximum utility is guaranteed—namely, what is called the "transitivity of preferences": if I prefer chocolate to coffee, and coffee to strawberries, I must then prefer chocolate to strawberries. This may seem trivial, but when such a clause is not respected we simply cannot determine what maximizes utility.[14]

Certain people will say that humans are often irrational because their preferences are not transitive. This is more complex than it seems. For example, let's imagine that Albert prefers chicken to eggs, and prefers eggs to fried fish, but prefers fried fish to chicken: a clear violation of the transitivity of preferences and a self-declaration of irrationality. But in fact, in the first preference the eggs are prepared as an omelet and in the second they are hard-boiled—which means it is no longer a question of three but of four compared items, and that the question of transitivity no longer arises. Alternatively, when someone prefers fried fish to omelets, omelets to burgers, but burgers to fried fish, we can refine the description and say that it's one particular burger that is preferred, and that others are less appreciated. Finally, if the items are exactly the same, it's still possible to say that the compared items, when the agent fails to satisfy the transitivity of preferences, are temporally situated. In that case, we are no longer talking about a "burger," but instead a "burger at 12:17"—which means that there is no issue of transitivity since it's perfectly rational to have placed a higher value on a "burger at 12:17," but to ultimately prefer "fish at 12:33" to a "burger at 1:12." And given the fact that no actual series of choices takes place instantaneously, this strategy always works.

And so it is often easy to show that the cases presented as transgressions of the transitivity of preferences can be redescribed as standard cases. We must insist on this point because it leads to a thesis that is somewhat trivial but important: if we can constantly ask and often discover why people do what they do, it is because we assume them to be rational. Only this supposition allows us to move from actions to motives, to say that someone broke several eggs to make an omelet because omelets were at the top of their list of preferences. Yet this robustness in the transitivity of preferences, which most of the time can be saved by redescribing the basket of choices, is an epistemic problem: there may not be a way to show that an agent is irrational, which deprives the concept of rationality of any empirical content (since no empirical data can inform an attribution of rationality). Therefore, this renders the principle of rationality into an a priori principle like that of the principle of inertia—which share this same impossibility of being disproven while also providing a structuring role for science.[15]

Why Did Mickey Mouse Open the Fridge?

The Rationality of Economists and The Three Musketeers

Historians who examine documents from the past to understand who did what and why implicitly make this supposition of rationality. Up to a certain point, it allows one to imagine that people in the past acted much like we do; and that if one therefore reconstructs the nature of their preferences—which may be very foreign to us—we can understand their reasons-for-action. The principle of human rationality is at the root of our ability to understand others, to reconstruct the past, and to generally follow a narrative. For this type of understanding, it plays the same role as Leibniz's principle of reason ("everything has a reason"), which we encountered earlier when we were discussing the justification of beliefs and the explanation of events. Conversely, if we did not presuppose this and we could thus not conclude from our knowledge of someone's preferences or utilities that they would aim toward a particular goal (or rather that they did a particular action with this goal in mind), we could neither explain nor predict the actions of others—which would make our social lives much more problematic. And more broadly, since we could no longer make sense of our actions based on our goals or act on the basis of our preferences, we simply would not be able to understand ourselves.

Of course, what we have been dealing with so far concerns a minimal form of rationality, which includes the transitivity of preferences. The nature of preferences themselves, or of utilities, has not been discussed; and it is entirely possible to have preferences that many would deem unreasonable. For example, the Nobel Prize–winning economist Gary Becker's work on addiction considers certain subjects to be rational when they prefer shooting heroin to anything else and explain their behavior on this basis.[16]

Such a minimal rationality calls for three remarks:

- Beyond this rationality, we can distinguish a rationality of higher degree that concerns the preferences themselves. It is generally considered more reasonable as a preference to seek satisfaction by learning a musical instrument instead of consuming heroin (there are numerous criteria for this—sanitary, social, etc.). It is worth noting that this kind of rationality (which is probably best classified as a moral or political rationality) is less formal than that of the principle of minimal rationality.

- In this way, we better understand the difference between understanding and justifying an act (which was indicated above). Understanding means reconstructing the set of preferences of the agent—as well as their beliefs—so that the act effectively appears as the maximization of the agent's utility. Nevertheless, these preferences themselves can be considered more or less good in terms of exterior moral criteria, or even in light of their later preferences. When the minimal rationality we have been discussing is supposed, identifying an agent's preferences means characterizing their reasons; while justifying means evaluating these preferences as being more or less reasonable—in other words, showing that the agent had good reasons. The latter is related to a rationality of higher degree (sometimes called "practical," in Kant's terminology) concerning goals or preferences.

- In the end, this duality of degrees implies that the question "Why are they doing that?" can receive a dual response. It becomes, first, a question of reconstructing beliefs and desires (in ordinary language) or beliefs and preferences (in the language of economists). "Mickey took the orange juice from the fridge because his ultimate preference was for orange juice instead of water, milk, or Coke." But besides that, one can always then ask why these preferences were what they were. Here, another order of considerations comes into play. Beyond the agent, they concern the agent's society, and the historical world to which the agent belongs. In what sense?

Let's open *The Three Musketeers*. At the start, d'Artagnan comes across one musketeer, then a second, and then a third (Athos, Porthos, and Aramis)—each of whom in turn behaves in a way that d'Artagnan considers offensive. He challenges them each separately to duels in a nearby meadow and confronts them. Just as the first duel is beginning, the king's guards come and try to arrest them for illegal dueling, a fight ensues, and thus begins a long friendship between our four musketeers.

This novel's famous opening is crystal clear: d'Artagnan instigates the duels because he considers himself insulted (belief) and wants to defend his honor (desire, intention). Among his preferences, defending his honor is placed above his health and well-being. We thus understand d'Artagnan because we perceive his desires and preferences, but at the same time these seem absurd or unseemly. If I ask why d'Artagnan provoked a duel, I arrive at the notion of *honor*—of which I can then ask why it has so much importance for these people. This is a question about the formation of the musketeers' preferences. It lets us see that preferences are always historically anchored. If we have difficulty understanding the past, if its customs seem strange or unreasonable or even crazy ("What a bizarre phenomenon dueling was!" "What possessed those Aztecs to perform human sacrifices?"), it is not because they were irrational—since a minimal rationality is supposed in order to be able to give meaning to their action—but rather that their preferences seem unreasonable in terms of second degree, or practical, reason. Yet people do not choose their preferences the way a child would choose one or two treats in a giant candy shop. If d'Artagnan demands a duel, it is because duels were a solution to conflicts of honor at the time—even if they have been forbidden by order of the king in the novel; and more profoundly, it is because honor was considered an essential virtue that had to be defended at all costs, and that it was lost precisely by refusing to defend it. The very essence of duels conveys the idea that one values certain things even more than one's own life, which means that one proves one's honor by defending it at the risk of death. Today, duels are no longer even in the register of possible preferences; and honor now vies for priority among many other common preferences (well-being, personal fulfillment, human dignity, health, etc.). The fact that they were socially valued to the point of becoming a norm at the time of the musketeers thus reveals that for many—as with d'Artagnan—defending one's honor was at the summit of personal preferences.

This story illustrates a more general idea: if we want to reconstruct the preferences of agents, and thus say why they have the particular goals that they are pursuing, it is necessary to identify which preferences are available and socially valued in their world. On this point, the question "Why are they doing that?" leads us to sociology. I am by no means claiming that historical sociology fully explains the goals of agents according to their social group and historical background, but simply saying that it allows us to understand the horizon of possible preferences in which the agent will "choose" their own—with these preferences thus explaining their choices and their actions. Today, d'Artagnan would not fight in a duel because duels are no longer available at the preference store and honor is no longer a dominant social norm. Maybe he would sue for defamation; maybe he would launch a wave of hurtful messages against Aramis and Pathos on Twitter; maybe in the end he would go back home thinking of other things, like planning a squash match with friends or scheduling a yoga session. In any case, *The Three Musketeers* would not exist.

The Infinite Regression of Means and Ends

In this chapter, we have been deliberately vague about terms: desire, will, and intention are different things but all have an intentional structure—that is, a structure which aims toward a nonexistent state of the world (a goal), whose representation and valorization are a reason that the agent acts in the way that they do.[17] The causes of events respond to a particular why-question; while goals, desires, and intentions respond to a different kind of question that could be formulated as "What for?" (*Pour quoi?*). These two responses to different "why?" questions present an important structural analogy: they define concept pairs. On the one hand, we have cause and effect; on the other, we have the goal and its means. The cause causes the effect; the means produce the goal—but in addition, the goal is what motivates the means to be implemented. This second clause radically distinguishes the pair goal/means from that of cause/effect.[18]

By pursuing this parallel, we see that the goal, just like the cause, gives rise to possible iterations. Indeed, in the two cases, when someone responds "because" if we ask the question "why?", we can always keep asking "why?" The cause of the fire was lightning, the cause of the lightning was the state of electricity at that particular moment in the clouds, the cause of the state of electricity was a previous meteorological state, and so on perhaps to infinity.

We also saw above, in similarity to the language of economists, how the structure of the reason-for requires being divided into two distinct levels, two types of rationality, and two why-questions—with one concerning what maximizes utility, and the other about the formation of preferences. But if we now leave aside this language and consider our daily language and its references to goals and means, it is clear that the goal can always be the means of another goal, and so on. For Mbappé, dribbling the ball is a means of scoring a goal. Scoring a goal is a means of winning the match. Winning the match is a means of winning the World Cup. Winning the World Cup is a means of being among the best players in the world. And so on.

Like cause, the reason-for as a response to "Why are they doing that?" can be iterated in an infinite number of ways due to a purpose's reversibility, which allows it to become a means toward a broader end. But do we really mean "infinite"? Or does this regression stop at some point? Kant gave the name of an "end in itself" to those goals, which are both ends from all points of view and which are never a means to anything else.[19] For him, only a subject that is likely to follow a moral law that is given by their own reason—a human, in other words—would be such an end in itself. Before him, Aristotle—especially in his *Nicomachean Ethics*—suggested an analysis that is probably closer to what I am describing here. We have intentions and desires that—once they have been satisfied—become means to other ends in turn; but ultimately these goals are in the service of our own fulfillment, or what we sometimes call (along with Aristotle) "happiness."[20] Happiness in itself is supposed to be universal, but the subjective determination of happiness varies just as preferences vary according to subjects. However, the fact that all our different goals are ordered in the pursuit of happiness constitutes the ultimate term of the regression from means to end that we have been discussing, and which is therefore not infinite. In addition, the language of economists on the subject is almost identical: after all, what is the maximization of utility, which is what guides our actions and our choices, if not another name for "doing what makes us happy" (even if this happiness is at the cost of our well-being, our health, our comfort, our reputation, etc.—since the preferences of the agent, like those of the heroin addict, can be logically contradictory with these same values).

Perhaps the term "happiness" is inappropriate here, especially if we think of all those cases where utility is maximized but the agent looks very unhappy from the outside. Indeed, one of the lessons of psychoanalysis consists in showing that these "unconscious desires" that push us can be relatively indifferent to what is generally called happiness. Freud devoted his influential text *Beyond the Pleasure Principle* (1920) to his discovery that what he called the "pleasure principle" (*Eros*), which is ultimately driven by erotic gratification, does not govern all of human psychic life. He then went on to make a startling argument: one of the drives that governs humans is that of succeeding in dying one's own death, which he calls the "death drive" (*Thanatos*).

But let's not go further into these difficult subjects and instead highlight this simple result: questions along the lines of "Why are they doing that?" must receive answers in terms of reasons-for, or goals—which are ultimately linked to each other and articulated in one final goal, which varies from individual to individual, and whose general concept is not uncontroversial.

Why Did Mickey Mouse Open the Fridge?

Why? or What For?: Intentional Bias

I emphasized earlier the parallel between causes and reasons-for/goals; I also indicated that two different "why?"s were at play. Nevertheless, the confusion of one and the other, of "why?" and "what for?" occurs regularly in many diverse contexts. The denunciation of this confusion is even a recurring trope in philosophy.

Confusing "cause" and "reason-for" goes back to responding to the question "why?" with an intention instead of a cause, and thus of supposing that there is an agent at work who is responsible for the phenomenon that interests us. This confusion is present in many religious notions—such as all those concerned with atonement and the retribution of actions by God. Saying that someone has fallen ill because they sinned essentially explains their sickness as a punishment, and thus as the intention of a divine agent (since by definition a punishment implies someone having a will to punish).

Psychologists sometimes call this tendency of looking for intentions when causes explain phenomena "intentional bias." And if we look at the psychological development of a child, and particularly from the perspective of Jean Piaget, we know that small children respond to "why?" with intentions and agents in a rather generalized way. This Swiss psychologist also spoke of the "animistic stage"—in the sense that animism is a religion that attributes desires and goals to natural entities (plants, animals, etc.).[21] Becoming an adult thus involves progressively discerning the two registers of response to "why?" and the occasions in which one (cause, if not scientific explanation) or the other (intention, goal) must be invoked. Intentional bias thus illustrates the difficulty of separating these two registers of "why?"—even at an adult age.

The very idea of God in Judeo-Christian religions, just as much as the gods of polytheistic religions, proceeds from this kind of confusion in the grammatical registers of the question "why?" In the Old Testament, God is explicitly represented as a moral agent who is often angry, or who sometimes simply wants to put his followers through trials in order to test their degree of faith—as is the case with poor Job, who has to suffer the death of his children, the loss of his home, and physical deformation so that God can verify that he believes in God more than anything and despite everything. "Why did Job's crops go up in smoke?" would require an answer along the lines of "Because God wanted to test Job." Whether it is Poseidon vindictively pursuing Odysseus with tempests in order to prevent him from returning home, or Zeus unleashing hurricanes and lightning, the confusion between intentions and natural causes that presides over their invention is striking.

The critique of "final causes" is an essential part of the general critique of religion and morality in Spinoza's *Ethics*. In the famous pages of Book One's Appendix, he rejects all forms of explanation by intention on the basis of an ontology in which everything is effect and cause—flowing necessarily from what he calls "substance," or the reality of nature. He further maintains that the prejudice of most humans in favor of final causes creates the main moral concepts that structure their lives. He writes:

> Now all the prejudices which I intend to mention here turn on this one point, the widespread belief among men that all things in Nature are like themselves in acting with an end in view. Indeed, they hold it as certain that God himself directs everything to a fixed end; for they say that God has made everything for man's sake and has made man so that he should worship God.[22]

He continues:

> Further, since they find within themselves and outside themselves a considerable number of means very convenient for the pursuit of their own advantage—as, for instance, eyes for seeing, teeth for chewing, cereals and living creatures for food, the sun for giving light, the sea for breeding fish—the result is that they look on all the things of Nature as means to their own advantage. And realising that these were found, not produced by them, they came to believe that there is someone else who produced these means for their use.[23]

Why Did Mickey Mouse Open the Fridge?

The very usage of the concept of goal and its corollary, means, ends up occupying, in the elementary psychology of humans, all forms of relationships that they experience—often instead of the link between cause and effect.

> For looking on things as means, they could not believe them to be self-created, but on the analogy of the means which they are accustomed to produce for themselves, they were bound to conclude that there was some governor or governors of Nature, endowed with human freedom, who have attended to all their needs and made everything for their use. And having no information on the subject, they also had to estimate the character of these rulers by their own, and so they asserted that the gods direct everything for man's use so that they may bind men to them and be held in the highest honour by them. So it came about that every individual devised different methods of worshipping God as he thought fit in order that God should love him beyond others and direct the whole of Nature so as to serve his blind cupidity and insatiable greed.[24]

Spinoza's analysis only goes on to enrich the denunciation of what we have been calling a grammatical confusion by providing an anthropological explanation of this confusion and its consequences. We move from intentional bias (what Spinoza calls a "prejudice," i.e., a preference for the means/goal explanatory pair) to "superstition" as a grounding force in ordinary perceptions of the world.

> Thus it was that this misconception developed into superstition and became deep-rooted in the minds of men, and it was for this reason that every man strove most earnestly to understand and to explain the final causes of all things.[25]

But this confusion denounced by Spinoza goes far beyond religion, since it gives rise to a set of very general moral concepts that are supposed to explain everything.

> When men became convinced that everything that is created is created on their behalf, they were bound to consider as the most important quality in every individual thing that which was most useful to them,

> and to regard as of the highest excellence all those things by which they were most benefited. Hence they came to form these abstract notions to explain the natures of things:—Good, Bad, Order, Confusion, Hot, Cold, Beauty, Ugliness; and since they believe that they are free, the following abstract notions came into being:—Praise, Blame, Right, Wrong.[26]

This generality of superstition is not specific to the distant time when the Dutch philosopher was writing—one which we often associate with being rather distant from the rays of the Enlightenment. Indeed, it is not uncommon to read that "the markets are afraid" as an explanation for worrying developments concerning stock indexes, or that "capitalism is aiming toward world domination." Yet these entities—whether markets or capitalism—are not agents endowed with intentions. They are above all else the name of a number of complex and intertwined causal processes. One may say that they are only metaphors; but when they persist and settle within our discourse, they illustrate that the confusion or elementary grammatical error expressed by Spinoza had a bright future ahead of it even in the secularized West.

In other words, there is a guiding thread that runs from the child (and sometimes adult) who calls the door on which they have just banged their head "mean," to the faithful who ask God to bring them success and prosperity, to the economic journalist worrying about the markets becoming upset at the indictment of the head of a major corporation; and this thread could be described as covering up the language of causes with the language of intention. In the following chapters, we will explore how intention and causality can still, despite their differences, be articulated in subtle ways; and can sometimes produce legitimate knowledge, especially in the case of biology.

To Sum Up

This chapter focused on the third meaning of "why?" (*pourquoi?*), which could be rephrased here as "what for?" (*pour quoi?*)—i.e., in the sense of for what purpose or intention. Formulated in ordinary psychology in terms of belief and desire, or in a more sophisticated and operational way by microeconomists in terms of utility and preferences and beliefs, goal-based explanation specifically applies to human agents. It usually comes in the form of an attribution of beliefs and desires. It requires a principle of minimal rationality, which supports both the understanding of myself and the understanding of others and the past—as well as all forms of narrativity. But this minimal rationality says nothing about the rationality of the agent's preferences; and understanding others around us as well as understanding our predecessors is possibly the proper identification of preferences that seem opaque or bad at first glance.

This language of goals or reasons-for-action contrasts with the language of causes and combining them together is problematic. When we confuse them, we often produce absurd explanations.

TWO

Fusions

4

Why Do Triceratops Have Horns?

"TO DEFEND THEMSELVES FROM THE T. REX OF COURSE!" A fairly spontaneous response like this should intrigue us because it sounds like tyrannosaurs had goals in their lives. Yet we have just seen that goals and reasons-for relate only to actions taken by humans. This was not the case for tyrannosaurs, and it is doubtful that they were rational agents. Yet this language concerning living beings is generalized: the peacock's tail is there to attract females, the skin tissue between the legs of the flying squirrel is precisely used to fly. And even in regard to plants, it is said that sunflowers seek out the sun, and that flowers attract insects to their stamens so that they cover themselves in pollen and thus fertilize other plants. Discourse about purpose, utility, and more technically "function" (eyelashes have the function of protecting the eyes, kidneys have the function of eliminating toxins) is consubstantial with biology. But is it a good answer to questions about flower stamens or the horns of the triceratops?

Animals, Plants, and Machines

In regard to why-questions, it seems that living things do not behave like the rest of nature. The paradox did not fail to preoccupy thinkers from the Scientific Revolution such as Descartes—who were the very people who theorized the restriction of science to efficient causes, and thus excluded final causes from "natural philosophy" (as the science of nature was called back then). Descartes is famous among French high school students for having developed the so-called "animal machine" concept, according to which animals follow the same laws of mechanics as machines and nothing else. Usually, students are somewhat shocked by this: "My cat is not a machine, he understands me and has emotions!"; "My dog feels guilty when he does something stupid!" There is nothing to suggest that Descartes was less sensitive than these teenagers, but his argument responds to a central conceptual need: reconciling the illegitimacy of final causes in science and the appearance of goal-directed behavior seen in animals. Since machines are also oriented toward a goal (that which is programmed by their designer) while clearly not having a will or intention of their own, they provide a good model for thinking about animals.

A simple example is enough for us to understand the Cartesian line of thought. Traditional thinkers, following the original driving forces of physiology and medicine (the Greeks Aristotle and Hippocrates, and the Roman Galen), believed that animals contained a specific internal heat source that was essentially different from any form of physical heat, and that it came directly from their immaterial soul and allowed them to move. Descartes disputed the fact that this fire had anything exceptional to it:

> Thus, I say, when you reflect on how these functions follow completely naturally in this machine solely from the disposition of the organs, no more nor less than those of a clock or other automaton from its counterweights and wheels, then it is not necessary to conceive on this account any other vegetative soul, nor sensitive one, nor any other principle of

> motion and life, than its blood and animal spirits, agitated by the heat of the continually burning fire in the heart, *and which is of the same nature as those fires found in inanimate bodies*. (Descartes, *Oeuvres Complètes*, AT XI, 202, my emphasis)

Descartes is often presented as a foil to those who argue that biology is a truly special science that cannot be understood by physics and chemistry alone—these "vitalists" or more generally "anti-reductionists" (since they did not want to reduce life to matter, even if they often thought that the idea of an immaterial vital principle was excessive). But Descartes actually believed in two related ideas. The first, in connection with metaphysical reasons, was that everything in living bodies operated under the laws of mechanics (which he moreover helped in developing). But for Descartes, secondarily, there existed a fundamental ontological difference between extension—which is the essence of what we call matter—and thought. There is an infinite difference between these two things, which were moreover for him the only two types of things that existed in the universe. As humans have both a soul and body, these things are somehow united in us but just how remains a great mystery. Animals do not think because they have no language (their not having a language being our reason for not ascribing thoughts to them); they are therefore entirely matter and thus entirely governed by the laws of mechanics.[1]

But the machines we make are a good model for understanding animals. With these machines, Descartes formulated a fundamental heuristic which modern biologists still discuss: the analogy with the artifact. In fact, each era has constructed a biology that resembles its techniques for explaining the world.[2] Thus, for Hermann Boerhaave—a major physiologist from the early eighteenth century—the universe of mechanical machines provided biologists with their lexicon: "We find in the body supports, columns, beams, bastions, levers, corners, integuments, presses, bellows, filters, channels, troughs, reservoirs. The ability to perform movements by means of these instruments is called function; it is only by mechanical laws that these movements are made, and it is only by these laws that they can be explained" (*Institutions of Medicine*, I, 121). In the nineteenth century, organisms were regularly considered through the lens of electrical machines, with a major interest in the role of the nervous system. This was the case with Claude Bernard—whose *Introduction to the Study of Experimental Medicine* (1859) became as we know the vade mecum for the empirical method in science. In the twentieth century, all of molecular biology and genetics bore witness to the power of computing, with most of its notions (code, program, instruction, memory, etc.) coming from the world of computers—which was in full development at the time of the discovery of DNA (1953).

This analogy with machines, or technical artifacts, indeed allows one to inquire about the nature of any structure since they generally always serve a purpose within a greater machine. The Swiss scientist Albrecht von Haller, whose *Elements of Physiology* (1755) is one of the classics of eighteenth-century physiology, declared that the physiologist's intellectual task was "anatomical deduction": to deduce a structure's function from its description.

In fact, physiologists have rarely been genuine *iatromechanists*—the weird name given to those who truly subscribed to Descartes's mechanicist ideas. *Using* this analogy is one thing (and an extremely common thing at that: who has never explained to a child asking "why do we have to eat?" that we are like cars and need fuel to in order to run?), but *justifying* it is something else entirely.

The goals of a machine don't pose any problems for us since we know that it was designed by someone: as such, they are the goals of the designer. But no engineer constructs living beings; and the fact that they grow by themselves constitutes, at least according to Aristotle, the difference between living things and technical objects. How then can we support this analogy with machines if not as a heuristic—an aid to understanding and discovery—that provides an often easy way to identify functions? But in this case, two big problems arise. First, why must this heuristic be limited to living beings? For example, we could clearly say that during the water cycle the heat of the sun tries to evaporate water from the oceans and that the earth has the function of absorbing rainwater and spreading it in groundwater. However, in our earlier examples, we saw that this language of utility and function seems to provide a fairly legitimate answer to the question "why?" in the case of the triceratops but rarely elsewhere in physics. Second, if the machine is only an analogy, can we really talk about the function of an organism's structure? The function is what the designer has planned for the machine and its parts; thus, in the absence of a designer, there would exist no function strictly speaking, thereby leaving only things that we humans see in our own functional way.

For Descartes, the justification of the machine analogy goes back to theology: God is the engineer who built animals and plants, like man with his machines. And his own system provides a proof of the existence of God—prior (logically) to the consideration of animals.[3] Even if Descartes's particular arguments for the existence of God and its truthfulness are not universally shared, this strategy—which consists in assuming that some divine architect has determined that every part plays a role in an animal or a plant—is common for classical rationalists.[4] Leibniz was one of the first to use the term "organism" to designate living beings or in any case the special form of arrangement that they represent;[5] he distinguished between "artificial machines" made by man and "natural machines" made by God—with the former resulting from a finite intelligence and the latter from an infinite one and therefore infinitely organized. Every part of an animal or a plant is in reality a small machine whose parts are organized *ad infinitum*, as is illustrated by the following famous sentence from his *Monadology*: "Each portion of matter may be conceived of as a garden full of plants, and as a pond full of fishes. But each branch of the plant, each member of the animal, each drop of its humors, is also such a garden or such a pond" (§67).

God and Russian Dolls

Writing at the time when the first microscopic observations were being made by the Dutch scientists Leuwenhoek and Swammerdam, Leibniz developed a metaphysical theory that appears strange to us but which makes it possible to understand the fecundity of the machine analogy: the so-called preformation theory; and more precisely, the version of it that is called the "preexistence of germs."[6] Since Aristotle, the formation of living beings has always been something quite mysterious. Observation under the microscope of the spermatozoa present in seminal fluid inspired several thinkers of the time—Leibniz being foremost among them—with the idea that these "animalcules" are what the organism will become in miniature. And, like Russian dolls, that these animalcules contain their own gametes in an even smaller version; and that the gametes of those even smaller animalcules will have in them a still smaller version, and so on *ad infinitum* for all of their descendants. God thus built all living beings at the origin of the world, endowing all their structures with their functions so that these living miniatures could develop throughout the whole history of the world without needing to add anything essential to the process that God had initially laid out.

The theory of the preexistence of germs perfectly justifies seeing animals as machines made by God, and thus endowed with many functions that all aim toward allowing them to exist and to reproduce (since it is necessary for the miniatures of their offspring, and the offspring of the offspring contained within them, to develop in turn). But many scholars ended up rejecting this dominant idea at the beginning of the eighteenth century, with the best known among them being Buffon and Maupertuis.[7] According to them, the structures of living things do not preexist within their embryogenesis and are instead constructed through a regulated exchange with the physico-chemical environment. This second theory is called *epigenesis*. We may note that the opposition of "epigenesis vs. preformationism"–in other words, the opposition between the idea of a preexisting form and the idea of the construction of form through the interplay of various forces (both chemical and physical) during their development—is a constant one in biology, just like the one mentioned earlier between mechanisms and vitalists.[8]

But preformationism is not as ridiculous as it may appear. Of course, no one believes in this Russian Doll theory anymore; and our best theory about how an organism develops involves genes and genomes. However, the most reductionist version of this theory—which was in vogue until the 2000s—described genes as a parentally inherited program or set of instructions present in the zygote that directed development toward adulthood. As such, it was a modern version of the preformationism of Leibniz and his contemporaries, where "shape" is replaced by "information."

Be that as it may, in the absence of a God who created the living (possibly in the form of Russian dolls at the beginning of time), the justification of the machine-like analogy is no longer self-evident. Are we really allowed to say that the function of the triceratops's horns is self-defense? Likewise, are we able to maintain that the goal of an eagle tearing through the sky toward a defenseless sheep is to capture and then eat it? Or that the dog that chews on our shoes or brings us its leash wants to go out for a walk? In our modern post-Galilean, post-Newtonian, post-Kantian science—a science in which God guarantees nothing—how is it that we can truly use these action verbs (hunting, gathering, fleeing, supplying, etc.) to respond to why-questions pertaining to the living world?

Darwin, Natural Selection, and Adaptation

In the end, wouldn't all of these statements and answers that invoke the function of wings or the kidneys, the courting strategy of the peacock or the hunting strategies of the cheetah, simply be opportunities to confuse causes (those that are necessarily physical) with goals or intentions—something which Spinoza so forcefully denounced? This is not the case, because we are all Darwinians, in the sense of the often-quoted aphorism from the Russian biologist Dobzhansky that "nothing makes sense in biology except in the light of evolution." But how could Darwin and the

Darwinians dispel our concerns here about a triceratops's horns, or the pistils of a flower, or how hawks hunt?

To better understand this, let's refer to the Reverend William Paley. Darwin was a great admirer of Paley's treatise on natural theology from 1802, *Natural Theology or Evidences of the Existence and Attributes of the Deity*. A natural theology is a theory that infers the indispensability of the existence of God from the complexities of the world—or what Kant calls "physico-theological proof." In nineteenth-century England, a place and time full of naturalists and bird connoisseurs, these wonders of the world generally belonged to the universe of the living. Paley thus knew how to very accurately describe the subtle mechanisms by which, for example, orchids ensure that the insects that feed off of them will also fertilize them. Yet if we look back at animal-machines and anatomical deduction, we see the same correlation of justification and explanation that was discussed back in the first chapter. Physiologists can infer from the shape of a wing that it is used to fly—and thus explain it—because they know that birds are machines built by God, and that He endowed his structures with specific functions. Conversely, natural theologians like Paley are justified in their belief in God because the observations that wings are used to fly, that the ball joint is used to rotate the knee, and that the eyes of vertebrates allow them to see (in other words, that everything in the living world seems to have a function or a utility) indicate an intelligent and benevolent cause—namely, a God.[9]

Of course, we do not need to wait until Darwin to see criticisms of this. Without being fierce materialists, many thinkers questioned these arguments of natural theology. In particular, in his *Critique of Judgment* from 1790 (one of the few major philosophical texts devoted to life before Darwin[10]), Kant advanced an interesting distinction between what he calls "relative" purposiveness and "internal" purposiveness (§63). When we say that grasshoppers are food for starlings, or that horse droppings are food for flies, we are establishing a relationship of purpose and utility between two different species. But ultimately, Kant says, these relationships can be arbitrarily drawn between any species and thus have no final cognitive value. Indeed, they hardly say more than Marcel Pagnol's joke that plane trees were made to provide shade for *pétanque (bocce)* players, or Bernardin de Saint-Pierre's apparently serious argument that melons had been previously divided into slices by God so that they could be eaten *en famille*.[11] These are the very same confusions that Spinoza criticized in the Appendix which was quoted earlier at length. But "internal purpose," according to Kant, is attributed only in relation to a given organism and its parts: a part, or an organ, seems to be there for a specific purpose. This is indeed a "final cause," since the effect explains the cause: for example, the mating success of a peacock explains why its caudal appendage is multicolored. But unlike relative purposiveness, it is very difficult for biologists to do without these kinds of statements—these functional attributions that make up a good part of physiology.

For Paley, these functions prove the existence of God. More fundamentally, they indicate in a general way what he calls "contrivances"—a term describing multiple parts that appear to be forced to fit together for one same purpose. To take up a classic example from Kant in a 1764 text called *The Only Possible Argument in Support of a Demonstration of the Existence of God*, the eye is composed of hundreds of separate parts (lens, retinas, muscles, nerves, corneas, etc.) and vision would be impossible if any of them were only slightly different. It is therefore difficult to think that this is all due to chance; for if we imagine being given all of these pieces and assembling them at random—regardless of even whether vision would be possible or not—the probability of ultimately having a functional eye in the end would be almost zero.

The contrivances appearing throughout living nature thus indicate that the parts of living things are "made for" something; and Paley, like all natural theologians, infers a divine intelligence from this since chance seems to be once again excluded. Moreover, these contrivances can be more or less complex; and obviously, with increasing complexity (like with the eye, for example), the inference toward divine intelligence only becomes stronger.[12]

This adjustment is not only internal to the organism between constituent parts and organs; it also takes place between the organ itself and its environment. Thus, among all possible colors, the polar bear is as white as the surrounding ice, which allows it to more easily stalk its prey. Cheetahs and lions are the color of the savannah. The dolphin and the shark—creatures which move rapidly under water—have similar hydrodynamic shapes even if they are not closely related (one is a mammal, the other an "elasmobranch" fish). This is what is traditionally called adaptation, in the sense that organisms are adapted to their environment. And adaptation is sometimes amazing: researchers recently understood that fish living in the Antarctic Ocean, where water is a cold as −2°C (salt keeps the water from freezing), are able to prevent ice crystals forming in their blood (which would mean certain death) by producing a protein that is similar to the antifreeze we put in our car engines.

The same theological reasoning as that behind "contrivances" would be applied by Paley and his contemporaries in regard to the polar bear. Among all the possible colors, the polar bear is white, which allows it to hunt more easily. How can we possibly explain this perfect coincidence when any other color had the same possibility of being produced? Here again, we are thinking in terms of final causes: the pairing of the bear and its outer appearance—an effect of it being white—is imagined to be the cause of its color: it is white *in order to* hunt.

Physiologists identify and dissect *functions*; seventeenth- and eighteenth-century naturalists like Linnaeus, Buffon, Jussieu, and Réaumur study the *adaptation* of organisms; while theologians are amazed by these things and use them to prove the existence of God. As was mentioned earlier, functions and adaptations seem profoundly finalist, or "teleological," as philosophers have pointed out repeatedly since Kant. Darwin, in his 1859 *Origin of Species*—which proved that species descend from one another—presented a solution to this enigma of biological finalism that did not resort to God and did not shock the scientific meaning of causality, as we will soon see.

It is often said that Darwinian evolutionism caused a scandal because it included man among the animals; Freud famously spoke of this as a "narcissistic wound."[13] Without denying certain resistances to the idea, we must note that Darwin's genuine novelty was the argument that natural selection (which he was the first to discover, along with the less well-known figure Alfred Russell Wallace) was responsible for the evolution of species—the very idea of an evolution having already been conceived of by figures ranging from Lamarck to Darwin's own grandfather Erasmus, and already had several followers. However, evolution could still be considered the result of a divine plan of improvement, thereby keeping it within the realms of acceptability for those with a theological mindset. Natural selection, on the other hand, broke definitively with the shadow of God in living nature. Indeed, with Darwin, the process he called "natural selection" explained both adaptation and the functions of organisms without having to resort to any form of divine intelligence while also avoiding the crutch of pure chance as an expository measure. How can this be?

The "Paramount Power of Natural Selection"[14]

In order to figure out the connection between natural selection and adaptation, let's imagine a population of a certain species, rabbits for example. All rabbits are slightly different from each other, as well as being slightly different from their parents; this is what we call *variation*. Rabbits produce offspring that look more like them than other rabbits but that do not copy them; this is called *heredity*. Now let's consider a particular property of rabbits like running speed. This influences the chances of survival for rabbits—because the faster they run, the less likely they will be eaten by foxes. Supposing that running speed is heritable (which is indeed the case[15]), rabbits who run fast will live longer and therefore produce more offspring, who will in turn run faster than other rabbits in their particular generation (because of heritability). Thus, in generation after generation, the proportion of fast rabbits increases in the population; and since a few of the young rabbits can be expected to eventually run faster than their parents, the average speed (as well as number) of these rabbits will also tend to increase. When someone says that natural selection explains the running speed of rabbits, they are talking precisely about this process. Rabbits are adapted to a world where foxes chase them; thus, *natural selection explains adaptation*. This is the major Darwinian argument about adaptation—and a key aspect of purposiveness in biology.

Let's note three things here. First, why would this running speed not increase infinitely? To answer this, it should be highlighted that the main frame of reference for competition for running speed is not that of the rabbit and the fox, but that among the rabbits themselves. As a joke much loved by biologists goes: "Two scientists are in the jungle. A tiger comes. One says, 'A tiger! Let's run!' The other replies, 'It's useless, he can run faster than us.' The first one responds, 'But I don't care about running faster than the tiger! I care about running faster than you!'" And since a rabbit that runs much faster than the foxes expends more energy than one who simply runs a little faster than them, it will have less energy than the latter to, for instance, produce offspring—thus leaving behind fewer offspring to fill the population with its genes. This same reasoning tells us that through natural selection the speed of rabbits has a tendency to stabilize at a rate that is slightly higher than that of foxes.[16]

Second, natural selection is fundamentally a population-level process, and not an individual-level one. As Darwinians say, *individuals* never evolve! They develop—meaning that they go from an egg stage to an adult stage. Only species evolve.

Last, simple variations (from one generation to another; for example, from adult rabbits to their offspring) are not spontaneously directed toward the traits that would be best for the organism. Our parental rabbits do not always produce rabbits that run faster and faster; they just produce rabbits that look like them more than others. If variation, on the contrary, produced rabbits that run faster than foxes for generation after generation, the "rabbit" species would not need natural selection to achieve a running speed that is adapted to foxes. Variation is random—or like biologists say, "blind." Despite this random quality (random in the sense that nature does nothing for the good of organisms), if given enough time, and enough variations, the process of natural selection ends up producing the adaptation of organisms to their environment.[17] A current major controversy in the area of evolutionary biology consists in discussing the extent to which some variation processes can be seen as Lamarckian, in the sense that they feature processes through which new variants tend to be better adapted on their own.[18] This is an ongoing scientific controversy, which does not crucially affect my cartography of "why?" and the way adaptation is a "why?"

When the adaptations are complex, the accumulation of selections will account for them. It is the selection of those variations that are always the best from each generation over a long period of time that allows for the production of an organ as sophisticated as the eye—to which Darwin devotes a passage purely with the intention of refuting the classic argument of those who believe that the complexity and the functionality of life require an "intelligent designer." Likewise, Darwin's argument was reinforced by an article in 1989 using a computer simulation to demonstrate that the production of a vertebrate's eye from small simple cells was plausible as long as they were slightly more sensitive to variations of light than other small cells and that development did not take an excessively long amount of time.[19] Paley's "contrivances," which were unattainable solely through chance and its aimless processes, are thus explained through cumulative natural selection. And Darwin will go on to devote an entire book to orchids in 1862 (*On the Various Contrivances by Which British and Foreign Orchids Are Fertilised by Insects)*, these flowers whose different reproductive systems present countless examples of such complex arrangements.

Even though natural selection is the major *explanans* of many features of the biological world (including *adaptation*, as well as species *diversity*—since a multiplicity of environments yields an even larger multiplicity of adapted species), there are still major controversies about such explanation. First, what does "explain" actually mean? And to what extent does selection explain? Biologists used to conceive of natural selection as a force or a cause. Thus, philosophers often inherited the view that selection is a force—for instance, Elliott Sober, in *The Nature of Selection* (1984), which was a milestone in the philosophy of evolutionary biology. Actually, the first modern evolutionary biologists themselves (who created the so-called Modern Synthesis—see below) oscillated between "forces," "causes" (e.g.,

J. B. S. Haldane, *The Causes of Evolution*, 1949), and "factors."[20] More recently, the so-called "statisticalist interpretation of natural selection," put forth by philosophers Mohan Matthen, Tim Lewens, André Ariew, and Denis Walsh, contested that selection is a cause. They contend that multiple interactions such as eating, dying from parasitic disease, and reproducing represent what is causal; and the "force of selection" is constituted by the aggregate of these interactions. However, nothing exists in addition to these causes that would explain the changes in traits within a population.[21] A second dispute concerns *what selection explains*, even if it's not a cause *proprio sensu*: the diffusion of a trait (which is the minimalist characterization of its effect), the spreading of an allele, or the arrival of a particular trait in a population.[22] These debates bear important consequences for the practice of science itself. For instance, if selection is not a cause of the emergence of novel adaptations, then their causes should be thought of at the level of individual developmental physiological processes—a position systematically developed by Denis Walsh recently.[23] But such controversies do not directly matter for the current issue of deciding to what extent answers to why-questions about biology should legitimately include intentional or teleological wording.

Natural Selection and Biological Functions

The Modern Synthesis unified the Darwinian theory of evolution with Mendelian genetics (Darwin did not know about genes, which were suggested by Gregor Mendel in 1880 and discovered as a material reality named DNA by Rosalind Franklin, James Watson, and Francis Crick in 1953). The natural selection process conceived of by Darwin thus received an explanation in genetic terms; evolution is shaped by changes in gene frequencies in populations, mostly under the effect of natural selection.[24] But the substance of the Darwinian argument—at least with respect to the explanation that it provides for biological adaptation—does not change. Granted, philosophers and biologists disagree about how exactly this allelic frequency change should be understood: is it evolution itself, or an effect of evolution, or its cause?[25] I won't delve into this problem here; it encompasses metaphysical issues about the proper theory of causation, as well as the biological question of whether selection targets genes or organisms.

Natural selection, the explanation of the sometimes complex adaptations of organisms, ultimately justifies these familiar yet scientifically shocking teleological statements that rely on purpose in the study of life. To fully understand it, we must remember that the very notion of biological "function" often has an explanatory use: to say that "the function of the kidneys is the elimination of toxins" explains why one has kidneys. It is even for this very reason that Spinoza would see a departure here from good scientific method since there is an apparent final cause: the effect of the kidney (the elimination of toxins) explains its cause, namely the existence of the kidney.

But we Darwinians have a scientifically acceptable reformulation of this. Indeed, the vertebrate kidney exists because it has been favored by cumulative natural selection—exactly like the running speed of rabbits or the structure of the eye—and the reason it was selected was that it allowed for the elimination of toxins. To say that a feature, a part, a behavior, or an organ has a function X is not an appeal to divine intention; it is a simple affirmation that the effect X is the reason for which this trait was selected as it gave its bearers a selective advantage (i.e., a longer life than others, more opportunities for reproduction, etc.). And this proposition reformulates the final cause in terms that are much more acceptable as they are based on a long-term scenario involving the history of the population of the first vertebrates—among which the kidney evolved. This idea—initially formulated by Larry Wright and called the "etiological view of functions"—makes "the function of the kidneys" something perfectly legitimate scientifically, since it encompasses a causal explanation of the kidneys.[26] Therefore, like all causes, functions are ontologically robust; they are part of the "furniture of the world," in the sense of Russell's old phrase. And functions encompass *norms*—since when something has a function (like the kidney or a tire), it can also malfunction while still continuing to have its function: flat tires, diseased kidney. Karen Neander and Ruth Millikan developed this realist view of functions (realist in the sense that functions exist in real-life terms) by emphasizing that norms set by functions exist in nature—which in turn allows us to posit epistemic norms (such as "truth") and to therefore naturalize epistemic concepts such as intentionality.[27] This is called the teleosemantic program, which was embraced by Fred Dretske, Daniel Dennett, and Ruth Millikan among others.[28]

Some philosophers disagree with this interpretation of functional statements. For these "causal-role theorists," "the function of the kidney is to eliminate toxins" does not explain the presence of the kidneys, but rather the evacuation process by which an organism gets rid of harmful substances. The question answered by functions is not "why do we have kidneys?" but "why are we able to get rid of these substances?"—which in turn is part of the general question: "why are we able to remain alive despite our intake of toxins?"; which is ultimately a sub-question of "why are we able to stay alive?" Different why-questions therefore license a different understanding of the concept of function: namely, a function is the causal role of kidneys within the process of toxin evacuation. More generally this means: "The function y of X is its contribution to a certain general process Y, proper to a general system S to which X belongs." This implies that whatever system S is chosen, there will be another function of X. Therefore, "functions" depend upon the choice of an explanatory system S, and are not something that exists in the world, as functions do within the context of etiological theories. This lack of realism implies that functional norms are only in the eye of the beholder, thereby preventing philosophers from using this account of functions to naturalize norms (as the competing account of functions does).[29]

I won't explicate these theoretical differences in making sense of biological functions any longer. The debates are still raging among philosophers; but it suffices to say here that function harbors both realist and less realist accounts, and has a legitimate status within biology.[30]

This debate—which relies on distinct ways of understanding the explanation required for questions like "why do we have kidneys?"—already indicates that there exist several ways of answering the question "why?"

in biology. Together with this duality of the question "why?" embedded within functional ascription, consider someone asking, "Why is my hair growing?" Two types of response are possible and both are correct. The first would list all the physical processes through which scalp cells secrete keratin that then becomes hair. The second would indicate that hair is a defining trait for mammals, and that it was selected because it offers protection against variations in temperature. Ernst Mayr, one of the architects of the Modern Synthesis, theorized this difference by speaking of *proximate* causes and *ultimate* causes.[31] The first response to "why?" discusses proximate causes—that is, causes that are specific to the existence of an individual of the given species; it states efficient causes in exactly the same way as chemistry does. The second response concerns ancestral populations of the species in question, and is "ultimate" in this sense; it essentially discusses evolution by natural selection. I used the example of the triceratops earlier because the first type of response is almost impossible since we do not know much about the physiology of the triceratops; this leaves us with ultimate causes (evolution), and there we can provide an answer. It is also in this kind of answer that living beings—from the scientific point of view—present interesting characteristics, such as functions and adaptations, which are not essentially found in physics or chemistry. Notice that the former way of understanding "why" allows one to talk about "functions" as causal contributions to a mechanism (for example, the function of secreting follicles in growing hair); and thus as "causal role" functions instead of "etiological" ones, which instead fit with the latter kind of why. Hence, discussions concerning function in biology can be divided into two meanings that correspond to the two kinds of causes as defined by Mayr.

Interestingly, the first answer encapsulates the mechanism of hair growth, while the second addresses its function—in the sense of the etiological account that was just sketched out. Mayr claims that only the second one is proper to what's alive, and epistemologically characterizes biology as a whole: evolution by natural selection is what distinguishes the living from pure matter. The mechanisms through which (etiological) functions are implemented are, at all levels, complex physicochemical systems. This latter claim is often challenged, especially by philosophers who argue that molecular biology is different from physics and chemistry because it features emerging properties. Others (e.g., Laland et al. 2011[32]) contest that the ultimate/proximate difference is accurate, because some phenomena occurring in the lifetime of an individual organism—such as its development (namely, the process through which it goes from zygote stage to adult stage)—have an evolutionary relevance and thus pertain to both ultimate and proximate causes. But in any case, this difference has an interest in classifying explanations; and therefore, the meanings of "why?" If it proves to be misguided, an additional layer of complexity would be brought into our cartography of "why?"[33]

Functions, Artifacts, Agents

Let's summarize: if there is a population of individuals who have heritable properties and who are variable in regard to these properties, if this variation is not directed toward what is adaptive, and if these properties give their carriers a higher or lower chance of survival and reproduction, then evolution through natural selection will take place in that population.[34] And insofar as living beings result from natural selection, they will be adapted to their environment. This means that there is no need to presuppose an infinitely intelligent engineer in order to see physiological functions in an organism's structure. The webbed foot of the duck has the function of water propulsion. This can be easily explained through the hypothesis of a selection of bigger and bigger interstitial tissue between the toes, as compared with the feet of the ancestors of ducks who lived outside of water. The features of organisms are thus both close to what an engineer would create—the wings of an eagle resemble those of an airplane, the shape of a dolphin resembles that of a submarine—and somewhat different; because, as was pointed out by François Jacob and Stephen Jay Gould among others, natural selection must always start from a previous state.[35] It is a "tinkerer" (Jacob), managing with whatever is at hand; and not an engineer, who can procure the best materials that may be required. This is why, for example, the eye of vertebrates is not perfect: it has a "blind spot"—namely, a point that is entirely unreceptive to light because the optic nerve occupies it, a result of the ancestral state from which this organ evolved. There is no doubt that an engineer with access to all of the materials they would have wanted or needed would have done differently and better.[36] Thus, one answers the question "why do eagles have claws?" by invoking their function and ultimately natural selection. However, the same response in a slightly modified way is also suitable for questions about apparently dysfunctional traits (or, as biologists say, "maladaptive") like, for example, "Why do we sometimes swallow the wrong way?" (Answer: Because the trachea and the esophagus lead to the same cavity—since, in order to "build" a trachea, natural selection had to graft it onto the already existing esophagus of aquatic vertebrates.)

But the explanatory capacity of natural selection does not limit itself to making rational this analogy with machines that physiologists have used since Galen; it can also justify an intentionalist or finalistic language in which goals are attributed to organisms without conscience or intellect. Let's look at birds, for example; their clutch size was one of the major themes of what is now called "behavioral ecology"—the study of the behaviors and traits of organisms based on the assumption that they result from natural selection.[37] For most species, this size varies little: each season, they lay around four to five eggs per nest. In the 1940s, the biologist David Lack performed in-depth studies of many bird species in England (great tits, starlings, etc.) and accumulated data in this way. He then wondered why the number of eggs was what it was.[38] One would imagine that natural selection would increase the number of eggs—since the more that there are, the more descendants there may be. But in fact if there are too many eggs, the competition between them becomes too high and the chances of survival suffer for all of them. In the end, the clutch results from a trade-off between these two tendencies—with the added consideration that a female bird that exhausts itself too much over the course of a season is at a disadvantage with other females that "reserve" their strength for the following season. This ultimately suggests that there is an advantage in the strategy of not laying too many eggs even if they all survive, and the size of the nest stabilizes at around 4–5 eggs per clutch.

Everything thus happens as if the bird were trying to maximize its number of healthy offspring over the course of multiple seasons—just like we saw with rational agents and how they maximize their utility, and how therein lies the matrix of responses to the question "Why are they doing that?" Natural selection thus allows for us to consider that poorly intelligent organisms like many birds (and even those devoid of cognitive abilities like insects or plants) behave like rational agents. However, instead of maximizing their utility, the former maximize, roughly speaking, their number of offspring—or, in the language of biologists, their "fitness." More generally, if animals seem to make decisions insofar as their decision-making mechanism has been forged by natural selection, it is legitimate to think that the decisions they make can be modeled as the choices of a rational agent maximizing a utility defined by its "fitness." This takes place without the animal in question having any awareness of it, since natural selection has "built" it that way. Thus, life itself is a domain where causes surprisingly look like purposes because of natural selection. But they are not, since we generally do not attribute cognitive capacities to dinosaurs, and certainly do not do so with plants, amoebas, or mollusks. And if one objects that only conscious beings can perform the complex cognitive operations required to execute rational decisions, they should be reminded that our brain constantly conducts very sophisticated cognitive tasks of which we are unaware.[39] Thus, the process of selection mimics the intentions of a cognitive agent at the level of a population across multiple generations, and then individuals in this population appear as cognitive agents.

Samir Okasha, in *Agents and Goals in Evolution*, recently examined the following two ascriptions of goals in evolution: organisms as intentional cognitive agents, and selection itself as an optimizing agent.[40] He argues that while the latter faces many theoretical issues, the former appears justified to the extent that a "community of purposes" between parts of the organism can be asserted. But the parallelism between maximizing fitness as a criterion for selection in choosing phenotypes, and maximizing utility as a criterion for rational agents in choosing options, instantiates a deep affinity between natural selection and rationality. Beyond the etiological account of function, which relies on a reference to natural selection, we see here (as Maynard-Smith famously wrote about in his seminal book about evolutionary game theory[41]) that there is a close connaturality between economics and biological evolution—which ultimately allows us, to some extent, to treat biological why-questions as intentional why-questions.[42]

The evolutionary viewpoint here supports an account of animals as somehow rational beings. This has been strongly and independently advocated by Susan Hurley, who inquired about the "space of reasons" possibly inhabited by animals; she claims that it is the "space of action," not of "conceptualized inference" used in epistemic frameworks.[43] Therefore, she argues that animals can be rational in the sense that they act *for reasons*, even though they lack conceptual abilities (and therefore can't represent their reasons). Their rationality is "context-bound": they can base their actions upon transitive preferences about particular things in a context, for instance mating, but can't generalize this transitivity across all contexts.[44] The idea that animals have some practical rationality appears as a point of convergence between Hurley's philosophical analysis of rationality, and an examination of the assumptions of behavioral ecology.

Organisms as Social Agents: The Extent of Altruism

Nevertheless, by providing a genetic understanding of heredity, modern biology introduced an additional subtlety. Sometimes, like bad economic agents, organisms act in ways that are contrary to their interests and in seeming contradiction with what we just claimed. Why do they do this? Why are most bees sterile? Why do male praying mantises let themselves be eaten? Why do vervet monkeys yell out loudly to warn the group if they see a predator (at great risk to themselves) instead of discreetly fleeing? The explanation lies in a somewhat esoteric formula called Hamilton's Rule, which is a mantra for biologists interested in cooperation and expressed as $br - c > 0$. In the equation, c is the cost for the individual, b is the benefit for another (the queen, for example), and r is a coefficient that expresses genetic relatedness.

The whole point here consists in taking into account not just the reproduction of the individual but also the impact that their actions have on those who are closely related to them—since there is a good chance that these relatives will pass on the same genes as the individual would (or, at least, more of these same genes than unrelated individuals). This is called kin selection, a concept introduced by William Hamilton in 1963 and perhaps the most significant advance in biology since natural selection.[45] Thus, being sterile while working to help the queen fertilize, the bee will leave more of her genes behind than if she produced her offspring (because in the unusual bee kinship system, a bee's sister is genetically closer to a bee than a potential daughter—even though "how close" depends upon which species of bee is considered, as there are hundreds of bee species and their kinship systems often differ).

In the living world, everything thus happens as if organisms were aiming toward maximizing their so-called "inclusive" fitness, which is defined in the Hamiltonian equation by the relationship of br and c (i.e., the genes left to the next generation by themselves and by their close relatives, linked by the degree r, that they help to reproduce). When someone asks "Why are bees sterile?", it is thus legitimate to answer that it helps the queen to procreate as much as possible—although bees obviously do not have cognitive abilities that would allow them to explicitly make such a plan. One can thus think of organisms as economic agents trying to maximize their inclusive fitness even if they are as brainless as an oyster or a plane tree.

Biologist Alan Grafen recently defended the legitimacy of seeing organisms as "maximizing agents" on the basis of a formal correspondence or "isomorphism" between models in behavioral ecology (which focuses on the evolution of the fittest phenotype) and population genetics models (which capture the dynamics of allele frequencies).[46] Such correspondences do not always hold; but in principle, it would provide behavioral ecology models (framed in terms of optimal responses to environmental demands) with a guarantee that they explain the result of an actual process of evolution by natural selection instead of a mere speculation about phenotypes. Those isomorphisms would therefore realize a mathematical proof of a correspondence between natural selection as a process involving *gene* change, and adaptation as a concept concerning *organisms.*

Granted, the quest for a mathematical justification of the idea that natural selection in principle creates organism *design*—as long as all circumstances are satisfied—is as old as Ronald Fisher's work in population genetics. For him, in his *Genetical Theory of Natural Selection* (1930) a "Fundamental Theorem of Natural Selection" is proven, which states that the fitness increase due to natural selection between two generations is always positive; and thus, selection by nature increases fitness.[47]

In practice, fitness may not increase if the environment deteriorates enough at the same time to counterbalance it, for example when the selected traits themselves change the environment in ways that harm their capacities for flourishing.[48] Fisher's theorem was met with much opposition.[49] By integrating kin selection Grafen's view takes into account those cases where selection is frequency-dependent, which can appear as improving the prospects of Fisher's project.[50]

Notwithstanding the ultimate limitations of using it as a justification, the maximizing agent analogy brings our attention to agency as another aspect of the conflation of two meanings of "why": the cause, and the intention. Determining to what extent the 'maximizing agent' is an analogy remains an open question. Some philosophers adopted a very different perspective than the Darwinian view put forth by Grafen or Okasha, and argued that agency is a major ontological category required for understanding what organisms are and do. Walsh's *Organisms, Agency and Evolution* (mentioned earlier in this chapter) develops a view that is far more realist regarding agency than what Grafen proposes, since for him agency is more than an analogy. If organisms are indeed agents—which would result in the ontological category of agency being far more widely distributed—major ethical consequences would follow. The jury is still out on the exact ontology required for the use of agency concepts in biology.[51]

Limits to Purposes and Agency in Biology

The illusion of final causes that Spinoza denounced therefore has no place in biology, even though biologists constantly use apparent final causes and would find it very difficult to formulate their speech differently. However, natural selection and Hamilton's Rule (which states that, considering an allele, adding the payoff it provides to its bearer to the one it provides to the others, mitigated by their degree of relatedness to the former, determines its being selected when it is positive) underlie a legitimate language in which both the analogies of the machine and of the economic agent are authorized and thus allow science to say the why of phenomena—even though the proper metaphysical interpretation of such agency is still disputed.

It should not be inferred, however, that final causes are completely authorized in biology and that living beings are therefore here for some purpose. The German poet Angelus Silesius said as much three centuries ago: "The Rose is without why." How can we understand it? How can this rose—which I look at, whose perfume I smell, whose variety may have received the name of a famous actress or tennis player (as is common among thousands of existing breeds of roses)—be without a why? On the contrary, it seems like we know very well why roses exist: we can reconstruct the ancestors of the species and their evolutionary history; for the same reasons, we know why roses have thorns (protection against fragrance-attracted herbivores) and why petals are arranged the way that they are (pollination). The life cycle of the rose, the way it reproduces, and the way its flowers bloom and wither annually are all well-explained through evolution by natural selection. These traits can be compared with conifers like fir trees, whose leaves do not fall because the high mountain environment where they live imposes very different selective pressures on plants. In the case of our rose, let's attribute some of its specificities to its gardeners—

who through techniques such as hybridization, stem cuttings, and artificial selection created the rose that they had been wanting. Finally, in a broad sense that is becoming increasingly precise, we can also explain how a rose seed develops into a rose given the right environmental conditions by tracing how the seed's genome responds to environmental stimulation by triggering a certain number of embryogenetic processes (cell divisions and differentiations, morphogenesis, etc.). According to the two registers of ultimate causes and proximate causes that Ernst Mayr distinguished (respectively represented here by evolution and development) we thus have a substantial set of answers to the question "Why *this* rose?" So was this Silesius just a crank?

In reality, the Silesius's *warum* deals with something else. Roses bring happiness: some sing odes about them, and others want to share this joy and offer them as gifts. This has reached a point where they have become a symbol of love—or rather of all the variants of the feelings of love, namely passion (red) and tenderness (pink). That a flower can bring so much happiness thus suggests that it is there precisely for such a reason—whether to sing the glory of the Creator, as generations of theologians maintained; to satisfy our aesthetic appetites; or to help people seduce each other if we believe books about popularized evolutionary psychology. However, this intuition must be resisted, which is what Angelus Silesius understood: the rose is there for nothing, without aims nor whys. The fact that it blooms and enchants us simply comes as a free extra, a supplement to the long evolutionary and developmental process that led it to our eyes and nostrils but that was directed by no external goals.

But Wait . . . Why Life?

We have just seen that the living world authorizes a more flexible application of final causes thanks to Darwin's theory of natural selection. Rival ideas, which are sometimes called "intelligent design," have become unnecessary in accounting for the functions and purposes of animals and plants.

Why Do Triceratops Have Horns?

But as a modern Paleyan might retort, if final causes for living beings belong solely to a purely natural order of things that is without intentions or goals—like we see in physics and chemistry—why does life exist? Is this life, where purposes and functions are only natural properties without an intentional agent to explain them, not the result of a project or goal similar to that of a divine creator? Although natural selection may explain the horns of the triceratops, the wings of birds, or the size of nests, it can hardly explain life. After all, even with the existence of heritable traits through reproduction, "before" life there was no reproduction and thus no natural selection! And regarding the basic facts of living—for example, the fact that a cell reproduces and harbors a metabolism that requires a plethora of coordinated and simultaneous molecular operations—are they not so complex that their appearance simply due to chance is unthinkable? And despite the vastness of the known universe—with billions of galaxies hosting billions and billions of stars, many of which are accompanied by exoplanets whose number, for us, has multiplied by twenty in recent years—we have not found any sign of life on any other planet (although our ability to detect life on exoplanets remains limited). Doesn't this Fermi paradox, as we call it, prove that the unique life seen on this planet was infinitely improbable? And doesn't this improbability require an explanation?

Honestly, the Paleyan scores a few points here. In his book from 1971, *Chance and Necessity*, which is an essential text for anyone interested in biological theory, the molecular biologist and Nobel laureate Jacques Monod concludes that the two fundamental theoretical advances of the past century—namely, molecular biology and the modern theory of evolution—come up against two unknowable things (for now): the emergence of thought in the brain, and the origin of life. Decades later, all of our research programs into the origin of life—whether by reproducing it *in silico* or *in vitro*, by looking for it in exoplanets or in the multicolored hot springs at the bottom of the ocean—have not yielded a consensus. The few extant Darwinian theories concerning the evolution of prebiotic molecules have not been unanimously accepted.[52] Should we thus interpret the question "Why life?" as "What is life for?" given the absence of scientific theories that incontestably explain its origin?

But the Paleyan asks his question poorly here. We know a great deal about the horns of a triceratops, or why a duck has webbed feet; we know much less about the exact nature of life. Without going into too much detail, I will simply indicate that even the cardinal properties of metabolism and reproduction are perhaps poor characterizations of life: mules, which are sterile and thus do not reproduce, appear as being very much alive; and viruses—which are strands of DNA that some say are alive—have no metabolism (it is activated by entering a host cell). Additionally, if all life on Earth is composed of molecules of carbon, oxygen, hydrogen, and nitrogen, does this make them necessary conditions for life? Similarly, since genes are made up of DNA, should we expect a different form of life to also involve this molecule as the foundation of its heredity? There is a whole scientific field called "Artificial Life" where researchers look for what life *in general* would be like if it were independent from the contingent fact that it is implemented in these C, H, O, and N–based molecules. Artificial Life operates mostly on in silico models but also includes research done on "protocells," which are chemistry-based.[53]

The problem here is that there is no definition of life. Moreover, some Darwinians think that just as a "cow" is defined as "any individual that descends from the first cow," living is defined as "any individual born from the first living cell"—which effectively excludes the possibility of "life" on a different planet. Others adopt the ideas of François Jacob, who wrote the following famous sentence in his groundbreaking book *The Logic of Life*: "We no longer question life in laboratories," implying that questions about the nature of life were no longer a matter of true science and were instead purely metaphysical rambling.[54]

Granted, molecular biology superseded all speculations about the nature of life, restricting scientific inquiries to explanations concerning the interactions between DNA, RNA, mRNA, as well as other molecular vehicles. This bears a striking similarity to when psychology emerged as a science in the nineteenth century by focusing on the dispositions and operations of the mind while getting rid of the notion of a "soul." The fact that "bio" figures in the word biology does not mean that life exists any more than "psyche" remaining in the name psychology proves the existence of a *psyche* (a term generally translated as "soul"). And some philosophers subscribe to this idea, arguing like Edouard Machery that the question of the definition of life is poorly constructed.[55] Others like Christophe Malaterre argue that the question of the nature of life as deciding between life and nonlife is ill defined; we rather have a set of marks of life that may be found together, but often are not satisfied at the same time—along the lines of Wittgenstein's idea of a "family resemblance" that he used to make sense of concepts like "game," which can't be defined by an appeal to necessary and sufficient conditions for being a game.[56] (This view is probably the closest to what derives from the perspective I will argue for now.)

In any case, these issues are fiercely debated. For our purposes, I would just like to highlight that occurrences of life in the universe strongly depend on what we mean by the word "life." As a result, the very question of the frequency of life in the universe—and from there, that of the probability of life and its common or unique character—is not just a matter of fact but instead depends on conceptual suppositions concerning the very notion of life, suppositions that for the moment cannot be confirmed or invalidated since they condition the only facts that are likely to test them.

I call this problem "definitional fragility," and it has its roots in the philosophical issue of the reference of terms. Let's give an example by taking a common object like a motorcycle. I can give several definitions of a motorcycle: a motorized vehicle with two wheels, a two-wheeled vehicle with a combustion chamber larger than 50 cc, a two-wheeled or three-wheeled motorized vehicle, a motorized vehicle with saddle and handlebars, etc. Each vehicle that is considered as a motorcycle may be a little different from the others. For example, three-wheeled scooters and motorized bicycles may count as motorcycles according to certain definitions but not according to others. Some may even consider the Renault Twizy—an unusual vehicle with four wheels and a convertible hood—to be one. But overall, the cases that vary according to different definitions are quite rare when compared with the mass of things that are universally considered to be motorcycles. In this sense, the concept of the motorcycle is definitionally robust. On the other hand, where "life" is concerned, modifying the characteristics involved in its definition greatly changes what we will consider living or not. Let's explain this in more detail.

One often distinguishes between two families of definitions of life, with each emphasizing one of two salient properties of most organisms we know: *metabolism* and *inheritance/evolution/information* (these three things go hand in hand: evolution assumes inheritance and relies on gene changes, which in turn embodies information, in some sense).[57] This partition is often used to classify projects about the origins of life, depending upon whether they have to account first for metabolism (the circular process that handles external materials—turning them into the organism itself while keeping its major physiological parameters stable)—or evolution.[58] If metabolism is used as the essential definition, viruses (or the internet) may not seem alive, but ecosystems or Earth could; if evolution is used as the key notion in the definition, then viruses and the internet might be alive[59]—but not Earth[60] or termite mounds, which nevertheless regenerate themselves in such a way that the idea is not so absurd for some biologists.[61]

This is definitional fragility: changes in the definition excessively affect the extension of the concept—that is, the range of things to which we ascribe the defined property (in this case, life). Definitional fragility here entails a major consequence: it is not possible to robustly estimate the extension of "life" in the universe. Is it really extremely scarce, as Monod asserted? If this question can't be answered, then the claim that life is extremely improbable makes no sense either. To this extent, all explanations of life that refer to some design which operates on the basis of an impossibility to explain a phenomenon that is extremely unlikely within the laws of nature are not sound since they explain an unestablished fact. Under these conditions, our Paleyan—who argues that there is an intelligent design behind not only living forms but also behind life itself—is not able to assert unconditional premises in support of his inference of a creative intelligence.

Why Do Triceratops Have Horns?

Additionally, definitional fragility raises conceptual issues for exobiology—since this discipline assumes some idea of life in order to recognize living things when we are exposed to them. It raises similar issues for Artificial Life, because there are many options for research programs that aim at fabricating life in general (since the reference point "life in general" appears fragile).

In the end, "Why life?" now seems like a poor question; and by extension, questions along the line of "Why X?"—where X presents an elevated degree of definitional fragility—no longer count as legitimate why-questions.

To Sum Up . . .

Living beings are adapted to their environment: why are they adapted? We explain why they have their parts by assigning functions to them, which places them in the domain of final cause. Is this possible when nonhuman nature has no intentions or purpose? Can this be explained through a simple analogy with machines, or a metaphor? The concept of natural selection justifies this way of describing nature: a function is a selected effect. It explains the adaptation of organisms to their environment. It legitimizes how we use the analogy with machines, as well as the metaphor of the rational agent when applied to mindless creatures, even though some would confer a higher metaphysical weight to this biological agency. On the other hand, to say that life on Earth has a purpose or a function *simply does not make sense.*

5

Why Did World War I Happen?

"BECAUSE ARCHDUKE FRANZ FERDINAND WAS ASSASSINATED in Sarajevo on June 28, 1914." High school history books generally answer with something like this. However, there is a problem with this response despite the subject being so well known: many historians highlight the fact that the war would have happened regardless of this event. Does this mean that it is really the right answer?

Historians and Their Quest for Causes

World War I perfectly captures the essence of what a historical event is: occurring at the scale of several entire societies, it had major consequences that reverberated throughout the rest of the twentieth century. It therefore typically represents an object of study for historians, and the question that opened this chapter has motivated many of them. Philosophically speaking, it is a singular fact and one can reasonably think that history is primarily concerned with singular events (the French Revolution, the collapse of the Soviet Union, etc.)—even if a better familiarity with historians will let one see that they often go on from there to study more general things, such as "How do revolutions happen?"; or to analyze the long-term course of a subject like "the evolution of the West's relationship to death."[1] A singular fact is distinguished from general or universal facts like "a stone will fall if you drop it"; asking "why?" about the former will thus largely differ from "Why do stones fall?", whose answer allowed for us to study the scientific way of responding to the question "why?"

From the outset, the answer to "Why a singular fact?" can hardly be a nomological deductive explanation showing how the fact follows from the laws of nature. Even if this explanation existed—showing, for example, how the initial conditions of the universe and the laws of nature led to World War I as a logical consequence—it would doubtlessly be too complex for us to understand, or to even be stated. Of course, the principle of rationality—which is not exactly a law but still appears as a universal statement—is involved in all understanding of human action; but even if it plays the role of a law in deductions based on historical facts, in which, for example, the preferences of the agents would play the role of initial conditions, far too many other facts that are independent of human rationality come into play and prevent us from being able to formulate a good *nomological* explanation.[2] It is thus more natural to assume that "Why did World War I happen?" will receive an answer based on certain *causes* accompanied by mentions of the beliefs and desires of certain actors.

Is the assassination of Archduke Franz Ferdinand on June 28, 1914, such a cause? The arrest of conspirators and then the discovery of the involvement of the Serbian government resulted in an ultimatum issued by Austria-Hungary (whose emperor was an uncle of the murdered archduke) to Serbia. War quickly ensued; and the strong alliances between the many surrounding countries plunged Europe into a conflict that was initially specific to Serbia and Austria-Hungary. It seems fair enough to say that the assassination caused World War I.

With different alliances, however—if, for example, Serbia had had the same allies as Austria-Hungary—the war would have been different or nonexistent. It is thus easy to see that the assassination of Franz Ferdinand would not necessarily have led to a world war on its own. On the contrary, a whole precise geopolitical configuration was needed to create such massive and disastrous consequences. As such, the Sarajevo assassination could not have been the cause of world war without the existence of certain geopolitical conditions provided by the era.

This example illustrates a major distinction that is very useful if we want to account for both the fact that World War I happened because Franz Ferdinand was murdered; and that if the world had been different, the murder would not have had this consequence. This distinction is that of "triggering causes" and "structuring causes," which Fred Dretske introduced in his book *Explaining Behavior* (discussed in chapter 3). The latter represent those conditions that allow for the former to have the effects that they do. Thus, the spark created by the firing pin that ignites the gunpowder tucked inside the shell casing of a bullet—which is then projected at great speed and distance—is a triggering cause; the design of the gun itself is a structuring cause. Without the structure of the gun—if, for example, the barrel were a hollow sphere or a very short pipe—there might be a pop or an explosion but a bullet would not be successfully fired. The question of knowing which causes are important does not make much sense in this respect: without triggering causes, nothing happens; without structuring causes, the triggering ones do not trigger anything. And so with our question about why World War I began, we must respond by indicating the two orders of cause: the attack itself and the geopolitical structure of Europe on the eve of the war—the trigger and the structure.

The Return of Possible Worlds: Contingency, Destiny, and Martina Navratilova

But once this is stated, things become a little complicated: the assassination itself, in this context, turns out to be a rather anecdotal cause. At the time, the major European powers had traversed so many profound mutual antagonisms—ranging from territorial issues (especially in regard to their various colonies around the world) to economic concerns to historical bad blood (such as an underlying French resentment toward Germany)—that the Sarajevo shooting was, as the French say, *La goutte d'eau qui fait déborder la vase* ("the drop of water that made the vase overflow"). Yet this implies that if the assassination had never taken place, a similar event would have created the same catastrophic consequences.

In this sense, if we recall the definition of causality in the counterfactual sense from chapter 2—"if there had not been A, there would not be B"—the attack was not even a cause of the war since this definition is not satisfied. If the attack had not happened, there would still have been a war because we would have found another pretext to butcher each other. And if we use the terms from above, the structuring cause was thus so conducive to war that the triggering cause was no longer a cause at all since almost anything else could have played that role.

To understand this apparent paradox, we must look into the metaphysics of events and facts.[3] Metaphysicians distinguishes between "fine-grained" and "coarse-grained" events.[4] What do they mean by this? World War I fits at least two descriptions: "The War of 1914" (after all, a war between the same protagonists starting a little before or a little after the real date would still be "World War I"), and "the war started on June 28, 1914, by Austria-Hungary's declaration of war." These are both the same event of course. But the second description is defined with a much higher degree of finesse since it is distinguished from all other wars that may have been started at different times—while the former is differentiated only from peace in 1914. This first event is "coarser," covering a much broader portion of time, and potentially corresponding to many "fine-grained" events. We can go on to imagine still coarser-grained events (like "war in Europe") that enfold the coarse-grained event in question among other similar events.

These differences somehow overlap with the differences between contrast classes found in chapter 1 when we dealt with the semantics of causality. Here the fine-grained event "World war started on June 27, 1914" would contrast in some inquiries with other fine-grained events such as "A world war started on September 1, 1914," so that the Sarajevo assassination, cause of the fine-grained event, answers "Why World War I at this moment rather than later?" In turn, the coarse-grained event "World War I in 1914" contrasts with coarse-grained events such as "no war in 1914," and a cause of such coarse-grained event (namely, the geopolitical situation that rendered it almost inexorable) would answer "Why a war in 1914 rather than peace?" And the most general why-question here would be "Why war in general?", and would bear on a very coarse-grained event (namely, "a war"). This question could be an issue addressed by social scientists rather than historians.

Thus, the Sarajevo assassination itself in no way causes the coarse-grained event "First World War in 1914." Whatever may have ultimately been the trigger, it was essentially caused by the structure of European geopolitics. For its part, the fine-grained event "World war started on June 27, 1914" was indeed caused by the shooting in Sarajevo; if it had not taken place, the war would have presumably erupted but on another day and thus this specific fine-grained event would not have occurred. I am aware that all of this may sound like byzantine or scholarly subtleties. But the stakes are high. Grammatically speaking (in the sense of our "why?" grammar), "Why this war?" or more generally "Why such a singular event?" can receive different answers depending on the granularity of the event and whether it is considered fine or coarse. From a metaphysical stance, we are dealing with what is called inexorability. The 1914 war such as it took place (the fine-grained event) seemed to have been a case of bad luck: if Gavrilo Princip had missed his target, the Kaiser would not have wanted to punish Serbia, the infernal machine of alliances would not have been set into motion, and there would have ultimately been no such war! In line with Pascal's aphorism about Cleopatra's nose—which claims that if it had been shorter the course of world history would have changed—the twentieth century would have been entirely transformed if the trajectory of a tiny piece of metal had deviated by one centimeter. Certainly. We are after all in the realm of the absolutely arbitrary and the totally contingent. On the other hand, the "coarse" event—namely, the 1914 war in general—seemed inevitable; anything could have ignited it. There are thus degrees of necessity, which make it so that events seem increasingly necessary as their grain becomes coarser.

Why Did World War I Happen?

On a much larger scale, this world war resembles what is happening in our own lives—not to mean that life is war (although this may depend on who you talk to), but rather that it is sometimes difficult to defend one's self from a dizzying sense of contingency: "If I hadn't missed my train, I wouldn't have met that Russian on the next one; he wouldn't have lent me his chess set; I wouldn't have learned how to play chess; and I wouldn't have become Bobby Fisher." (It is possible I made this story up, but it illustrates my point well.) But other times we feel that in one way or another our lives would not have been fundamentally different if certain important encounters had not taken place: "If I had taken the train as planned, I would have arrived at Freiburg im Breisgau; at the central station, I would have seen Iranians playing chess; because of my clear fascination with the pawns as they slowly moved across the chessboard, one of them would have asked me to play," and you can guess the rest.

This feeling of necessity corresponds to what is sometimes called the "nature" of a being—a nature that is assumed to express itself very similarly in a broad range of different situations. Some philosophers talk equally of an *essence*. For the phenomenologist Edmund Husserl, the *essence* of a thing is seen when we imagine different changes affecting this thing.[5] The changes that transform it into a thing that we no longer recognize thus indicate, through the negative, what makes up its essence. A black swan is still a swan; a featherless swan remains one too. But a scaled swan that lives underwater contradicts a swan's essence. Likewise, the nature of a thing is what determines that its behavior remains relatively identical across a wide range of possible situations. Let's look at another, and more interesting, example: Martina Navratilova, who once dominated the world of women's tennis. If we were asked "Why did Martina train so many hours a day? And why did she keep competing? And why did she keep winning?", the answer "it was in her nature" may seem empty, but it expresses a necessity (namely, her being the best in the world) that is quite distinct from contingent events such as winning at this or that tournament against this or that player.

Contingency ("It came close to . . .") and necessity ("Whatever happens, this would have taken place") thus go hand in hand here. And to understand it, as well as the meaning of "because of its nature," it will be useful to look at this notion of possible worlds that we owe to Leibniz and David Lewis. A *necessary* event in this framework—namely, one that cannot not take place—is therefore an event that occurs in all possible worlds, or rather in all those that share the same natural laws: stones fall if they are dropped, the Earth's sky is blue. An event that would take place in a very wide range of possible worlds similar to ours would not be necessary strictly speaking, but would inspire a fairly legitimate impression of necessity that we could call *inexorability.* A contingent event is an event that takes place in our world (the so-called "actual" world) and perhaps in a very small number of possible worlds: the jacket I am wearing today is blue, Donald Trump became president of the United States. More precisely, inexorability means some kind of uniformity across close possible worlds, with respect to coarse-grained events (for example, all the possible worlds close to the actual world in which a "first world war" happened). If we know that an inexorable set of events is taking place, we also know that in almost any of the close possible worlds it is also taking place; whereas a contingent event is such that it may or may not happen in a close possible world (see fig. 1). There are ways of providing formal analyses of this notion that would use the mathematical theory of measure (Lebesgue-Borel) and state criteria to formalize the meanings of "almost any" and "close possible world." This is not the place to delve into such technicalities. It should suffice to say that this mathematical measure theory is also the basis for the formalization of probability theory; therefore, one can see how these considerations about modalities—possibility, inexorability, and contingency—will stand in accordance with probability calculus. In fact, they are more general, and may even hold when the requisites for applying probability calculus are not met.[6]

Why Did World War I Happen?

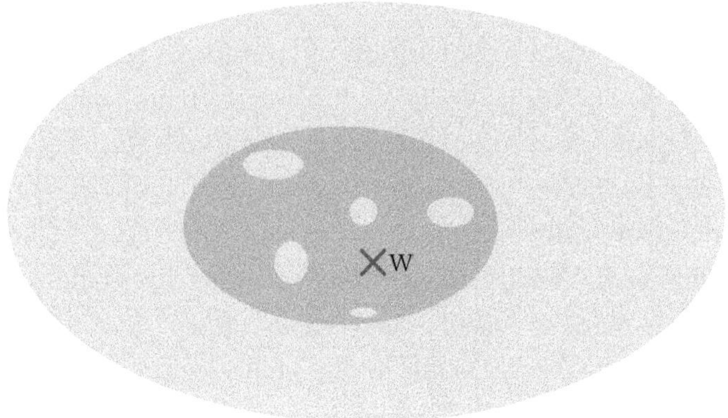

Figure 1. **A representation of the inexorability of an event X occurring in the actual world. The plane stands for a universe of possible worlds around actual world W. In the darker inner oval, worlds where the focal event X occurs; in the lighter outer oval, worlds where X does not occur. (Each world is a dot in the space.) Around W, the set of worlds is darker almost everywhere.**

Inexorability, Natures, Essences, and Kinds

As we saw with Martina, inexorability may ground the concepts of "nature" or "essence." Granted, many philosophers since Frege have dismissed the notion of essence. Assuming that the essence of something X (in the sense of an answer to the question "what is it?") really exists bears a heavy metaphysical weight. Some would reject it as a hidden form of idealism: in addition to the particular thing X, the essentialist philosopher posits an idea that exists by itself and that is instantiated by this thing. In any case, the fate of "essences" depends upon one's understanding of the status of the question "what is X?", and therefore engages questions concerning *the reference of terms* (here, the name X).

But by talking here about *natures*, and the nature of particulars (events, things, persons), I am not committing to any theory about essences: "natures" refer to a specific structure of the set of possible worlds within which something X is referred to. It might be that some natures are also what is meant in certain philosophical accounts by "essences"; but if one denies any essentialism, "nature" is still a term that can be used. Moreover, there exists a major debate in philosophy about the meaning of "natural kinds" existing in the universe, and how we can identify them (that is, a property P is a natural kind if it captures an ontological feature of the world—like "to be a stone" or "to be in gold"—and not just a conventional assemblage—like "being-a-truck-or-a-garden").[7] If some properties are natural kinds, then they should relate to general natures in the way that is sketched here; namely, they should feature the inexorability-style structure of possible worlds I highlighted. But I leave the exact account of "natural kindness" open within this particular framework.

My account is also neutral regarding biology: the "nature" of Martina Navratilova is not necessarily some set of biological properties, or her DNA, or her genes plus a few other factors that are supposedly less bound to environmental vagaries. Many nonbiological things could be robust across possible worlds; and the question of what constitutes such a nature in each case and for each particular is an empirical one, which can be addressed through our knowledge of natural and social regularities.

Back to Inexorability and Contingency

So what does my portrayal of contingency in Martina Navratilova's life ultimately convey? Her winning Wimbledon in 1982 belongs to the current world and to a very few possible worlds (as soon as we modify certain events connected to our world that pertain to this event, it no longer takes place). But if we now look at the set of possible worlds that are similar to our own—where Martina Navratilova has a similar origin and education, where there are tennis tournaments, where the rules of tennis competition and rankings are unchanged, and where the pool of other tennis players is the same—she will end up atop the world tennis rankings for a similar amount of time because she will have won many other tournaments (often against Chris Evert Lloyd in finals or semifinals). The feeling of contingency thus concerns the realization of a fine-grained event (e.g., winning the French Open in 1985 after a hotly contested final with Chris Evert Lloyd) in our unique actual world; the feeling of inexorability concerns the fact that the coarse-grained event of remaining a top player over such a long period of time—which contains the particular fine-grained event in question among other possible end results—is realized in most parts of the possible worlds that are close to our own. The two feelings coexist because they translate two distinct orders of metaphysical modality, and because they concern two different structures of the set of possible worlds. Regarding contingency, we focus more on fine-grained events—which means that the pattern of inexorability described above, tied to the corresponding coarse-grained event, no longer holds.

Thus, in the next chapter, we will be discussing a very different situation where contingency and inexorability are completely disconnected—a situation that will ultimately give rise to the birth of the metaphysical idols that were presented at the beginning of the book.

To Sum Up

Explaining a singular event implies identifying the triggering causes and the structuring causes. The event may be fine or coarse, and the causes will not be the same. A coarse-grained event that would be identical in a large zone of possible worlds due to the constraining power of structuring causes is inexorable. A very contingent fine-grained event takes place in a very small zone of possible worlds surrounding our own, but can realize a coarse-grained event that will itself be inexorable.

6

Why Did Napoleon Lose at Waterloo?

"BECAUSE MARÉCHAL GROUCHY, WHOM HE WAS EXPECTING on the western front, arrived late due to a poor transmission of orders, which allowed Blücher's Prussian army to safely come to the assistance of Wellington's British forces that were already engaged against the French empire's army." This is the common answer summed up in a few words, an answer which admits a fundamental property found in intentions and goals: namely, that they can fail. Napoleon, one of the greatest military strategists in history, had devised a remarkable battle plan; but this single detail about Grouchy's delay (as well as some others that we will go into) thwarted it and Napoleon lost. Any historical narrative must come to terms with this possibility and thus retranscribe and reconstruct intentions in order to measure their effectiveness—their rate of success, so to speak—in the world. Napoleon's defeat can be understood by the arrival of Blücher's reinforcements for Wellington, as well as by the too important role that Grouchy's troops had within Napoleon's own battle plans.

Chance, Causes, and Plans

We must note that there is an asymmetry here in the answers to "why?" When an intention is realized, it seems to be a sufficient answer unto itself. But when it fails, what is happening is not explained; and on the contrary, it is necessary to resort to explanatory causes (in this case, namely, to ask what events could have undone the Corsican emperor's plans).

After the case of Sarajevo from the previous chapter, we now find ourselves in another entanglement of the necessary and the contingent within a narrative. Grouchy's delay is paradigmatically contingent: it might not have happened if we trust the various arguments about the different forces and strategies at play presented by historians; however, the problem (for Napoleon) is that it did. The contingent seems to have no "why" from the point of view of reasons-for-action; instead, it features a poor connection between intentions and sets of natural causes. In a more general sense, the case is as follows: a near infinity of events happens every second; among these events, we notice Grouchy's delay because it ran counter to Napoleon's plans and incurred terrible consequences for the empire's army. It was bad luck for the emperor. To call something "chance" or "luck" thus does not mean that there is no cause (after all, everything has causes); but rather that this supposedly random event has a strong link with what interests us (Napoleon's battle plans) while not having causes that have a direct physical or logical connection with it. This is why, when commenting on Aristotle, Antoine-Augustin Cournot—a major contributor to the early philosophical understanding of probabilities—viewed chance as an encounter of independent causal series.[1] Of course, this very independence is not absolute or metaphysical since all causal series go back to the origin of the universe as their common beginning; but it remains in any case an independence within the time scale that concerns us here. And better still, according to this definition, causal series encounter series of reasons-for-action without a logical connection. Here, independence is thus metaphysical because reasons-for and causes are heterogeneous: reasons-for are ideas (beliefs, intentions, etc.); causes are facts or events in the world. Thus, these two things can't be mixed, and their independence means something more than the lack of a direct causal process that connects them.

To say that "chance caused Napoleon to lose" is obviously a misnomer since chance is neither the name of a force nor the name of an event. But such an expression does mean something—namely, this precise complex structure that intermingles multiple causes; intentions; and the expectations of whoever is telling the story and describing the events, and who is thereby selecting certain events and certain intentions as being significant rather than others.[2]

The Map and the Territory of Waterloo

Of course, the defeat of Napoleon is complex and Grouchy's delayed arrival is only one aspect of it (otherwise, the many historians of the period would be out of a job). Specialists enumerate many other facts that contributed to it; and one of them in particular seems to be a perfect example of the role of contingency in the fabric of history. The Battle of Waterloo took place on the plain beneath Mont-Saint-Jean, and Wellington's forces were positioned on the mountain near a farm of the same name. Another farm called La Haye Sainte was situated one kilometer to the south. The map used by the French was of poor quality, and the Mont-Saint-Jean farm was mistakenly indicated as being where La Haye Sainte was—resulting in major consequences. With the extra distance created by this error, the French cannonballs that were aimed at the British soldiers systematically fell short since they had a margin of error that was less than a kilometer.

We can thus see how a single detail—a minimal cartographical error—played an enormous role in Wellington's resistance to the empire's army, and thus in the final victory of the British and Prussian forces. We can imagine how different the world would have been if Napoleon had won at Waterloo, continued his second conquest of Europe, and perhaps forced the Prussians to surrender and the British to agree to an armistice. This cartographical mistake is a typical contingent fact: a reproduction mistake is a detail, and there exist many possible worlds that are very close to our own in which everything is exactly the same at the moment where Napoleon entered into battle except for the map. In all of these possible worlds, the rest of the battle would have resulted differently. This contingent fact thus had disproportionate consequences.

Formally speaking, the defeat at Waterloo thus differs from the case of World War I. The latter enveloped a certain form of necessity, or what we called earlier an "inexorability." In the case of Waterloo, things are clearly not the same. In numerous worlds that are very close to our own, the map of Mont-Saint-Jean was correct, and Napoleon won instead of losing. In others, the information arrives to Grouchy in time, and the emperor wins again. In a general manner, the "structuring causes"—namely, the situation of the belligerents—are not as restrictive as they are in the case of World War I. Changing the details of certain events—the map, the information given to Grouchy—would possibly change the outcome of the battle; but this is something that is difficult to estimate. In the end, while World War I—with its particular circumstances—presents a clear case of inexorability, this is not the case with Napoleon's defeat at Waterloo. If we want to specify this difference, we see that the group of structuring causes from World War I (alliances, conflicts of interest, etc.) contributed in making war imminent, thus meaning that anything could have ultimately triggered it. In the case of Waterloo, there are as many causes that are conducive to Napoleon's defeat as there are that are conducive to his victory. If we modify the state of the world in our minds to imagine other possible worlds, then—depending on whether we address one series of causes or another—we will end up with possible worlds where Napoleon wins and others where he loses. We will not end up with a set of possible worlds that are close to our own, where the outcomes of the battle are almost all similar to each other—as is the case with World War I, which makes this fact inexorable.

Let's be clear: in the two cases (Napoleon's defeat at Waterloo and World War I), there are contingent events that play the role of being the (or one of the) triggering cause(s). But the articulation of the contingency of these causes and of the necessity of the event itself is very different. For those of World War I, there is an inexorability at play that can be conceived of within the framework of possible worlds. With Waterloo, this is not the case. There is a contingency in the event of the "defeat at Waterloo" itself—a contingency in the "coarse-grained" event (to use the categories from the previous chapter, where the coarse-grained event "1914 World War" was inexorable while the fine-grained event was contingent).

Mapping the Structure of Contingency

Contingency and inexorability therefore correspond to two distinct structures of the set of possible worlds around ours. When event X occurs, its being contingent means that X happens in many possible worlds close to ours—but not in all (or almost all) of them. If we had a closer look at those two subsets of possible worlds—the one in which X happens and the ones in which it doesn't—we would see that they are intricate, and that it would be impossible to single out a small homogeneous subset of worlds close to ours where X happens in all of them (see fig. 2).

This is a fact about the topology of possible worlds: "contingency" refers to a pattern where changing one detail in a nearby possible world W′ (like Napoléon's map, for example) may preclude the occurrence of X in W′; but changing another detail in W′ would lead to W″ in which X ultimately happens, and thus we have a topology of the set of possible worlds where X-worlds and non-X worlds alternate infinitely. In any region of the possible worlds close to the actual world W, there is at least one possible world in which X does not occur. (Notice that among the events we also include the intentions of the agents—for instance, Napoleon's desire to dominate Europe. Even though intentions sometimes don't lead to events that are similar to them, they are crucial in determining what our actual world is, and which possible worlds are close to it. In other words, a world in which Napoleon decided to become a ballet dancer is very far from our own.)

If one would like to develop this view, degrees of contingency would need to be defined. The highest degree would be a total intrication between X and non-X worlds, such that there is a non-X world in between any two X worlds. The concept of fractals would describe such sets.[3] This would mean that the size of the largest homogeneous non-X worlds would define the degree of contingency. The lowest contingency would be defined as pure inexorability; inversely, and according to the "size" of the zone of possible worlds where the event in question is constantly taking place, inexorability would come in different degrees.[4]

We thus see the differences between two types of modalities: real contingency (Waterloo) and inexorableness (World War I). This difference moves between two very different structures in the universe of possible worlds around the actual world when we consider the event in question.

In cases that are logically or causally similar to World War I, we discussed the notion of "nature"—understood as an affirmation of what seems

Figure 2. **Structure of contingency. In the set of possible worlds, W is the actual world where an event E happens. Each pixel represents a possible world. Black pixels are worlds where E happens, light pixels are worlds where it doesn't. Whichever neighborhood of W one considers, there are light and black pixels, that is, worlds where E happens or doesn't happen.**

constant across different possible worlds in spite of dissimilar potential triggering causes, representing a subtle articulation between contingency (triggering causes) and necessity (structuring causes). Yet in a case like the battle of Waterloo, this notion of nature and this subtle articulation prove to be irrelevant.

Contingency, Inexorability, and the Formalisms of Complex Systems Science

What is relevant, however, is the fact that this characterization of contingency can map onto a partition of the systems in terms of their *predictability*, which one could infer from an examination of classes of models of physical systems. Since the 1980s, it has been common to talk about unpredictability in regard to those systems that are labeled "complex." I won't delve into the complexities of the meaning of "complex." My point here is that predictability is an objective property of systems; that it is distinct from determinism; and that different kinds of predictability map onto my partition between degrees of contingency and degrees of inexorability as defined in terms of possible worlds.

Considering only deterministic systems (namely, those systems in which the state at instant t is wholly determined from instant $t - dt$ just before t), we can't state that the behavior of the system at future time T is always predictable even though the common intuition about this determinism is that it renders systems wholly predictable. Why? Because of a property that has been crucial in the study of complex systems, named "extreme sensitivity to initial conditions" (ESIC).[5]

Determinism, in principle, states that once the laws and the initial conditions of a system are given, its behavior is wholly determined until it achieves a final state—which is often an equilibrium state. To say that the system is not sensitive to initial conditions means that given initial conditions I—after which the system reaches a behavior F at time T—a small modification di will change the trajectory, and its behavior will be a small modification $F + dF$ at T. Thus, the system is predictable because someone who knows I, with a small error margin di, will be able to predict the final behavior F, since the error margin dF on F will be small. But what if this condition does not hold? In this case, if the initial conditions change from I to $I + di$, the final state F can change to a state F' which is very different from F.

This extreme sensitivity constitutes a problem for any prediction for the following reason. Any determination of the initial conditions I is a physical measure, and thus a finite measure with error margin di. In other words, it's actually an interval of value (granted, a small interval, $[I - di, I + di]$).[6] But if there is sensitivity to initial conditions, then the final state reached by the system at time T can be anywhere between F or F', which are very different from each other; and because—from the viewpoint of our measurement—I and $I + di$ are not discernible, we can't decide what the final state of the system will be with a decent error margin.

This ESIC may happen in apparently very simple systems—as the French mathematician Henri Poincaré already demonstrated in 1890 with the "three bodies problem."[7] Think of the moon, the earth, and the sun. They follow trajectories wholly determined by the law of gravitation. Given their current situation, Poincaré shows that the ESIC holds; and that in a very long time (in the range of billions of years), one will not be able to decide whether the moon will still orbit the earth or not.

This historical example offers us two additional lessons. First, the unpredictability only applies in respect to a certain time range. The three bodies problems is fortunately very predictable in all time periods of interest to us; and whenever the moon may diverge, humankind will have probably already been gone for millions of years.

Second, Poincaré's mathematical demonstration explains why this may occur: in all differential equations describing actual physical systems, there are terms one neglects when solving these equations[8] (for instance, the action of the gravitation of the moon upon the trajectory of the earth impacting the earth's relation to the sun, which modifies the sun's gravitational force, and then the trajectory of the earth, and then the effect of the moon at the next instant). Those are indeed nonlinear terms. Ordinarily, they are so small that we can neglect them with no impact on our predictive abilities. However, they may make a difference upon the trajectory of the system when two initial conditions are extremely close. With time, this aggregates and may lead to a divergence between the system starting at conditions I and the system starting at condition $I + di$—even though the equation dictates, mathematically, the position of the three bodies at each instant. Yet the prediction—which is always based on physical measures, which are themselves finite—can't discriminate between these diverging trajectories over a very long time lapse.

This situation formally defines contingency. Logically, it shows that there are two elements in the concept of contingency: the fact that an event would be different or would not have taken place if another event had not also taken place (something which is met by the phrase "contingent upon"); and then epistemologically, the fact that with respect to our cognitive abilities, the system (or the world) could be very different—and this is due to the fact that the system, even when wholly determined, starts with conditions that can't be infinitely measured, and is thus ESIC.

Yet this has another consequence. It may happen that not only given close distinct initial conditions, the system ends up in the same state; but also that given very different initial conditions, the system still ends up in approximately the same state. It's easy to think of an example: picture a bowl. Have a ball roll from the top to the bottom of the bowl: wherever you drop it, it will still end up at the same point.

States like this are called "attractors." The spaces of interest may not be made up of real bowls, but can instead be an abstract space in which each state of the system is figured by a point whose coordinates are the values of the main parameters describing the system (e.g., position and speed, or pressure, temperature and energy, etc.). In such a space (called "phase space"), the behavior of the system appears as a trajectory. An attractor would be a shape in this space around which the system evolves so that the system ultimately tends toward this shape whatever its initial state. Obviously, if there is an attractor for the behavior of a system—at least given a range of initial conditions (which is called the "basin of attraction")—then the trajectory is predictable. If there is an attractor, then the system faces an inexorable destiny since its state will end up "in" the attractor wherever it starts.

Contingency and inexorability map onto these two kinds of dynamics: those which are unpredictable because of ESIC and those which are predictable because of attractors. The sets of possible worlds in which an event X occurs, when it comes to assessing the degree of inexorability of X, correspond to the basin of attraction defined by the occurrence of event

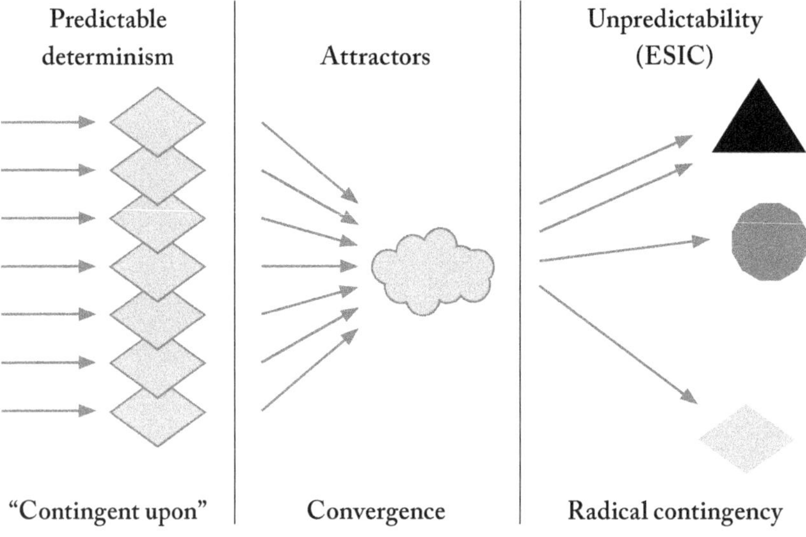

Figure 3. Three kinds of deterministic systems. To the left of the arrows: range of possible initial states; to their right: values of final states. (a) Predictable determinism: range of final states varies smoothly like values of initial states. (b) Attractors: whatever the value of initial state, the system ends up in the attractor state. (c) Unpredictable system (ESIC): very small variations in the initial states lead to very distinct final states (represented by distinct shapes). Attractors is a case of convergence of various causal paths and corresponds to an inexorable outcome; unlike (b), (a), namely predictable determinism, is a system type where final states are contingent upon initial states. The (c) system type is radically contingent.

X taken as the attractor of many processes occurring in the world. There is a correspondence between metaphysical concepts of necessity and formal notions in nonlinear dynamics that parallels what we previously saw when discussing ordinary goals and beliefs, and the formalized rational choice theory used by economists.

Measuring the degree of inexorability of an event would therefore correspond to the size of the basin of attraction. I will leave out the details of this account, but still wanted to show how the semantics of possible worlds and the formalism of complex systems provide concurring coherent tools for making sense of the intuitive notions of contingency and inexorability.

Epistemology: Knowing about Contingency

Nevertheless, a question is left unresolved: how do we know if an event belongs to the "Waterloo" type or the "World War I" type? In other words, how do we know what is happening in these possible worlds that are close to our own? We must distinguish here what happens in these possible worlds (what we will call *counterfacts*) and *our access* to these possible worlds. The fact that we may not be able to know what happens there is distinct from the fact that things are determined there in a certain way or not. A world where Princip shoots at Archduke Franz-Ferdinand and misses is determined at least in part: this miss results in many possible consequences, which will define just as many possible worlds. Yet up to a certain point we know certain things about counterfacts; and it is precisely because of this that we can make causal inferences, which suppose that we are able to tell what would have happened if the putative cause were not there.

For example, we know what would happen in the worlds where Princip missed Franz-Ferdinand. Because of our awareness of certain laws of nature, as well as of the economic and geopolitical regularities of the time, we can claim that Europe would have exploded into war regardless of whether his aim was true or not. Briefly, our knowledge of the laws of nature and social regularities allows us to know things about the possible worlds surrounding our own (but not everything, of course); and it is this knowledge that justifies the argument that World War I was inexorable, as well as many other things. It also justifies that we can correctly maintain that a given event is contingent because we see through the same method that there exist many possible worlds around our own where one or two previous events have not happened and this event did not have taken place.

The contrast between the contingent defeat at Waterloo and World War I inexorability is a metaphysical contrast between two structural types for the sets of possible worlds under focus when dealing with each event. In these two cases, by considering each of these events, we know enough about sociology, politics, economics, and nature to say to which structure each of them belongs. Of course, I deliberately chose these examples; yet in many cases, we cannot know what would happen in a large variety of possible worlds because we know too little about laws, regularities, etc. Consequently, for any given event, we will not often know whether it is contingent or inexorable; but this is a question of *our knowledge* and not the event itself—of which it is reasonable to think, metaphysically, that it belongs to one of the two types, since counterfacts are determined in one way or another. We just don't have access to them.

This epistemic opacity, however, implies that an apparently contingent event can in reality be inexorable, since we only have a limited and ultimately erroneous knowledge of the group of regularities that underlie it. It could therefore be that certain "Waterloo" events prove to be, metaphysically, "World War I" events. Hence the temptation to wrongly think that *all* events are in reality "inexorable," and to reify or personify that inexorability. This can then lead to what we are going to consider now—an entirely illusory ideal construction that we will call a metaphysical idol, and which will play a conceptual role that is analogous to that played by the idea of the *nature* of a thing.

The idea of destiny is one of the figures of this idol. What is called the destiny of an individual is realized in events, even if these are not included in the individual's plans—and a fortiori when they are not. Someone could, for example, say that it was Napoleon's destiny to lose at Waterloo because he had conquered too much, because he had been too ambitious and too greedy. This argument would be supported by a kind of moral vision of the world that is somewhat similar to the Hindu idea of karma—according to which, in basic terms, humans ultimately pay for their actions in a following life; and which can also be found in the biblical aphorism that is well known to all the characters in the cowboy comic *Lucky Luke*: "who lives by the gun dies by the gun." With the idea of destiny, we thus create a short circuit between causes and reasons in the independent series of causes that Cournot conceived of. The poorly reproduced map of the Mont-Saint-Jean farm was of course a contingent fact; but in the light of this notion of destiny, it becomes the thing by which Napoleon's destiny was realized. Unlike the case we discussed in the previous chapter, we are not dealing here with the expression of an event that would roughly be the same in all the possible worlds close to our own. On the contrary, this event is contingent (in other words, in very similar possible worlds, the event would sometimes be different)—a fact that the idea of destiny aims to erase.

When talking about destiny, I do not want the reader to imagine an obscure mystical or religious idea, even if it is integrated into a great number of myths and stories from all cultures. The simple practice of narrativity—of telling stories—produces the device from which the notion of destiny emerges. I will explain this in a few words, and will then turn toward the myth of Oedipus and psychoanalysis—two examples of how a metaphysical idol is constructed.

Chekhov's Gun and Destiny

Imagine you are at the movies. The camera follows a young man; he is walking in a crowd while a woman with slightly red hair wearing a white fake fur coat advances toward him from the opposite direction. The man sees her; and at the moment where they begin to cross the street that separates them, he smiles at her. Because of this, he does not see the car bearing down on him from his left, and which hits its brakes too late. The man barely has enough time to throw himself backwards, falling hard on the pavement. The people around him are of course very frightened by this, the young woman included—who approaches him and helps him to get up, now smiling back at him. And then she leaves to go about her business, as he does as well after a deep breath. *Voilà.*

After this scene, you expect something. These two will surely meet again, share a life story, fall in love, have children and terrible fights and go through crises; perhaps they will die together, or save the world, or spend all their time in cafes having irritating and depressing conversations while listening to Tindersticks playing in the background and smoking *many* cigarettes (especially if the film is French and dates from before 2000). Everything depends on the film's genre, where it comes from, and its director.

Your expectations here are fundamentally linked with narrativity—with our ability to listen, read, tell, and love stories.[9] In a narrative, things necessarily happen in one way or another because of how the different causes and effects are linked together. The structuralists, following the Russians who laid the groundwork for these ideas (such as Vladimir Propp and his *Morphology of the Folktale*, 1928), maintained that there are major articulations in all folktales, and even in all narratives. They tried to extract them from the immense multiplicity of existing stories and novels; more recently, scholars have referred to the "narrative arc" when discussing these general structures of narration (which are now taught in film schools to young people mostly aspiring to write screenplays at Netflix or HBO).[10] However, I would like to talk about something that is much simpler and more primitive than that—something that Chekhov expressed best in the idea now referred to as "Chekhov's gun." This idea is simple: in a play, if a gun is mounted on a wall in act 1, it must be fired by act 5.[11]

What does this mean? In the real world, each event like each intention will have innumerable causes and innumerable effects. Only certain ones among them interest us—namely, those that we control and those which influence our lives. If a narrative was forced to account for all the causes and effects of all events, it would be impossible to follow: infinite, too dense, with no principle of hierarchy between the different elements. On the contrary, the causes and effects that are generally presented are those which have causes and effects that are directly relevant to the major events and characters of the story. The infinite clutter of events thus becomes manageable. For this reason, details are rarely given at random in a narrative; and this is what is illustrated in Chekhov's idea.

The criteria for event selection in narration thus becomes the opposite of the notion of efficient causality: they are there *because of the effect they have* on important things and characters in the story (such is the case with Chekhov's gun), while other events that are the effects of internal events in the story but don't impact relevant people are excluded from the narration. This is the basis for what I will call the "principle of causal saturation" in narration.

What does this mean? In our daily lives, we cross paths with hundreds of people every day; we step on their toes or we smile at them or we steal their bags; and then we never see them again and nothing happens. Or perhaps something will indeed happen as a result for one of them: his foot needs a bandage; he goes to the pharmacy and meets a teacher who is there to buy medicine for her sick dog; later they have a child together. But we will never know this. In the film that I was imagining, the young man will see the young woman again—simply because, like in those children's maze games where you have to help the mouse find the right path to the cheese among the many different tangled routes—we have to start at the end to construct the story (in this case, that of the young man). Indeed, among the many different encounters of this young man the same day, the film focuses on this one in particular *because* he will later share a story with this woman—even if in the life that the film recounts, he does not meet her because he will share a life story with her.

From this, a good portion of the events that we see in the film—events that are present in the narration—are full of important effects for the agents in the story. This is what I call "causal saturation"; and this is what differs from reality, where events lead to a myriad of effects that affect millions of individuals in billions of possible situations that all belong within the same causal framework.

More precisely, causal saturation can be defined as follows: given two successive events in the narration, A and B, most of the effects of A that are causally very far away from B will not figure in the narration, along with many events that are roughly contemporary with A that don't connect causally with B (either as obstacles or as facilitators or as accelerators or as any other way of modifying the nature and the time and location of B). As a consequence, the causal space of the narration is saturated, meaning that most of the causal chains therein are related to A or B; while in the "real" world, these chains are much more diversified in terms of the events/facts they relate. Now, if I introduce other events C, D, and E, they will be selected for their connection with the causal pathways already there connecting A and B. And if I add F and G, that are not events but people, the same principle of event selection holds, and the same effect of saturation emerges and is reinforced (see fig. 4).

This causal saturation thus produces in the reader's or spectator's mind the effect of destiny: the events seem to have the function of leading toward a certain conclusion—a very understandable effect since they were chosen in the narration specifically for this. This leads us to the formulation of a very simple hypothesis: the causal saturation belonging to the structure of narration—whether it is found in fairy tales, novels, or a narrative that we make about our own stories or history in general—creates a feeling of destiny. In an imaginary tragic play cowritten by Dostoevsky and Chekhov, the gun which Dimitrius ultimately uses to kill Svidrigailov is a tool of destiny: "It was there for that purpose." More generally, for the playwright and spectator alike, the feeling will form that all the facts of the world—and in particular the actions of Svidrigailov himself—contributed to his violent death.

Briefly, this is what is conceptually happening here when "destiny" or kindred notions are introduced: within the narrative, the Waterloo-type situation (in which we can conceive of nearby possible worlds that indifferently include Napoleon's victory or defeat) becomes a World War I–type situation (in which all possible worlds close to our own include the eruption of this war). Indeed, if we exclusively consider the causes and effects that are present in the narration, and if we respect the constraint

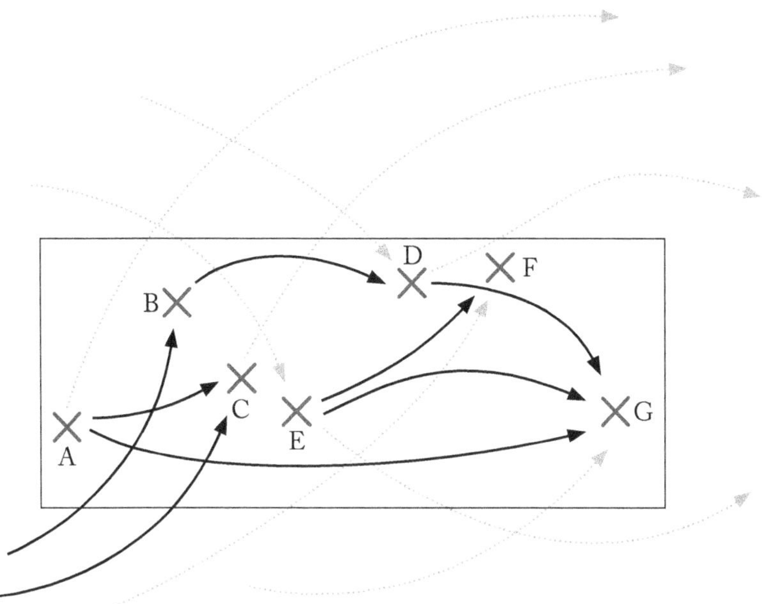

Figure 4. Representation of the structure of causal saturation proper to narrativity. A, B, C, D, E are events or facts, F, G are people. Arrows indicate causal connections. Plain lines are relations that are told in the narration; dotted lines represent causal relations that do not take place in the narration, and that connect all events and characters together, including A, B, . . . G. The black square is what is in the narrative. It appears full of causal relations between A, B, . . . G, namely, plain black arrows, with no represented causal line telling anything about other events and people.

of causal saturation in all of these worlds, the possible alternative worlds constructed exclusively based off of this become very similar to each other with respect to the central characters in the narration and what happens to them. Why so? Let's consider again our romantic chance encounter between the red-haired woman and the distracted young man and suppose a possible world close to the world W that they inhabit. (W is defined on the basis of the requisites for narration, as sketched above.) Because of the structure of narrativity, most of the causes that could exist and have led to their not seeing each other again won't be there, since by definition they would lead to effects and assume causes that are not in W. If a world W′ must be close to W, then it will very probably not include such causes; therefore, the two young persons will meet again. And this reasoning applies to all the key events in the narration; as a result, most of the worlds close to W will be such that the characters meet again, go through the several stages of the nascent love story, and end up in the final situations chosen by the screenwriters of our movie.

Thus, the impression of inexorability—inexorability being by definition the constancy of an event through a very large set of possible worlds that is close to our own. Through the effect of causal saturation that is unique to storytelling, Napoleon "had" to lose in the same way that Martina Navratilova had to end up as one of the most important tennis players in history. It was their destiny.

In his major opus *Temps et récit*,[12] Paul Ricoeur insisted on the affinities between writing history and writing fictions.[13] In addition to all the affinities he listed, I want to emphasize the fact that causal saturation as a key feature of narrativity impinges on any attempt to tell a story, whether the subjects of the story actually occurred or not. This is one reason why written history looks like stories; and perhaps more strikingly, why our own way of telling our story to ourselves—and thus our own self-understanding—often appears to be shaped through this causal structure. In addition to how we have seen that two meanings of "why?" emerge in two sorts of discourse—namely, justifying (one's action or one's belief) and explaining (the world)—and thus two sorts of linguistic practice, it appears that a major figure of the confusion between the meanings of why (as we have seen with the notion of destiny) stems from a third major linguistic activity among humans: telling stories, or narrativity. And because we tell ourselves the story of our own lives and constantly use narration to understand our own lives and the lives of others (both alive and dead),[14] the notion of destiny (or kindred notions) will always be available for the better understanding of ourselves and others.[15]

Oedipus and Failures

Of all the contributions of Freudian psychoanalysis, the use of the mythical figure of Oedipus is perhaps the most famous: after all, who has not heard of the Oedipal complex? But beyond the illustration of the Freudian theory of everyone's ambivalent attachment to the two parental figures through the myth of Oedipus, psychoanalysis also reactivated a major idea concerning Greek myths—namely, that of a hero's destiny. Generally speaking, destiny is a way of aligning a chain of contingent events so that they become the manifestation of a profound necessity linked to the essence of a person. In particular, the random events that thwart an individual's plans prove to be the mainsprings of the realization of their destiny.

The story of Oedipus illustrates this perfectly. At his birth, an oracle predicts that he will kill his father and marry his mother—the royal couple of Thebes. The credulous parents decide to kill their newborn son through exposure in the countryside. Thanks to a shepherd who takes pity on the wailing child, Oedipus survives and reaches adulthood but decides to visit an oracle when someone tells him that he is a bastard. After learning about his terrible destiny and fleeing from the people whom he believes to be his parents, Oedipus roams out into the countryside, randomly killing an old man who refuses to get of his way on the road (times were rough back then and people got worked up easily, especially behind the wheel). He then arrives at Thebes, where the famous Sphinx has taken control of the city and created a terrible epidemic as punishment for the assassination of King Laius—who of course turns out to be the rude old man who had refused to budge on the road. He learns that whoever can solve the famous riddle of the Sphinx will free the city from its curse and marry the now-widowed queen to become king. Oedipus comes up with the answer that everyone now knows and marries Jocasta, who is none other than his mother. Sophocles's legendary play, *Oedipus Rex*, retraces the detective-like investigation that Oedipus then undertakes to find and punish his predecessor's murderer—an inquiry that the prophet Tiresias advises against, as it will lead him to discover the terrible secret about the death of his father and his own true identity. A foundational myth in Greek culture, Oedipus is far more than what I have described in these few sentences; but what is interesting for us in our particular context is simply that the original prediction concerning Oedipus comes true in spite of the plans that were specifically conceived to prevent it from happening. The chance encounter with Laius on the road is the means by which the oracle's vision is realized, since it is from that point that everything unravels. This combined with Oedipus's intelligence in resolving the riddle of the Sphinx leads to his downfall—and by that we mean, his destiny.

The randomness presented here is not simply random; on the contrary, it is the manifestation of a destiny laid out by the oracle, and thus a necessity that is in some way superior. Once again, the situation is different from the case of World War I, where the chance assassination of the archduke in Sarajevo was simultaneously the cause of the war as it took place and a manifestation of the inexorability of this war in general. Here, if Oedipus had not met Laius, it would have been very unlikely that he would have ended up killing his father and marrying his mother. But the idea of destiny—an idea conveyed by myth that everything is converging toward the realization of a particular end—makes the story of Oedipus in some way similar to that of World War I, as it evokes the same impression of inexorability.

Psychoanalysis does not just cite the story of Oedipus. Under the name "unconscious desire," it constructs an avatar of the mythical notion of destiny. Let's look at what Freud tells us about what we call today more casually a "failure neurosis."[16] A patient had been named to the highest job in his own professional hierarchy—something that he had wanted for a very long time. In the three months that followed, he got sick repeatedly; lost valuable personal objects; disputed with his team; argued incessantly with his wife; and ultimately got fired and divorced. Freud interprets the case: the man in question was having a very difficult time accepting the success that he had been seeking for so long; deep within himself, "unconsciously," he thought that he did not deserve it, that he was usurping this position. Or rather, he unconsciously felt that he had gone beyond the level of his father, thereby engendering a feeling of guilt about having transgressed the natural hierarchy between father and son. The fall down the stairs and the virus caught in autumn are certainly coincidences; but ultimately, they are the means by which this desire to be punished—to spoil the sense of achievement that comes with success, to pay off the debt, to sanction the filial transgression—is realized. As in the case of destiny, acknowledging an unconscious desire combines a group of random events, tying them together in a way where they appear as the manifestation of a consistent and meaningful desire.

Destiny is thus not fixed by the gods or chanted by an oracle. On the contrary, it exists in the form of unconscious desires that analysts can decipher by listening to the dreams, associations, and words of the patient. But as for its structure, it is the same as that destiny found within myths. Since psychoanalysis developed its founding theories by keeping a watchful eye on these myths (Oedipus, Electra, Orestes, etc.), and since myths are a canonical form of narrativity, it is not surprising that a new avatar of destiny was produced—one whose source depended on the very nature of narrativity.

Let's go back to Napoleon and Waterloo. From the perspective of Oedipus or Freud (a bit more modern), the poorly rendered map was purely bad luck at a certain level. But on another, it realized the unconscious desire of Napoleon to see himself punished for his hubris. An original sin according to Ancient Greek wisdom, *hubris* makes mortals believe themselves to be capable of crossing the boundaries that nature has imposed on them. *Hubris* is always ultimately the reason for one's terrible destiny because all forms of *hubris* must be atoned for. Here, psychoanalysis is essentially a figure—one that is certainly culturally powerful—of the notion of destiny.[17]

Because of their essential affinity with the nature of storytelling, novels and narratives can be viewed as so many opportunities to think of existence as destiny—following the very precise articulations of contingency and necessity that have been under discussion since the preceding chapter. Within them, contingency is manipulated into becoming a necessity.

Why Did Napoleon Lose at Waterloo?

But if, as René Girard said, there exists "fictional truth," this is because successful novels allow for us to see a dialectic between inexorability and contingency in individual lives. In the following chapter, we will consider another figure—one that is very different—of this feeling of inexorability according to which chance does not exist.

To Sum Up

Narration intertwines natural causalities—both successful and failed intentions. Some events are contingent because it is difficult to isolate an area of possible worlds close to our own where they would inexorably take place. Under various guises, the idea of destiny transfigures this contingency into a sort of inexorability; many ideas and narratives, as ancient as myth or as modern as psychoanalysis, give substance to this concept. By inducing this specific organization of causality in the framework of a narrative that I have named "causal saturation," the very nature of narrativity contributes toward inducing the idea of destiny—an idea to which we are well disposed by our deep familiarity with narratives, since we tell our lives to ourselves and others throughout the course of our lives.

THREE

Limits

7

Why Were There American Soldiers on the 15:17 Train from Amsterdam to Paris on August 21, 2015?

ON THAT DAY, THE THALYS AMSTERDAM-PARIS TRAIN WAS the scene of an attempted attack so spectacular in nature that none other than Clint Eastwood made a film based on it featuring some of the actual people who were there that day. A 26-year-old Moroccan man boarded the train with a Kalashnikov and some automatic pistols with the aim of massacring the other passengers. We later learned that he was a radical Islamic terrorist with links to the ISIS group responsible for both the Bataclan attack in Paris and afterwards the coordinated bombings in Brussels. Almost immediately after he began his assault, he was brought down by three weaponless American passengers who were returning from vacation—two of whom were in the military. As it is difficult to picture civilians overpowering an individual armed with multiple handguns, we can easily imagine the terrible toll that this attack would have resulted in if these young men had not been there.

But what a coincidence! Right at the moment when a terrorist boards a train to commit his crime—something that is happily quite rare—there are soldiers in the same train car. It seems to be pure chance; but couldn't there be another reason for their presence than this banal story about going home after a vacation?

Defining Conspiracy Theories

Of course, as was the case after the September 11 attacks, speculations immediately appeared about a possible coup, the actual role of the Moroccan, the event being staged, etc.

The leitmotif for all conspiracy theories can be ultimately summed up by the two following sentences: "It is not by chance that . . ." and "Who benefits from the crime?" As such, the identity cards left behind by the Kouachi brothers—the notorious assassins behind the *Charlie Hebdo* massacre on January 5, 2015—were not forgotten out of negligence; just like the unusual presence of an extra police officer at the Federal Building in Oklahoma City right when Timothy McVeigh was leaving after having positioned his bomb (this attack remaining the most deadly instance of domestic terrorism in the history of the United States) was not merely a coincidence. At the behest of the *Charlie Hebdo* attack's mysterious sponsors, the documents were intentionally left behind in order to leave a trail for the police. And these sponsors are necessarily the ultimate beneficiaries of this horrific act: not the terrorists—who will spend the rest of their lives in prison, or who are already dead—but the enemies of Islam in France, or the partisans of war in the Middle East. After all, as September 11 showed the world, these kinds of events can potentially accelerate military intervention.

No matter how one defines them, conspiracy theorists stand out through their extreme attention to details that don't "match up" with the "official version."[1] A strange reflection in a rearview mirror in the video footage of the Kouachi escape; or, to use one of the most famous conspiracy theories, the position of the flag planted into the lunar ground by Neil Armstrong as we see it in the photos of the 1969 moon landing ("there is no wind on the moon and so the flag cannot be floating like this") allow them to cast doubt on what everyone thinks they know: that the Kouachis were responsible for the *Charlie Hebdo* massacre, that we landed on the moon.

This taste for detail must intrigue us somehow; after all, this is precisely how the character Sherlock Holmes operates. Where a normal person would see the suicide of a desperate painter, the great detective would notice photos of the deceased showing that he was left-handed—and that the revolver at the scene of the crime was being held in his right hand. "Staged," the detective would say, rushing out to find the murderer afterwards. This is how many detective novels have been structured ever since the presumed invention of the genre in the nineteenth century by Edgar Allan Poe with his extraordinary tales about Dupin—a figurehead for almost all the murder mysteries that continue to enthrall us.[2] The official version is never correct, and we must be suspicious of coincidences to understand what is really happening in the world around us.

But how does a conspiracy theory differ from a police inquiry? What distinguishes the "*9/11 truther*" who refuses to accept the standard narrative about Al-Qaeda's attack on the World Trade Center and the Pentagon from Hercule Poirot or Philip Marlowe?

To answer this, we must first agree on what "conspiracy theory" means. And likewise, while we generally agree that the idea of the Illuminati is pure fantasy, or that the theory according to which Paul McCartney died in 1964 and was replaced by a doppelganger (a theory called "Fake Paul" for the true believers, and which is undeniably my favorite one of all) is the stuff of crackpots; in other words, while we know how to intuitively recognize a conspiracy theory, it is very difficult to produce a set of general criteria by which one can decide whether an explanation of a given event is a "conspiracy theory" or not, and thus to define this type of theory in itself. The history of intelligence services and even democratic governments is actually paved with hundreds of more or less successful conspiracies, whether they have been discovered yet or not: the CIA plots to overthrow the government of Salvador Allende, among many others; the British and American lies about weapons of mass destruction to justify the invasion of

Iraq, etc. After all, is it unreasonable to see conspiracies everywhere? And conversely, when—after having highlighted the secret involvement of biotechnology giants in the financing of studies on the safety of GMOs—one argues that these products are indeed poison, are they giving themselves up to the world of conspiracy theories? Or are they practicing a healthy criticism of science that is a thousand miles away from the Illuminati, 9/11 truthers, and those who think they know the truth behind the Kennedy assassination?[3]

One useful definition of conspiracy theories argues that they characteristically assume an unnecessary hypothesis concerning the involvement of a group of responsible agents that remain hidden while malevolent acts are carried out.[4] However, since one cannot define what makes a hypothesis "necessary," this definition is hardly operational. For example, our "truther" will rightly point out that it is necessary to invoke the actions of the CIA when trying to account for facts that are inexplicable without it, particularly those "disturbing coincidences" which the "official version" doesn't bother to explain: how is it possible that members of the American military were returning from vacation on the Thalys train between Brussels and Paris on the day of the attempted massacre? If we let conspiracy theorists ask why-questions, they will quickly assume that the involvement of conspirators is a necessary explanatory hypothesis. To this extent, conspiracy theories can be recognized by the fact that they tend to ask why-questions that are not necessary for the ongoing investigation. But in fact, why are they unnecessary?

Negligible Details, Weird Coincidences, and Reverend Paley

These why-questions that motivate conspiracy theorists in discrediting the "official" story are generally of two different orders: troubling coincidences (like the American soldiers on board the train or the extra police officer stationed in front of Timothy McVeigh) and inexplicable details (like the identity cards of the Kouachi brothers or the unfurled American flag on the moon). These two types are not unrelated since in both cases the official narrative does not try to provide answers. I will now lay out an argument that conspiracy theorists are wrong to demand that facts be more coherent, consistent, and rational than they can actually be. As a consequence, their hyper-skepticism regarding the "official version" is combined with a hyper-rationalism regarding the state of the world.

What does this mean? To begin, try to narrate the day before the day before yesterday to a friend, and then to another, and then to another. It is strongly possible that certain details will shift between the three different narratives and that the versions will not be entirely identical: Marilyn's dress, initially red, will become green; the restaurant where you had dinner will change names from Basilic to Estragon; and so on.

We are dealing with more here than the reliability of memory. When scientists measure something, they know that there can be fluctuations. The measuring devices, the observation conditions, the thermodynamic fluctuations of the air, an entire group of things implies that there will be "noise" in the data (as computer scientists and physicists say)—which means that what interests us, the "signal," is not clearly given. For example, Kepler's observations about the positions of the planets allowed for him to detect elliptical orbits; however, all of the measured positions were not exactly following an ellipse. As a result of this, if we had wanted to account for each movement of the planets through each measured position (which would not trace out an ellipse), Newton's laws would never have been discovered (which do indeed predict an elliptical orbit). To know how to distinguish the signal from the noise, and to not look at all forms of data as being a signal, is thus as essential in science as it is in everyday life. In other words, it is reasonable to expect mismatched details in a narrative and in data; and therefore, unreasonable for a conspiracy theorist to imagine that everything coheres.

This is where the nonnecessary character of a conspiracy theory's hypothesis becomes demonstrable: when one tries to explain inconsistent details and needs conspirators to do so, one is making an unnecessary hypothesis precisely because it is not necessary to explain these details from the outset; and it is on the contrary rational to simply ignore them. Understanding the rationality of the world does not mean that its smallest details must be rational. Hegel illustrated this point by imagining a natural philosopher who wanted there to be a reason for why the exact number of parrot species is what it is—when of course this number is entirely contingent in regard to reason, and there is no rational explanation for why there are 52 instead of 53 of them.[5]

And so, we have a criterion for determining conspiracy theories and a reason for finding them irrational. This criterion primarily concerns the notion of chance. In which way? To say that everything tallies up means that the causal series at play merge or conspire (in the strictest sense of the word), which runs contrary to the Cournotian definition of chance given earlier. And this assumption also governs conspiratorial attitudes regarding those "disturbing coincidences" mentioned above.

To make a conspiracy theory, one must find a reason why the supposed Moroccan terrorist and the three Americans were in the same train car. Hence, "the four of them were part of a plan." With this link, we go beyond Cournot's notion of chance, where causal series are independent from each other—ending up in a situation exactly like that of Oedipus, whose idea of destiny made it so that a random encounter with Laius contained a direct link with the fact that he was subject to a terrible fate as the son of Laius and Jocasta. The divergent series of causes can indeed be united if the question is transformed from the causal "Why were there American soldiers on the train?" into "There are American soldiers on the train! What for?" To which one can of course respond: "To stage a fake attack."

The conspiracy theorist thus mobilizes reasoning that is similar to that of Reverend Paley when he was confronted with the complex adaptations proliferating within the living world: such an assembly of parts was so improbable that it could not have been there by chance, meaning that a divine design presided over its construction (at least according to him). Similarly, it was so unlikely that American soldiers would cross paths with the terrorist that it simply could not have been by chance; and thus, they were part of a plan. Asking who benefited from this crime will reveal a beneficiary, who thereby appears as the instigator of the plan. The conspiracy theorist of course commits here a logical imprudence in moving from the existence of a beneficiary—the group that objectively profits from the Thalys attack—to the assertion that this beneficiary *intended* to reap this particular benefit. Like losses, benefits are often accidental, meaning that they are not wanted by the agents. Benefit and intention are two distinct concepts, even if both envelop the idea that something or some event is good for someone.

Let's note a small difference from Paley's case. The human mind is not very gifted in the art of calculating probabilities. Cognitive science has shown that we have a tendency to overestimate minuscule probabilities (for example, we are afraid of airplane accidents and sharks even though the frequency of deaths due to one or the other is infinitesimal) and underestimate higher probabilities (for example, species extinctions or car accidents). Now let us suppose that you are at a dinner with twenty other guests. One of them was born on February 28, exactly like you. What a surprise! You see an "incredible coincidence," in the sense of the realization of an extremely unlikely event—even though, mathematically speaking, the probability that someone has the same birthday as you in a group of *n* people quickly grows higher as *n* increases. Chance itself is thus not an easily managed idea. In other words, the inference that "American soldiers could not be there by chance, and thus they were part of a plan" ("by chance" taken in the sense that "it was very unlikely that they would be there") is based on a false premise: it could even be that their probability of being in the train with the terrorist is not as low as one might think.

It is thus often necessary to accept contingency—to accept that things can be there or happen by chance, in the sense of independent causal series whose probability of crossing paths is weak but not zero. By definition, low probability events can occur and this is nothing surprising. But in spite of this, dissatisfied with the various possible enumerations of different causal series, the conspiracy theorist looks for a "why?" along the lines of a "what for?" He (and it is generally a "he") thus imagines the existence of a plan that generally corresponds to his own prejudices—antisemitism, anti-

Islam, anticommunism, hatred (that is sometimes justified) of agricultural and pharmaceutical lobbies, etc.

While it is indeed legitimate to think that everything has a cause, it is not always necessary to ask "why?" about something that appears to be an extraordinary coincidence in order to form a response that sounds more satisfying than "these three soldiers were on vacation in Amsterdam, a charming city; they were returning home; the train company had assigned them their particular seats." But precisely, why is this response not enough for certain people? When one is not satisfied by the ordinary explanation as to why American soldiers were present on the Thalys train on August 21, 2015—namely, that they were returning home from vacation—it is because they are actually expecting a certain proportionality between cause and effect. Whenever an effect is massive (like a massacre in a train) we all have the tendency to more easily accept a "big" cause than a series of bland events—an attested bias in how we handle the concept of causality, which we find at work in many conspiracy theories. Such is the motivation behind the reactions to the deaths of JFK and Lady Diana, as well as to the arrest of IMF leader Dominique Strauss-Kahn among many other examples (in regard to the latter, a French poll done just after his arrest showed that a majority of French people believed this to be a set-up): that an event which affects powerful people or the order of the universe could be caused by a simple armed fanatic, a drunk chauffeur, or the unrestrained sexual desires of someone well on their way to becoming president of a large country is shocking to our implicit sense of causal harmony. This inability to accept such a disproportion between cause and effect ultimately leads us to seek out more sizable and powerfully situated causes, such as a CIA conspiracy, the Queen of England, or President Sarkozy. If certain people think that something is missing in the investigation of the Thalys attack and in all the explanations of it that they read, it is because the only cause that would satisfy them would be one that is equal in importance to the effect which intrigues them. The dissatisfaction when confronted with a series of explanatory causes that we discussed earlier can thus also take the form of a disappointed expectation concerning the harmony between a cause and its effect.

Give Chance a Chance

Actually, "chance" deserves a far richer exposition than what I have described up until now. The notion of chance is not very consistent: it aggregates several meanings that can lead to distinct rigorous or formal expressions, and this also explains why it's hard to defend a strong stance about chance and why-questions.

Let's first note that there are many words in many languages used to talk about chance, which are partly synonymous. For instance, in English, randomness, luck (which means something positive but implies chance), and fortune are all good examples. Scholars of Aristotle know the distinction he makes between *tuchè* and *automaton*, two terms whose translation depends on the translator and their view of Aristotle's ontology. In French, one can say *hasard, chance*, or *aléatoire*; as well as the old word "*heur*" (which is the root of *bonheur* and *malheur* and could be translated as "luck").

Let's try to make sense of this linguistic plurality. When I say "I ran into her by chance," what do I mean? First, it does not mean that there is no cause. Her standing at the bus stop and me going to the same bus stop both have causes and reasons (in the sense of reasons-for-action). But the two sets of reasons are not connected. Thus, when the conspiracy theorist says, "There was a cop waiting for him there, this was not just by chance," he clearly means that there should be a connection between the causal history of the presence of the cop (including his reasons for why he was there) and the reasons why the terrorists came out of the Oklahoma federal building on that day.

Now let's again consider the chance meeting with my friend. Suppose I learn that she comes every day at the same time to catch a bus: in this case, I would not be able to say so easily that I saw her "by chance." Why? Because this habit of hers made it more probable that I would meet her there.

Thus, besides a lack of apparent reason, we see that there is a meaning of "by chance" that envelops the notion of "low probability," since raising the probability of meeting my friend makes me less likely to say it's by chance. This does not mean that there is no determinism in the world: for instance, if I say "it randomly snowed in April," I don't deny that there is a determinism supporting weather; it's just that it's very unlikely for it to snow in April, and so I ascribe this unlikely event to chance (or Prince). And this holds for the conspiracist example: he says that the supposedly low probability of the cop being there is not so low, because—given that the cop had the intention to be there (in order to perform the false flag operation)—the probability of him ultimately being there was in fact very high.

Yet this does not exhaust the meaning of chance, whose relationship with probabilities is much more complex. In fact, chance does not pertain only to low probabilities but also to probabilities nearing 1/2. How so? Let's imagine a tennis match between two major tennis players (say, Martina Navratilova and Chris Evert Lloyd) in the final of some Grand Slam tournament. The score is one set for each, and it is 6–6 in the third set. The last match point is harshly fought, and finally the ball launched by Evert Lloyd hits the top of the net and slowly falls to its base on Navratilova's side. At the moment of contact with the net, there is a subjective probability of 1/2 that it will come down on either side. Some would correctly say that luck made Lloyd win the match. Clearly, there is a determinism for all physical motions; and so the ball, given the state of the world at that precise moment, had to fall on Navratilova's side. From the viewpoint of the equations of physics, the probability is 1, since, if one commits to determinism, anything that actually happens must have a probability of 1. But we still say that it's luck, or chance. Chance therefore can also apply to situations where the subjective probability is 1/2 (for instance because, as here, we have no reason to say that the ball falls on one side rather than the other). The intuition is that if the game were replayed—or more generally, if we consider a possible world immediately close to the actual one—the ball would often fall on Lloyd's side.

This case of chance should be distinguished from cases where certain scientists or philosophers claim that there is actual indeterminism—namely, that an event is not determined by the instantaneous state of the world just before the event. I won't take sides on this issue; the question underlying the whole debate touches upon the interpretation of probability concepts, which are notoriously intricate and subtle.[6] In general, quantum physics provides most of the cases of purported indeterminism. In physics, the notion of half-life means that a substance made of certain radioactive atoms such as U235—which lose neutrons spontaneously—will lose half the quantity of atoms after a period T. This T characterizes the nature of an atom. However, in regard to one particular atom, it's not possible to say when exactly a particle will be emitted; and this impossibility does not depend upon our knowledge but is instead radically grounded in the nature of the atom (at least according to many physicists). Here, there is no reason for a neutron in a given atom to be emitted at a given time. Thus, this is a case of pure objective chance that is unlike all my previous examples where chance concerns our appreciation of events which in themselves have reasons and causes.

We should also note that ascribing chance requires us to specifically characterize the events in question: "losing a neutron at 5:46 a.m." is a chance event; but the quantity of atoms left after T—and thus the fact that after T a certain amount of neutrons is lost—is fully determined. And this holds not only for quantum phenomena but also for ordinary ones: suppose that Serena Williams, ranked number one in the world, beats some player ranked fifty-fourth by a final score of 6–3, 5–7, 6–2. She lost the second set because of the same net scenario described above. One would say that losing this set, and the resulting final score of the match, was bad luck and thus due to chance; but the final result, Serena's win, is not chance (given her ranking and that of her adversary, Serena's victory was expected). This means that chance could answer a question about why the final score was what it was; but the respective skills of Serena and her competitor were the true explanation for the overall outcome of the game. Chance or not chance: this depends upon the precise thing one considers.

Why Were There American Soldiers on the 15:17 Train

As a result of this short inquiry into our ways of talking, we see that "chance" includes two conflicting kinds of events: low probability events and half-probability events. This indicates a lack of internal consistency in the notion.

To some extent there is, however, a strong connection between this weakly robust notion of chance and the ideas I considered above—such as the notions of structuring/triggering causes, and the idea of contingency. Contingency—when understood in terms of possible worlds and the size of subsets of the set of possible worlds that include or do not include a focal event—matches with those notions of chance explained either in terms of low probability or of half-probability, since these two measures can be mapped onto measures of subsets of possible worlds. And when I think in terms of structuring causes, I can translate chance talk into causal talk in the following way: saying that top-ranked Serena won against our imaginary fifty-fourth-ranked player means that there were structuring causes, mirrored by the ATP ranking, such that Serena had to win. But the score itself must be explained by an appeal to triggering causes (for example, during the second set, Serena felt a little tired or stressed about the perspective of winning her nth Grand Slam title and breaking Martina Navratilova's record; or any other small event that would trigger her slightly less efficient first serve and the almost equal number of games won by each player in this set). In contrast, think of Serena playing against me: not only would the structuring causes explain her victory; but those same causes, which include our relative skills in tennis, would also explain the final score (a crushing and swift 6–0, 6–0 defeat).

These last considerations make clear why it is still possible to say that chance explains some events and answers why-questions. Chance explanations refer to the need to place triggering causes in the foreground of an explanation, and indicate a specific setting of possible worlds that features some degree of contingency. And there is even a way to integrate these chance explanations into science, which I will now illustrate with evolutionary biology.

We saw in chapter 4 that the intensity of natural selection also depends upon the size of the population where it occurs, and is inversely proportional to this size. The population geneticist Sewall Wright in 1932 (cited in that chapter) coined the term "random genetic drift" to name this effect, which is in essence an effect of "stochasticity" (or chance): the smaller the population, the higher the chances that the traits that should be selected (due to the higher chances of reproduction they confer to their bearers) are not selected. This occurs exactly like in a coin toss: if you toss a coin three times, you are likely to end up with "heads" three times; but if you toss it 1,000,000 times, you are likely to yield two almost equal series of heads and tails. This is called the *law of large numbers*, a law in probability theory that was demonstrated in the eighteenth century by Bernoulli. The objective chance of falling on heads or on tails is 1/2,[7] but this does not determine respective frequencies in small series: random genetic drift is about these latter frequencies.

One should also notice here that random genetic drift comes in two modes. When two traits with distinct chances to reproduce (named *fitnesses*, and written w and w′), are different, drift means that the trait with $w < w'$ outcompetes the other one in small populations. Whereas when two traits have the same fitness $w = w'$, the fixation of one at the expense of the other is also called drift. This duality reflects the exact duality we just discussed while analyzing chance between low probability and half-probability.[8]

The Japanese evolutionary biologist Motoo Kimura, who designed extremely sophisticated mathematical models of population genetics in the spirit of Wright, is famous for having elaborated the so-called *neutral theory of evolution*. Here, drift explains much of the architecture of our genome if one looks at genotypes at a minute level, nucleotide by nucleotide. In addition to Hubbell's dual theory that explains biodiversity in a neutralist way (see chapter 2), this shows how mathematical modeling can confer a rigorous meaning to the idea that chance can explain certain facts, patterns, or events.

Yet the final lesson of this short analysis of chance leads to an explanation of why conspiracy theories have such a mass appeal. The idea of chance is weak in the sense that even if some aspects of it can be mathematically formalized into theories intended to explain a specific set of phenomena, it still aggregates several distinct meanings (low probabilities, lack of intention, independent causal series, half-probability, etc.). Indeed, there are a few parallels with the notion of contingency; but there is no one-to-one correspondence between the mundane/colloquial notion of chance and the concept of contingency—with the latter being more likely to support a conceptual analysis and a formal characterization.[9] It is therefore easy to be dissatisfied by an appeal to chance as an explanation; and in turn, it is easy to think of some alternative explanation that would overcome chance by referring to an underlying plot or intention. This is exactly what conspiracy theories do. For the same reason, ideas of destiny or any other predetermining form (like preformationist theories in biology) are generally more likely to convince us to adopt them instead of appeals to chance—which, in the end, acts as a placeholder for too many disparate things.[10]

Contingency and Conspirations

The refusal of contingency thus generally characterizes conspiracy theories. Many of the sociologists and psychologists who have studied these representations have emphasized how they satisfy a need to give meaning to a chaotic and disjointed set of events, as well as to a world that seems to have lost its traditional order. Major waves of conspiracy theories appeared after the French Revolution (where we see the first appearance of the Illuminati in a 1798 work by Abbot Augustin Barruel entitled *Mémoires pour servir à l'histoire du jacobinisme (Memoirs Illustrating the History of Jacobinism)*, just after a book by John Robison, *Proofs of a Conspiracy against All the Religions and Governments of Europe, Carried On in the Secret Meetings of Free Masons, Illuminati, and Reading Societies*, published in Edinburgh in 1797) and after the fall of the Berlin Wall—two moments where the world lost an organizing principle. Whether one judges them to be good or not, these principles allowed for one to easily give meaning to events. These theories illustrate the pathologies that are linked to following the principle of reason too systematically, extending its application from the domain of signals to the field of noise.

But such speculations have a supplementary interest: they show how our use of the principle of reason can follow systematically erroneous pathways that correspond to what psychologists sometimes call "cognitive biases"—namely, spontaneous systematic flaws in our cognitive apparatus.[11] We already discussed the fragility of our understanding of probabilities and chance. The parallel with Paley and intelligent design also highlights how conspiracy theories demonstrate that a powerful "intentional bias" is at play—a tendency to systematically attribute causal roles to intentional agents, which can be viewed as modern facets of the belief in final causes that Spinoza denounced long ago. Ultimately, these half-baked ideas very clearly show the prior and unjustified belief in a symbolic proportionality between causes and effects—whose consequences are widely felt in our lives.

To Sum Up

Although they are difficult to define, "conspiracy" theories introduce interesting pathologies likely to affect the reasonable search for "why?" Their irrationality consists in refusing all chance and lending too much rationality to facts—which involves looking for reasons behind those details that should be considered "noise." In their refusal of chance and in their search for beneficiaries who are later transformed into sponsors, they bear certain similarities to the reasoning of those who support intelligent design. They show various cognitive biases regarding chance and causation—especially when in connection to intentional bias and the expectation of a proportionality between the importance of the effect and that of the cause.

8

Why Does Romeo Love Juliet?

"LOVE STORIES END BADLY, IN GENERAL." TO ILLUSTRATE their claim, the famous French pop group Les Rita Mitsouko had a whole galaxy of stories to choose from in classic Western literature. Tristan and Isolde kill themselves, Anna Karenina throws herself in front of a train, Woyzeck kills his unfaithful wife and then drowns himself, Madame Bovary takes arsenic, Werther shoots himself, Donna Elvira goes insane while her seducer Don Juan is dragged down into hell by a statue. Things don't go any better in the movies: Jean Seberg rats out Jean-Paul Belmondo, who is then killed by the police in *Breathless*; Bonnie and Clyde are mowed down in a hail of bullets (also by the police, who seem immune to all forms of romanticism); and as for *Titanic*—well, the boat sinks.

But among all the competing tragic love stories, none is as arguably emblematic as *Romeo and Juliet*. Made eternal through Shakespeare's poetry, the play recounts the story of these characters as they fall madly in love although they come from families that hate each other to no end. "And Romeo wanted Juliet, And Juliet wanted Romeo," as Lou Reed phrased it with his trademark dryness. Events then swoop down on these poor lovers; and as is often the case in theatrical tragedies as well as in historical ones (such as Waterloo for certain French royalists, who do indeed exist), the details and misunderstandings act as demons: Romeo believes Juliet to be dead when in fact she is deeply asleep from a drug; he stabs himself and dies; and when Juliet awakens and finds Romeo dead, she takes his dagger and stabs herself in turn.

But why? What can explain a love that is so overwhelming as to go against the order of the world and all familial tradition—one that ends in a double suicide because the two lovers feel that they cannot go on living if they are not able to openly share their love? Shakespeare does not provide an answer to this, as the mutual love of Romeo and Juliet is the simple driving force of the play. Romeo and Juliet kill themselves because Romeo wanted Juliet and Juliet wanted Romeo, as the song goes. But why does Romeo love Juliet? And why does Juliet love Romeo?

The Poverty of Causes and Sociobiology

If Shakespeare begins by showing us the love between Romeo and Juliet, it is perhaps because there is nothing else to say about it. It is a primitive fact—just like how gravitation was an irreducible and primitive fact about matter for Newton, and like how roses have no why in the writing of Angelus Silesius. But this seems to be a lazy argument. On the contrary, it seems that there are plenty of potential answers to the question "Why does Juliet love Romeo?" But are they real answers?

Traditional philosophy and then psychology have offered up various hypotheses about love. Plato—the most famous of all philosophers, and the one concerning whom Whitehead could jokingly say that all other philosophy is a footnote to his work—wrote a remarkable and much-commented-on dialogue about love called the *Symposium*. Its most famous moment is the myth that we were once doubled individuals who were punished for our joyful pride by the gods, and that we are now forced by this catastrophe to search the world for our other severed half. The Platonic vision of love is an extension of Platonism in general—a theory that only the soul can know those things that it has forgotten, which the philosopher calls Ideas. Likewise, one falls in love with those who were joined to them at the beginning of all souls—just like Platonic Ideas are joined to the original knowing soul.

But this does not help us very much: after all, to say that Juliet loves Romeo because they were originally one joined entity at the beginning of time sounds more like a beautiful myth or a metaphor for their emotions than a concrete answer to the question at hand.

Other thinkers of the human soul—such as Schopenhauer, Pascal, Kierkegaard, and Freud, for example—developed interpretations that relied less heavily on myth. A young and somewhat romantic philosophy student will pour over the supplement to Schopenhauer's *World as Will and Representation*—a 500-page masterpiece that is reinforced by 500 additional pages of equally brilliant supplementary writing—that is called "On the Metaphysics of the Love of the Sexes." With this promising title and the assurance that Schopenhauer was a great philosopher (revered by Nietzsche, Tolstoy, and Wagner to name but a few), the reader expects an arsenal of luminous concepts. This same reader is generally disappointed: we learn that men love women because it is through their love that the human species reproduces—which means that love is nothing more than the means by which the human species assures its own perpetuation in the best conditions, since no one can procreate robust humans with just anybody they meet. As such, the amorous instinct thereby acts as a discriminating agent. The species is thus more powerful than the individual; and as a result, the individual can suffer the worst torments connected to love.

This theory of course now seems rather naïve, and similar to the expression in simple metaphysical terms of what we find today in treatises on evolutionary biology. When the eminent evolutionary biologist Richard Dawkins says in his famous *The Selfish Gene* (1976) that organisms are "robots" that allow for genes to perpetuate themselves under the best conditions—because these genes have replicated themselves since the dawn of time and have been optimized by natural selection to replicate themselves in the best way possible—he is more scientifically formulating an idea that seems merely trivial and intuitive in the German metaphysician's words.

In the end, whether it is coming from Schopenhauer or a modern biologist, we can explain the instinct or drive that pushes humans toward each other in a purely sexual sense—with reproduction not having to be the conscious or unconscious goal, although it is statistically associated in a not insignificant way with the sexual act; but we still cannot explain much about this love between Romeo and Juliet (who, moreover, most likely did not have many occasions to satisfy this particular drive).

Evolutionary biology says more, however. It claims to know how to distinguish love and sexual desire, and strives to demonstrate that the amorous bond and the aspiration of one person toward another can also be explained through behavioral dispositions that are already present in the human species—dispositions that come from a complex game pertaining to the evolutionary interests of men, women, and their possible children ("interest" being used here in the sense of biological evolution, where it is measured in terms of the genes likely to be left to subsequent generations). The emotional involvement of the parents would thus allow for real parental care and increase the chances of survival for their offspring, who will also inherit this capacity for loving relationships and will transmit it to their own offspring—and so on according to the process of evolution by natural selection that we have already discussed. The human species thus prolongs the forms of pairing that we already find in some primates in a specific and sophisticated way (e.g., chimpanzees experience something like jealousy, since the females of dominant males hide to copulate with other males).

Based on evolutionary biology, so-called "evolutionary psychology" took over "sociobiology," which in the 1970s was intended to be a Darwinian science of human social behaviors.[1] This psychology progressively refined its favorite explanations: not only does it claim to show that women and men have divergent sexual interests because of the difference of their gametes (the female's one large egg makes her more limited and selective in terms of the frequency of copulation; the male's billions of spermatozoa make him far less so); it also distinguishes between long-term and short-term "sexual strategies" in humans. In the long term, the female will look for a partner who is likely to take good care of her offspring; but she may also want partners with "good genes" for short-term relationships in order to guarantee the genetic quality of their offspring—the very ones who, being highly valued on the sexual market, have an interest in dispersing their genes widely. Women may very well practice this strategy since they have been conversely shaped by evolution to know how to discriminate the (supposedly) secondary signs of good-quality genes (prominent chins, symmetry, square and pronounced features, deep voices, etc.).[2] From the point of view of biology, this line of thinking thus demonstrates a kind of "Madame Bovary effect" where a woman seeks a good man for a husband—one who may not be the most attractive but who is present and responsible (Charles Bovary); but tries to have intercourse with "high-quality males"—such as nobles, princes, and aristocrats (Rodolphe)—during periods of high ovulation activity in order to produce offspring with good genes (who will themselves thus be able to reproduce abundantly) that will be raised by our hapless Charles.

As one can imagine, there have been numerous critiques of these claims. Many point out their total neglect of all social processes and constraints; others often note the lack of methodological care in evolutionary psychology—particularly when compared with the work of evolutionary biology itself. I won't explicitly comment here on the validity of these explanations beyond stating the pure fact that they exist, especially when the other so-called human sciences offer different ones about Romeo and Juliet that are worth going into. Sociologists show how romantic choices are always made in a specific social context in which the desired partner is already selected from a group of socially acceptable partners, which is also measured against the possibilities of the social trajectory that the potential partner would allow. After all, it could be argued that love as it is found with Romeo and Juliet is a luxury; and that for a good part of the world and for a very long time there only existed two forms of heterosexual relationships: purely sexual ones; and legal unions that existed for descendants to be born and cared for, as well as for economic legacies to be properly transmitted. As Apollodorus once wrote, "For we have courtesans for pleasure, and concubines for the daily service of our bodies, [and] wives for the production of legitimate offspring and to have a reliable guardian of our household property." This striking phrase, which Michel Foucault was fond of citing, summarizes the affective and sexual division of labor in ancient Greek society.

With all these explanations, and adopting the idea of contrast classes from above, we are able to answer the question "Why should Romeo love Juliet rather than no one?" But this does not tell us why Romeo loves Juliet *and not Annette*, her (hypothetical) sister. Theories—whether they be mythical, metaphysical, evolutionary, or sociological—make sense of generalities about love in an often interesting way; but one cannot avoid the impression that individuals escape them—and that "why (the individual) Juliet rather than (the individual) Annette?" will always be left unexplained.

Proust against the Psychologists

But of course, I can hear you say, biology and sociology are not sciences concerned with the individual and so there is nothing surprising in how they have no say about Romeo. What would a (real) psychologist say about the most famous Capulet and Montague in history?

A psychologist would probably examine the childhoods of Romeo and Juliet—how they interacted with their parents, their friends, and the social world to which they were gradually exposed; how they built defenses against those anxieties that were particularly strong, systems of narcissistic gratification, identifications, and projections. Just as, according to Hempel, a physicist can deduce the behavior of a system in a particular state if they know its laws, a scientific psychologist would be able to deduce from their research that Romeo would fall in love with Juliet the moment that he met her.

This sounds particularly naïve to our ears. Simply put, there is something about love that feels entirely new, that defies expectations and routines and what has been patiently and lengthily constructed in the individual over the years. Gustave Flaubert (again), when describing how the hero of *L'Éducation sentimentale* (Frédéric Moreau) meets Madame Arnoux—who will be his great love, and to whom he will share his feelings only after fifteen torturous years—writes in his brilliantly concise way: "It was like an apparition."[3] The word "apparition" describes a rupture, a form of breach within the regular sequence of facts, anticipations, events, and readjustments that make up what is ordinary in one's personal existence. If love were a Hempelian system, we could, for example, expect it to rise and accelerate at a particular speed (and this is exactly what Hempel calls "an explanation"); but if something so mathematically predictable happened between Juliet and Romeo, could we really call it love?

Such reflections are not coming from a gratuitous and romantic appreciation for paradox. Novelists are probably much better than philosophers in understanding what is at stake in these determining and singular encounters. In *Swann's Way*, Proust recounts the love story between his childhood neighbor Swann and a young disreputable woman named Odette de Crécy. Their relationship goes through all of the phases of passion: seductions, fervors, outbursts, separations, spoiled reunions, separations, jealousies, reproaches, anxieties, moments of forgiveness—and so on. And then, because it fails to end badly, the love story simply ends. After going through all of this agony, Swann realizes that he no longer loves Odette. They meet again by chance sometime later on courteous terms; and Swann, suddenly realizing the mystery that had sustained this drama throughout its entire arc, exclaims: "To think that I wasted years of my life, that I wanted to die, that I felt my deepest love, for a woman who did not appeal to me, who was not my type!"

Far from being paradoxical, this statement has much to bear on our question: a psychologist or a sociologist would certainly be able to explain which kind of women Swann would like; but in the end Swann loves Odette, who is not his type! This is a good illustration of the gap between the disruptions caused by love stories and scientific explanations—even when the latter are focused on individuals.

Why Does Romeo Love Juliet?

Causes of Love and Reasons of Love

"Because it was he, because it was me," Montaigne famously said when explaining his friendship with La Boétie in a phrase that resembles anything but an explanation. Does this declaration mean that there are no reasons for love and friendship and their other shared feelings?

Let's imagine that Juliet said to Romeo, "I love you because you are six foot three" or ". . . because you make excellent cookies"; or that Romeo said to Juliet, "I love you because I have never seen a woman run as fast as you." The explanations sound immediately absurd. After all, what would they mean if Juliet discovered she enjoyed Mercutio's cookies as well? Or that Annette was in fact a secret Olympic runner?

In addition, Juliet would have cause to wonder: will Romeo still love her if she can no longer run the 100 meters in less than 12 seconds? The word "because" indeed seems to bear a conditional character: "If you are polite and muscular, I will love you; if not, it's over." But things are not like this. To adopt the language of logicians, "I love you because X" is neither a necessary nor a sufficient condition for the love between Romeo and Juliet. Nonnecessary: if Juliet ran less fast, it is very plausible that Romeo would love her all the same; nonsufficient: it is possible that Annette runs just as fast or faster than Juliet but Romeo will not fall in love with her.

A brilliant anatomist of the soul, Pascal took account of the inscrutability of the object of love in one of his most famous "thoughts":

> But does he who loves someone on account of beauty really love that person? No; for the small-pox, which will kill beauty without killing the person, will cause him to love her no more. And if one loves me for my judgment, memory, he does not love *me*, for I can lose these qualities without losing myself. Where, then, is this Ego, if it be neither in the body nor in the soul? And how love the body or the soul, except for these qualities which do not constitute *me*, since they are perishable? For it is impossible and would be unjust to love the soul of a person in the abstract, and whatever qualities might be therein. (*Pensées*, 688–323)

This incongruity of "I love you because . . . you are X or Y" is easily illustrated by recalling the common oddities found in romantic life. If Juliet stops running faster than everyone else, it is probable that Romeo will continue loving her; conversely, it could happen that Juliet would stop loving Romeo even though he continues to make outstanding cookies—the very virtue that was her declared reason for loving him.

Thus, although we can make a list in the style of "Romeo loves Juliet (rather than Annette) because of x, y, and z," none of these explanations based on a scientific study of Romeo—his history, environment, education, and even his genome—fully grasp why Romeo loves Juliet. It is this gap between the *fact* of love and the "why does he love her?" that will be the major lesson of this chapter. Let's expand on it a little bit.

If we return to our tripartition of reasons—reason as cause, reason for believing, reason for acting—we can perhaps clarify why the question "Why does Romeo love Juliet?" is causing us so much trouble. After all, up until now, we have been putting how a sociologist or a psychologist would respond on the same level as what Romeo himself would say. But are they answering the exact same "why"?

The scientific "why?", which is most often oriented toward causes, is disappointing here. Let's imagine that a psychologist with biological inclinations explains that Romeo's love for Juliet is entirely due to a concordance of pheromones—these olfactory molecules that individual animals secrete which are genetically determined, and which serve as signal attractors in courtship behavior in many vertebrates. This can certainly play a role in the love between Romeo and Juliet; but again, how can we prove that this hormonal concordance is unique? Are there not other pheromones from other women that may have the same effect on Romeo? And what if Juliet had the same pheromones but was suddenly given the voice of Gilbert Gottfried? Would Romeo continue to love her? Even if they allow for us to contribute a chapter about the scientific psychology of love between humans and even mammals, these causalities end up missing the mark on the singular love of Romeo for Juliet.

Must we thus understand "Romeo loves Juliet because she runs fast" as a first-person statement in terms of reasons-for-belief, as a justification that Romeo could give for his love? Not exactly. For that, it would be necessary for love to be a belief—for example, the belief that Juliet is lovable. In this case, our statement would be trying to say: "The reason that Romeo believes Juliet to be the most lovable person on Earth is that she runs fast." But of course, this does not justify Romeo loving Juliet. We can easily imagine cases where someone believes that Annette is very lovable, the most lovable, but they do not love her; or reciprocal cases where Annette is not lovable at all, and yet they love her. Rather than reiterating the tired cliché that "women like jerks," we could rather just take another look at Swann and Odette: he had no justification for finding her lovable, but he still truly loved her.

In the Woody Allen film *Hannah and Her Sisters* (I know, I know, but stick with me), Mia Farrow plays an intelligent, beautiful, understanding, kind, and simply perfect woman; and this is why her sisters—who are more selfish and anxious (or drugged)—find her rather annoying. Hannah is "too perfect," as one of them tells her, and is almost too lovable to be loved (her husband ends up having an affair with her younger sister). If "I love her because X" was a justification, this claim would in reality justify a belief along the lines of "Hannah is lovable since she is so perfect" but would not be able to justify that I truly love her. All of this occurs as if "I love her because X" slipped into a gap between the causes of love—which further explain a certain number of behaviors (being attracted to someone who emits a particular pheromone, who has a particular education, or who has certain tastes)—and justifications—which justify a judgment regarding the value of a person's likeability but not the love for that person. The same argument would convince us that "I love her because X," if understood this time as a reason-for-action, would not work either: X could justify a certain number of behaviors (courtship, sexual desire, etc.) but not love itself, since love is neither an action nor a behavior. In truth, we need to look at things inside-out here: love is ultimately a reason-for-action in itself, and not what is justified by a reason-for-action. It is because Romeo loves Juliet that he breaks with his family and ends up killing himself. He simply cannot live without her.

Love, the West, and Performatives

Montaigne's phrase "Because it was he, because it was me" can be better understood now. All the categories of why fail to truly answer this chapter's question. The only true answer that explains the love (and even friendship) between two people is the invocation of the singular fact itself—the double fact that Juliet is Juliet, and Romeo, Romeo. Does this mean that love is without reason, that it is irrational, that it is similar to Angelus Silesius's rose invoked earlier?

We could indeed understand Montaigne's statement as an admission that love is irrational at its core. This is not to repeat trivialities like "love is blind," but to indicate the existence of a *gap*. Here, causes and reasons cause or justify *in a general manner*: they could thus predict the nature of Swann's "type" or justify why Hannah is lovable. But there exists a gap between these causes and reasons, and the experience of a purely individual feeling.

A skeptic could deduce from this that the love between Romeo and Juliet evades all the orders of reason because it simply does not exist: it is an illusion, an empty space. Certainly, Romeo and Juliet believe that they love each other, and perform actions in the name of this love (defying their families, serenading each other, spending the night together, killing themselves). But how do they know that this is love and not just desire—the latter being a feeling or an emotion about which psychology and biology have much to comment on? Moreover, is it certain that this romantic love that the story of Romeo and Juliet has come to define in many cultural circles has existed always and everywhere? In a book called *L'Amour et l'Occident* (*Love in the Western World*, 1939), which is certainly old and outdated (although even Lacan admitted that it provided some remarkable insights on the subject), Denis de Rougemont indicated that something as obvious as love is in reality a historical construct that owes enormously to the literary traditions of courtesan love in chivalric societies—which incidentally encourages love to defy social taboos.

How does Romeo know that he loves Juliet? He can only tell the difference between love, friendship, and desire if he has access to certain criteria for this. And how could he know these except from having overhead others discussing them, as well as having been exposed to this imaginary world of love that Rougemont writes about at length? We now have our finger here on the pulse of what is called social constructivism—i.e., the thesis that many things which seem natural to us (family, emotions, virtues, and possibly even germs and stars) are actually involuntarily constructed through a long process whose nature is still debated by sociologists.[4] Love cannot be lived and experienced as such outside of a social world in which its behaviors and feelings (desire, lack, aspiration, fantasies, projects, tenderness, etc.) can be conceived of and experienced as what we call "love." And this construction is made thanks to *narrativity*—to being able to tell a story both to oneself and the other. This consists less in recognizing than in building a common story, a novel of one's own love that can be referred to during all of its phases, from its birth to its death, while moving through all of its possible transformations (conjugal, familial, grandparental, etc.). In the case of Romeo and Juliet, the fact of using their love to stand up against the eternal hatred between their two families becomes something of an alliance, a horizon on which their feelings can be felt even stronger since they contrast with such disdain. This combined with the fact that their relationship must both be kept hidden and fought for makes their love that much more manifest—just like how white is most visible against a solid background of black.

The experiences and feelings (emotions, desires, etc.) that are the basis of love seem less unruly in regard to causes and reasons than the love of Romeo and Juliet itself—since there exists a psychology of desire, a psychology of jealousy, a sociology of the family, etc. To know whether love exists in the same way that tables, chairs, and humans who desire each other exist proves to be undecidable. Or rather, one could argue that it belongs less to the order of observation than that of decision-making: to love is to decide (more or less explicitly) to construct the narrative which makes it so that one is in love, or experience themselves as a human in love; or, to borrow another linguistic concept, it is a *performative*. John Austin in *How to Do Things with Words?* (1962) famously distinguished declarative phrases that describe reality (like "There is a boat") from performative phrases that describe nothing but create something (such as "I christen this boat 'France'," when stated by the person officially entitled to do so). In this respect, Romeo's love for Juliet is less declarative than performative, with "I love you" sounding more like the statement "I christen you" than "Juliet runs really fast."

"Subjectivity"

To think more clearly about this gap we have been discussing—the one that sets Romeo's love for Juliet apart from the order of reasons and causes—we must consider certain forms of speech and practice as attempts to give meaning to the irrational core of this love. A good part of my examples comes from literature not purely out of taste, but also because literature is particularly excellent at putting into words what is at play here. Not explaining or justifying, but simply letting the reader see the love between Romeo and Juliet.

One can also recognize certain psychoanalytic tendencies from the same angle. Here, "subject" precisely names the gap between the order of reasons and causes and Romeo's love for Juliet. As a human with a particular personal history, education, and social environment, Romeo developed particular tastes and erotic choices that made him susceptible to one kind of reaction instead of another. But as the subject "Romeo," he loves Juliet.

In this sense, this love is explained not by the facts of Romeo's life (as they would be understood by an average psychologist or sociologist) but by the manner in which the subject "Romeo" is constructed in the lived experience of these facts—with this happening in an unconscious and undetectable way that surfaces in conscious life only in a diverted fashion. In one of his more diluted and rehashed lessons, Freud argues that the unconscious life of the subject can only be understood by the subject himself in a psychoanalytic context (that is, by addressing a neutral Other in dialogue) and through necessarily indirect routes (dreams, parapraxes, lapses, etc.). The subject lives their life as a subject but does not recognize themselves as such, thereby being condemned to repeat the same pattern endlessly—we can call these repetitions "symptoms," or insistent psychic motives—a pattern derived from their "desire" in the psychoanalytic sense: not sexual desire, but the tendency toward something that is unknown to the subject, and which forms the subject into what they actually are. (Even if Romeo, dead before 20, does not have much time to be repetitive.) The situation of interlocution specific to psychoanalysis represents exactly the intermediary between the "third person"—in other words, the knowledge of the sociologist or psychologist who is objectively considering present and past facts, and who is basing their reasoning on general regularities—and the "first person" (namely, those justifying sentences such as "I love him because . . . ," which have been shown to not provide satisfactory answers to the question "Why do you love him?"). We can thus see how psychoanalysis could aim to capture this core of irrationality on which the love between Romeo and Juliet is based. Characterizing the psychoanalytic attempt in this way also explains to us why the key source texts for psychoanalysis (ranging from Sophocles to Edgar Allan Poe to Hoffmann to Goethe) have placed literature in a position of priority for examples—with literature precisely exploring this core of irrationality.

But this irrational core does not just concern romantic love—as we have seen with Montaigne and his friend La Boétie—and there are other feelings that share the same status in regards to the question "why?" We can even go beyond the domain of feelings. With this idea of an "irrational core" that is embodied by the love between Romeo and Juliet, we encounter the same intellectual frustration as that which I described at the beginning of the book about the tree falling on the car in front of me. This frustration can also leave a Napoleonic historian speechless at the idea that a poorly made map changed the fate of Europe, or the overly skeptical reader of a newspaper announcing that American soldiers had coincidentally been on the same train as an active terrorist. "Frustration" is meant to be taken here in its most precise sense: we see the entanglement of hundreds of causes that lead to an event, but it seems that an essential why-question is not resolved by this. In any case, there is a gap between the expectation of a "because" that would satisfy us and an explanation that mentions a host of independent causes that can as well be seen as a coincidence. Nafissatou Diallo went into the room even though Dominique Strauss-Kahn had not yet left, the American soldiers took the only train bound for Paris that was not sold out in Amsterdam, and so on.

This parallel nevertheless has its limits. The conspiracy theorist we met in the previous chapter expects a "because" that is proportional to the spectacular event that intrigues him. But in the case of Romeo and Juliet, it seems that no "because" can come to terms with the singularity of their love. All of these whys are too generous and too vast—like a badly tailored suit, something ready-to-wear for an individual with an unusual physique; as if all the different "because"s were too standard for this subject.

The "why?" here seems to come up against the individual, as Aristotle already hinted at by noting in his *Metaphysics* that "there is no science of the individual." Of course, what we have seen regarding singular events and their explanation (and in particular, what we saw in chapters 5 and 6) tends to mitigate this statement. But those cases like Romeo's love for Juliet, Montaigne's friendship for La Boétie, and so many others involving pure subjectivity (rather than just particularity), seem to represent the genuine limits to the question "why?"

In this light, we better understand the meaning of the Platonic myth of the *Symposium*, which argued that lovers are in fact two halves of an originally separated soul. It is a way of giving meaning to this aspect of singular love (like that of Romeo for Juliet) that the causes and justifications by which one answers the question "Why does he love her?" do not exhaust. Understood in this way, the ideal of romantic love (the complementarity between two beings who finally find each other) constitutes an avatar of the *Symposium*'s myth, which was reinterpreted by an era of Western literature that invented love—namely, a form of relationship between two individuals that cannot be reduced to sexual desire, the patrimonial association of two beings in one economic household, or the more general alliance of two families within a marriage (which is how some anthropologists view the concept).

In this measure, romantic love plays the same role as that of destiny: substituting the group of causal explanations (which are at the mercy of the Cournotian view of chance) in order to produce an answer to the question "why?" which—when applied to the singular fact of Romeo's love for Juliet, Werther's for Lotte, Anna Karenina's for Vronsky—finally seems satisfactory; and by which the lovers in question can describe their own love to each other and themselves, thereby consolidating it and making it into a reason-for-action, a "why" for their subsequent actions. The myth of the *Symposium*, the romantic ideal of love, and the myth of destiny thus appear as three figures of this metaphysical idol that answers "because" to a why-question that has no answer in reality.

To Sum Up

The love between Romeo and Juliet is explained in different ways that seem to not take the singularity of this love into account. The phrase "Because it was he, because it was me" expresses the inability of the different responses to "why?" to provide a proper answer on the subject; it indicates the irrational core of love (as well as friendship, and other singular emotions and experiences). The gap between Romeo's love for Juliet and the order of reasons and causes has sometimes been understood as the place of "subjectivity" (in the psychoanalytic sense of the word). Just like the notion of destiny, the myth of romantic love turns this radical contingency into a sort of necessity—which is enshrined in an idea of love that is reinforced by a broad spectrum of novels, songs, and films that permeate our world. Lovers draw from this mythology the elements of self-narration that consolidate their love.

9

Why Am I Me?

WHO HAS NOT HAD A STRANGE MOMENT WHERE THE arbitrariness of being yourself leaps to your attention? Someone else does not have the feelings that I am experiencing right now; there are endless problems that I have accumulated or unwittingly created or that my complicity contributed to stationing around me and which I now need to confront. If I were someone else, none of this would exist—this feeling of heat that I am suddenly experiencing, the loud voices that are coming from the street below, my sudden craving for cashews, etc. I am just going around in circles! Why am I not someone else? Why am I me, and the other, another?

These sensations of vertigo are most often pejoratively called "metaphysics." Usually, they pass after a good night's sleep, time spent with friends, a hard-won victory in Scrabble, or a well-prepared *magret de canard*. But in reality, the phrase is not as pejorative as it may seem: after all, what is academically referred to as metaphysics actually concerns precisely these kinds of problems. In his metaphysical masterpiece *On the Plurality of Worlds*, David Lewis manages to dedicate ten pages to the question "Could I be a poached egg?" After everything we have seen in our adventures with the question "why?", we have enough resources to tackle this daunting question of "Why am I me?"—which we normally try to bat away like an intrusive housefly whenever it comes to bother us.

Evidence and Hinges

Why am I me? If the question arises in my mind, my next move generally consists in judging it to be absurd for rather logical reasons. How could "I" not be "me"? Isn't part of the definition of "I" to name "me"—so that whoever this "me" may be, "I" will always name "me" and thus I will always be me? Yet if I am always and necessarily me, the question "Why am I me?" has no possible answer. In order for the question "Why is there X?" to have any meaning, it must indeed be possible for us to imagine that X is not the case. Yet I cannot not be me; and this impossibility is not even a physical impossibility (like going faster than the speed of light). It seems nearly metaphysical, or even logical: whatever the laws of the universe may be, and even when imagining all the possible physical laws that could exist instead of the ones that currently govern our universe, I am always me. Should we then make peace with this person inside us that metaphysics is harassing and give up on the question?

I don't believe so. Even if such a question is impossible, it remains an interesting fact for us—just like how in mathematics impossibility results like Galois theory or Gödel's incompleteness theorem are often considered by connoisseurs to be the most interesting.[1]

"Why am I me?" indeed indicates a limit to the question "why?" With it, there is nothing to ask, no reason that explains why "I" makes "me," no justifying fact; and if we try to explain it away by saying that it is a particularity of Western languages that the word "I" designates the word's speaker (and thus "me"), we are thrown into the more profound realization that this is the case with every language—that the translation of "I" always represents the one who is named by the name by which the speaker designates oneself.

We can thus see that this question shares its status as the limit of "why?"

with other questions for which it is unclear how an answer could have any kind of sense. For example, "Why does Tuesday come after Monday?" has no other answer than "Because it's Tuesday"—which is not a real answer, or at least not a satisfying one.

These questions interrogate things that are self-evident, with "self-evident" meaning here: statements about X such that their truth is understood as soon as we know the meaning of the word X. After the *contingency* of the singular fact "Romeo loves Juliet," or of the randomness of a tree falling, *self-evidence* is thus the other limit of why. Seized with a frenzy of "why?", children at around three or four years old can ask truckloads of questions along these lines. When they ultimately stop asking questions of this nature, it is generally because they have implicitly understood that there is a range of facts, things, and events whose reasons for occurring are beyond the reach of our reason.

Certain among these limits precisely concern the definitions of words: insofar as Tuesday is defined as the day that follows Monday, Tuesday does not follow Monday "because" of something; it comes after Monday simply because it is Tuesday—just like how "I am me" operates on the basis that "I," by definition, names "me." These things and facts do not have reasons because they form in some way the linguistic framework for our understanding of the world. Some of them are pure conventions: it just so happens that in our language we happened to call the second day of the week "Tuesday." We could have done something completely different. There is an arbitrariness here that is the arbitrariness of language—as Ferdinand de Saussure, one of the founders of modern linguistics, referred to it. The words are a certain way in one language, and different in another; the same goes for syntactic changes and grammatical rules. It is all arbitrary; this is to be noted and there is nothing more to say about it. Any historical explanation of the formation of these words in a language, such as pointing out the connection between names of the planets known by the Ancients and name of the days, explains language itself, but nothing about the things—the days themselves—named by these words, and objects of a "why?" question here.

Why Am I Me?

This arbitrariness thus does not accept any reasons: things that are self-evident, like the fact that Tuesday comes after Monday, form a limit to the question "why?" because they are ultimately based on a purely contingent fact. The self-evident "no why" thus joins up here with the contingent "no because"; but there are other forms of self-evidence that limit the scope of "why?" in a different way. Indeed, in the same way that I cannot ask why I am me, I cannot sensibly ask why a thing is the thing that it is. "Why is this tiger a tiger?" runs into the same problems as "Why am I me?" If this tiger were not a tiger, it simply would not be itself. It is not as if it were some undifferentiated entity that decided one fine day to be a tiger for some reason, like Einstein deciding to be a physicist, as to which one can meaningfully ask, "Why was Einstein a physicist?" No, it is self-evident that a tiger is a tiger. There is no reason for this; there is no cause that makes this thing a tiger since it was already, above all else, a tiger before being anything else (ferocious, sick, solitary, etc.). We can ask why this particular tiger is thin (because of deforestation, its natural prey is much less plentiful) or does not have any offspring (the competition for females has become particularly intense because of the scarcity of resources), but not why it is *a tiger*. Or at least we could answer, "Because his parents were tigers," but then the same question could be asked once again, and finally there is something self-evident about the ancestor tigers being tigers.

Similar why-questions generally concern the *essence* of a thing. The notion of essence signifies whatever T (for the tiger) which is such that if our tiger stops being T it ceases to be itself—whereas it continues to be itself if I shave its fur, cut off one of its legs, or paint it green. There is thus a logical absurdity in asking why a thing has the essence that it has because this presupposes that we are starting out with an entity that has no essence, and that such and such an essence would later befall it. In other words, it is rational to ask why a tiger is *as* it is, but not why a tiger is *what* it is. This question returns to the child who has not yet understood the grammar of why, and asks why Tuesday comes after Monday.

Of course, as I indicated in chapter 5, many philosophers contest the idea that essences exist—in the sense that they are entities endowed with a real ontological status in the same way as my cup of coffee or the Grand Dukedom of Luxembourg. More precisely, there are certain philosophers who believe that essences are "more" real than this cup (they are sometimes called "Platonic realists"); others who believe that they are just as real; and others like Willard van Orman Quine who think that they have no reality and that they are only abstractions. This question forms part of the so-called problem of "universals"—which has occupied our greatest minds since Aristotle (or, more precisely, Porphyry[2]), and which concerns the central question of knowing whether anything besides individual things (this cup, my hand, our tiger) can exist. But there be dragons, as we say; and we will not start walking down this thorny path.

We will make use of "essence" here in its most deflationary sense possible. Whatever the decision may be on the ontological status of essences, the argument that "Why is X what it is?" is a meaningless question will continue to hold. If we imagine the entire group of possible worlds and if we call our tiger "Gagarine," we can easily conceive of certain worlds where Gagarine exists and certain where he does not; but in those where he does exist he is nothing other than a tiger.[3] In all possible worlds, Gagarine is either a tiger or does not exist; and thus Gagarine is *necessarily* a tiger. If we refuse to discuss essences, this reasoning about Gagarine should convince us all the same that the question "Why is Gagarine a tiger?" has no more meaning than "Why is water wet?" It is wet because wetness consists of being somehow full of water; and since water is necessarily water, it is necessarily wet. Along these lines, Gagarine is necessarily a tiger. In this book, the *nature* of Gagarine—a term understood in chapter 5 within the context of the semantic of possible worlds as a structure of the set of possible worlds close to the actual one—is under focus now; and the question I'm considering asks why Gagarine has the nature of Gagarine, which has no meaningful answer.

And so we arrive here: the self-evidence of a thing being what it is—either in the sense of the name that it bears (Tuesday is "Tuesday," and comes after Monday because that's what Tuesday means), or in the sense of its nature (Gagarine is a tiger)—constitutes a limit to the question "why?"

Wherever this self-evidence occurs, there is no need to ask "why?" Curiously, one of the limits sends us back to the arbitrariness of the word, and thus to a certain *contingency*; while the other sends us back to the absolute *necessity* according to which a thing must be what it is. Wittgenstein says in *On Certitude* that one cannot doubt everything because there must be certainties, comparing these to the hinges of a door. In order for a door to open, there must be fixed hinges; and in order to be able to doubt, there must exist certainties (along the lines of "I know I have a body although I do not see it"). Something similar is at play here: in order to be able to ask why, we need these limits of why—these self-evidences where the question is not necessary, and on to which all of our other "why?"s can be latched.

Disambiguation, the Principle of Identity, and Gravitation

It could be argued that I am acting in bad faith here. In the same way that "Why was there a fire?" was ambiguous—since we saw that the question examined the cause of the fire as much as it did my beliefs about it—the question "Why is Gagarine a tiger?" ultimately leads to a questioning of what justifies my belief that this animal is indeed a tiger. To this I would respond: because he is striped and orange, a carnivore, etc. This does not make him a tiger; but since these properties form a part of what a tiger is—and are certainly its most frequent properties if not actually being the animal's definition (some would say they belong to the stereotype of the tiger) —my recognizing it as such is justifiable.[4] In this case, the different domains of "why?" are being confused by whoever contends, as I did, that the Gagarine why-question isn't meaningful; there is an error in how words are being phrased, with "Why is Gagarine a tiger?" being confused with "Why do you think that Gagarine is a tiger?" Likewise, after such disambiguation, "Why does Tuesday come after Monday?" becomes a question that is no longer about the days of the week but rather about the use of the words "Tuesday" and "Monday," and why I say that today is Tuesday (namely, because yesterday was Monday).

Have we thus emptied the question "Why am I me?" of all its metaphysics? One would not be blamed for doubting this. This is first because the method of disambiguation seems precisely less effective when applied to this particular statement: can we really interpret it as a question about the reasons for believing that I am me? What would be the strange contexts in which this question might actually be asked? An experiment in cognitive science where it is being investigated whether or not I have the ability to recognize myself in a mirror or identify my own movements? The chances of this are honestly slim.

And conversely, our metaphysical vertigo is revived if I think once more about our tiger Gagarine and rephrase my question about his nature in a slightly different way: "Why is *a* tiger a tiger?" Let's disambiguate this statement: "Why do I believe a tiger is a tiger?" The answer here is perfectly metaphysical: I am justified in believing that a tiger is a tiger because logic as a whole is dominated by the principle of identity—namely, that for all A, "A=A". Everything is identical to itself, and is thus itself. One could say then that the principle of identity is derived from the principle of noncontradiction: "a thing cannot be and not be what it is (at the same time and within the same context)." In Book E of his *Metaphysics*, Aristotle explains that this principle is implemented by everyone as soon as they speak; without it, a word like "tiger" could also mean "non-tiger"—and could thus mean "table" (since a table is a "non-tiger"). In the end, this would mean that all words would say absolutely everything, and nothing would ultimately be sayable. The principle of noncontradiction is thus the basis of all speech and thought.

But we can take this another step further and challenge my initial claim about the nature of Gagarine being beyond all why-questions: isn't the fact that "a tiger is a tiger" real *in virtue of* this principle of identity? If yes, we must say that "a tiger is a tiger because the principle of identity is true"—and even more, it is necessarily a tiger (since the principle of identity is necessarily true), which makes "tiger" (part of) its nature (or essence). In other words, we have a firm answer to the question "Why is a tiger a tiger?" Of course, the principle of identity is not a cause—in the same way that Zidane headbutting Materazzi *caused* his expulsion from the 2006 World Cup Final, and perhaps France's loss to Italy minutes later. But let's not forget that we have already seen that the reasons for facts are not always their causes. Using a concept I already employed, we should say that the principle of identity is the *ground* for the fact of a tiger being a tiger.

This analysis reshuffles the cards. We thought we had reached a definitive limit of the question "why?" with our earlier questions about Tuesday, Gagarine, and myself—but no, this is not the case.

Science should have made us familiar by now with the idea that a limit to the question "why?" is not always absolute. Let's look at physics, for example. I explained in chapter 2 (perhaps somewhat long-windedly) how observations about falling bodies gave rise to important concepts from Aristotle, Galileo, and Newton among others. For Newton, the fundamental cause of these falling objects (as well as planetary motion) was universal attraction. In regard to this attraction, he explicated its mathematical law but was very careful to not explain *why* it exists. For him, this attraction defined an essential property of matter—similar to length, for example. It would be clearly absurd to ask why a body has length; after all, without length, width, and depth, it would simply no longer be a body (since area belongs to its essence in the same way that the essence or nature of a tiger is to be a tiger). For Newton, the force of attraction (like area) was an essential property of matter and it was thus meaningless to ask why matter attracts. "I frame no hypotheses (*hypothesis non fingo*)," he wrote on the subject in a well-known Scholium from his *Opticks*—a phrase that believers of the scientific method would repeat for centuries to signify their refusal to believe in metaphysical speculations about the ultimate causes of things. However, this limit to scientific investigation was not absolute. With his 1905 Theory of Special Relativity and then his 1915 Theory of General Relativity, Einstein profoundly transformed the fundamental concepts of Newtonian physics: space, time, speed, mass. General relativity's introduction of the concept of mass-energy equivalence (the famous equation $E=mc^2$) resulted in some truly counterintuitive ideas—with that of mass and space no longer being independent arguably the most revolutionary among them. Space could no longer be viewed as an absolute and infinite container in which bodies are like shoes in a closet. In reality, masses have an effect on space, bending the space-time in their vicinity. When a mass is big enough, the curvature of space is significant to the point that a ray of light pursuing a naturally straight line—following the "shape" of space—will have its trajectory inflected. Einstein derived from this the prediction that when the light of the sun passes next to Mercury, its point of contact on Earth does not reveal a straight line from the sun (which was later confirmed). This curving induced by mass explains what gravitation is: space being curved around masses, the trajectory of bodies approaches a substantial mass when there is one. Einstein thus answered the question "Why is there gravity?"—a question that was the limit of "why?" in Newtonian physics.

As far as the changing character of the limits of the explainable is concerned, biology is certainly far from stable. For a long time, we thought that death was an intrinsic property of the living, that it formed a part of the essence of being alive. "The living dies because it lives," Aristotle wrote in his lapidary way; and for a long time, mortality has been considered one of the properties that characterizes living beings—along with reproduction, autonomous movement, and metabolism. However, within the framework of evolutionary biology, certain biologists have dared to ask the question, "Why must we die?" How is it that organisms are not eternal or almost so (like certain unicellulars, as it has been believed until recently)? And these Darwinians have found an answer: in short, because natural selection is no longer active after the reproductive phase in organisms, harmful genetic mutations are no longer controlled and accumulate generation after generation in our genome, acting like long-term time bombs. Death from old age is now no longer considered a necessary and intrinsic property of living beings; instead, it is a property that occurs in many lineages of living beings (particularly multicellular ones), and there is a reason for this. In fact, the evolutionary biology of death—and especially of aging, this being defined by a rapidly increased probability of dying—is an expanding field of research.[5]

Why Am I Me?

The sciences show us that the limits of "why?" are always relative—relative, that is, to the progress or changes in these sciences. We will now see that the "metaphysical" limits of "why?" are also relative, as paradoxical as this may seem.

Transgressing the Limits?

Why am I thus me? We could now understand this question somewhat differently, from a less metaphysical angle: "Why am I like I am?" When phrased in this way, a whole variety of theoretical knowledge comes into play. Psychology would explain why I have my particular tastes and fears, sociology would show how my habits and tendencies are constructed, genetics would demonstrate why I have a tendency toward baldness and being overweight. There are a thousand explainable causes for why I am what I am. Earlier, we saw how we can ask why a tiger is as it is, but not why it is what it is. But is this distinction actually pertinent? Is there really something more to a tiger than simply being *as it is*?

Maybe no. Maybe when all of these domains of knowledge have finished explaining why I am as I am, there is nothing more to explain. We find here again the metaphysical problem about the story of Romeo and Juliet from the preceding chapter. When confronted with the causal explanations of the love between Romeo and Juliet and the "singular love of Romeo and Juliet" itself, the skeptical philosopher would deny that the latter actually means anything. These romantic killjoys are "deflationists," meaning that they want to minimize the number of types of things to admit within their own ontology. Our skeptics arrive on the scene once again (looking like Adorno): they reject the argument that I would be what I am in addition to and beyond the explainable fact of being as I am.

Let us be clear. We are not dealing with some sort of semantic dispute here, as was the case with the disambiguation mentioned above; and I am not trying to argue that there is a more intelligent way to phrase the question "Why am I me?" that would allow for a real answer. No: I am suggesting here that there is a radical way of understanding the difference between "*as* it is" and "*what* it is"—according to which the latter is devoid of meaning. Between this alternative way and that which has been in use up until this point, there thus exists a difference between metaphysical arguments. Just like how, depending on whether one is Newton or Einstein, the question "Why gravity?" will either have an answer or be a limit to "why?", the question "Why am I me?" will likely be subjected to either one reading or another—ultimately receiving an answer if the latter is adopted. Whether or not a fact—such as "I am who I am" or "Gagarine is a tiger"—is a limit to "why?" is thus not something absolute and depends on the metaphysics by which one considers it. We will look at this in more detail; and then we will investigate how this rivalry between metaphysics can be understood—a rivalry that is firmly distinct from the competition between physical theories. Indeed, unlike physics, competing metaphysics cannot be ordered in a historical succession where the most recent is truer, more probable, more complete, and ultimately better than earlier ones.[6]

But let's avoid an initial misinterpretation. When I say that certain metaphysics exclude "What am I?" questions in favor of only "How am I?" ones, I am not uniquely singling out theories like those of Nietzsche, Quine, or Whitehead mentioned above (who are incredibly different from each other, it is worth highlighting) according to which there are no essences. Even in a metaphysics where one allows for essences, one could make sense of "Why am I me?" and not see it as a limit to "why?", as I will explain now.

Origin Essentialism: An Explanation for My Being Myself?

There exists a philosophical argument about the essence of living individuals that is called "origin essentialism." Emerging from the reflections of Saul Kripke—whose text *Naming and Necessity* (1972) is sometimes considered to be the origin of the revival of metaphysics in the twentieth century—this argument presents something very simple. Who are you truly? You could have another job, have more children or no children, have different clothes, live elsewhere, or speak another language and you would be no less yourself. What then must be changed in order to be someone different? The philosophers who support origin essentialism say: your biological origin. If you had different parents who fertilized you at a different time, you would no longer be you. There are biological reasons as well as metaphysical ones to support this argument. Moreover, the connection between the nature of a thing and its origin forms a part of our ordinary conceptual apparatus (think of cheese or wine: a Chiroubles is a Chiroubles because it comes from the Chiroubles terroir, as does a Camembert from Camembert).

Now let's suppose that we accept this origin essentialism. "Why am I me?" thus receives an answer: "Because my parents met and I was conceived." An answer like this is not particularly exciting and sounds less "deep" than the question—but it does answer the question. We can of course reiterate this "why?" by questioning the origin of the parents, of the parents of the parents, and so on.

I am not arguing here in favor of origin essentialism. I just want to highlight that if we adopt this metaphysics—which by the way does not refuse the notion of essence, unlike the metaphysicians I cited in the previous section—then the question "Why am I me?" acquires meaning and allows for a possible answer. It is no longer a limit to "why?" All of these self-evidences that appeared as limits to "why?" are thus only so on the condition of subscribing to certain metaphysics. And as soon as we develop this somewhat intuitive idea that our biological origins define our essence, we end up being able to make sense of the initially nonsensical question "Why am I me?" and can even envisage answering it through other facts than the mere conventions of language.

Metaphysics and Mathematical Pluralism

To better understand what is at play here, another analogy might be helpful. It concerns mathematics (so buckle up). The start of the twentieth century was a crucial period for this discipline, and the often-used term "foundational crises" sums up why. Mathematicians such as Gottlob Frege,

Georg Cantor, and David Hilbert wanted to reorganize mathematics starting from the most basic things. Cantor pioneered what is known as "set theory." As its name indicates, this theory deals with objects called "sets" (like the set **N** of natural numbers [1, 2, 3, 4, and so on])—as well as relations of belonging to a set (4 *belongs* to the set of natural numbers **N**), and inclusion within a set (even numbers are *included* in the set of natural numbers **N**). These notions are so basic that these mathematicians dreamed of rebuilding mathematics on this new foundation. In particular, Cantor was interested in them because he wanted to explore the notion of mathematical infinity: the set of integers (the numbers with which we count) is infinite; the set of even numbers is also infinite (although "smaller" at first glance; however, it is in reality the same size because each even number is an integer multiplied by two); the set of real numbers (ones that are sometimes indicated by infinite decimals and which *measure* continuous magnitudes[7]) is infinite as well, but is intuitively much "bigger" than **N**. Cantor sought a theory that would give a precise meaning to all of this. In his theory, there exist infinite sets that are bigger or smaller than each other which can be ranked; it is also possible to add or multiply these infinite entities. (The technical term for the size of a set is its "cardinal"; when one considers the order of the members of a set, it's an "ordinal." Set theory allows for operations on ordinals and cardinals, as well as comparing them.)

Ever since Euclid and his *Elements* of geometry, we have conceived of mathematics as a set of *theorems* that are proven based on *axioms*. Axioms are primitive propositions that are posited (for example, "through any two distinct points there is exactly one line"), and not many are needed to define all geometric objects. Logical deduction then allows us to demonstrate theorems that specify the properties of these objects. Even to this day, the thirteen books that comprise *The Elements* are the paradigm of this axiomatized mathematical science (which also constituted Spinoza's model for philosophy, as is seen in his *Ethics*).

We can also axiomatize set theory. But between David Hilbert, the German mathematician who conceived of axiomatizing mathematics overall, and whose "Program" was meant to secure foundations for all mathematics, and the famous incompleteness theorems proven by the logician Kurt Gödel in 1931, mathematicians saw their dream of firmer foundations collapse.[8] What does this mean? In order for them to establish elementary arithmetic, on the basis of which the rest of mathematics could then be constructed, they identified very simple axioms, such as "There exists an element 0" and "The number formed by a number '+1' is a number." Among these axioms, there is one called the "axiom of choice," which states, "Imagine sets: I can always choose an element in each set; taken together, they form a new set." Although apparently obvious when it is a question of a finite number of sets (for example, 54 sacks of potatoes), it is much less so when this becomes an infinite number in the same genre of infinity as the set of points in a line (the so-called "real" numbers, in other words).

Alongside these axioms there is a proposition that was of major interest to Cantor which is called the "continuum hypothesis." It claims that between the set of integers and the set of real numbers (in other words, those for counting and those for measuring a continuum), there is no intermediary cardinal—a set that would thus be larger than **N** and smaller than **R**. Cantor thought that this was true and wanted to prove it.

Negative results such as Gödel's incompleteness theorem, published in 1931, established that we cannot in reality prove that all the axioms of arithmetic are consistent together, at least while remaining within arithmetic itself. And since, as Hilbert had shown, arithmetics is the basis of all axiomatic reconstructions of the whole of mathematics, this impossibility cast a shadow onto the idea that mathematics are a realm of absolute logical coherence.[9] They also established that there exist "undecidable propositions"—ones that cannot be proven or shown to be false based off of the axioms.[10]

The continuum hypothesis (hereafter CH, and whose undecidability was proven well after Gödel by the logician Paul Cohen in 1963) is one of these undecidable propositions along with the axiom of choice (AC). Therefore, axiomatized arithmetic with the axiom of choice—just like arithmetic without the axiom of choice—is correct. But it is not the same kind of mathematics; and with each of them, we can either add or negate the continuum hypothesis as an axiom. The situation is thus as follows, and we can now see why it was deemed a "foundational crisis": there exist at least four different axiomatics (with or without CH, with or without AC); none of them can be demonstrated as being truer than the others; and yet they are different because they include different true propositions (or theorems). This is why the situation differs from that of gravitation in physics: we cannot decide which of these forms of mathematics is "true"—whereas we have arguments for claiming that Einstein's physics is the truest (and moreover, Newtonian physics is included within it as long as the speeds concerned are well below that of the speed of light[11]).

I am not claiming that metaphysics is a matter of axioms; but simply that the way in which the plurality of metaphysics is in mutual competition may possibly be more similar to the plurality of axiomatic mathematics than to the diversity of true or false physical theories. To give an example of the kind of immunity to empirical data that characterizes metaphysics as well as mathematics, let's briefly consider a central contemporary controversy in metaphysics: the nature of time. It is often formulated today in the following way: does a thing (a car, a symphony, a storm) exist in another point of time before being here, different, as if it had "temporal parts" (before, then) in the same way it has spatial parts? Or is it all there in each moment of time, meaning that it does not have different temporal parts since it is identical to itself at every instant? We can easily see that all of the facts of the world support the first metaphysics (called four-dimensionalism) as much as the second metaphysics (called three-dimensionalism) and that there is no way of deciding between the two of them on the basis of facts in the world.[12]

A Little Bit of Metametaphysics

Metaphysics is named as such because after having written his *Physics*, Aristotle wrote a number of treatises about substance, being, principles, actions, and power among other very general notions which commentators then grouped together and named "Metaphysics"—since they effectively came *after* physics (in the Greek sense of the word *meta*). Contemporary philosophers (who are clearly as fond of neologisms as their predecessors) give the name of metaethics to that which concerns discussions about the status of ethical propositions, and, later, that of metametaphysics to the theory of how metaphysics should operate. What we are about to discuss falls under this idea of metametaphysics—a term that certainly never fails to make an impression on people in conversation.

We have seen that, against our first impression, questions like "Why am I me?" and "Why is a tiger a tiger?" are not absolute limits to "why?" If we change metaphysical frameworks, if we adopt, for example, origin essentialism concerning living individuals—or perhaps a metaphysics in which the notion of essence is proscribed—they can become reasonable and allow for answers.

But does "why?" have any kind of limit then?

This all depends on our way of conceiving the plurality of metaphysics. It could be the same situation as that in physics where one option is true and the others false (even though I have implied that this is not the case); or it could be something similar to Hilbert's axiomatics, where several options could be acceptable in the end, depending upon our requisites.

I am bringing up *different metaphysics* here because we are not examining theories about empirical facts; on the contrary, we are looking at fundamental and extremely general notions in our language such as identity, essence, myself, the possible, etc. The way in which the signification of these terms will be conceived and then lead to other fundamental significations will define a metaphysical option. On these grounds, the meaning or nonmeaning of questions that use or refer to these words will be determined.

Quine wrote an important article in 1951 called "The Two Dogmas of Empiricism."[13] In it, he rejected a cardinal philosophical distinction between so-called analytic judgments and synthetic judgments—that is, the distinction between a true proposition that is based on the meaning of words (like "a bachelor is not married") and a true proposition that is based on the state of the world (like "France is the world champion in soccer").

In Quine's perspective, it is up for debate whether the proposition "this tiger is a tiger" (which is apparently true based on the meaning of the words involved) is really so different from "this tiger is sick" (which is apparently true because of the state of the world). But if this difference is done away with, we could then find answers to "why is this tiger a tiger?" (on the model of what I was saying above concerning origin essentialism, for example) in the same way that we find empirical ones for "why is this tiger sick?" We thus see that the existence of answers to questions that apparently concern self-evidences depends on our acceptance or our rejection of the distinction between the analytic and the synthetic.

Let's go further. When I was talking about disambiguating questions, I argued that the provided examples were simply grammatical confusions when considered as limits for why because they were actually sound questions about the justification of beliefs. But we can conceive of a very deflationist metaphysical position that rejects the notion of essences, universals, and natures, in which all questions like those currently at hand are naturally interpreted as questions about the usage of words.[14] There would thus no longer be a limit to "why?"

We are thus approaching the crucial question: is one of these metaphysics correct? Of course, unlike the world of scientific theories, it is not possible (in a straightforward way) to say whether one or the other is "true."[15] This is, after all, why I used the analogy of mathematical axiomatics. But this doesn't mean that all metaphysics are equal.

Without going into sophisticated discussions about the philosophy of mathematics, we can already observe that mathematics does not allow the same things with or without the axiom of choice. The simple operation consisting of determining in a set E, for a subset F, the "infimum"—namely, the greatest element in the subset of elements in E that are all smaller than elements of F—for certain infinite sets is impossible without the axiom of choice. Yet, other more complex mathematical properties are constructed on the foundation of this notion of infimum. A mathematics without the axiom of choice is thus "poorer" than a mathematics that includes it. But at the same time, there is merit in being "poor" and hence simpler since this implies fewer axioms—following the line of logic of the eternally applicable Occam's razor, where parsimony is a virtue when applied to scientific theory. This example shows that even if neither is truer than the other, different mathematics fall under different epistemic values: fecundity on the one hand, simplicity on the other. One must find arguments to justify one or the other value when choosing between them. It would therefore be inaccurate to think that choosing a mathematics is pure convention since there are competing epistemological reasons for justifying one's choice.[16] For instance, one could argue that a certain axiomatic realizes the optimal trade-off between fecundity and simplicity. However, other epistemic values could be introduced (such as the availability of developing a mathematics that can be applied to physics or to biology, etc.).

The metametaphysical situation is not so different. Certain metaphysics are "richer" than others. In what way? In the prologue to *On the Plurality of Worlds* (1988), David Lewis reflects on the metaphysician's methods. As we have seen, his own metaphysics supports a radically counterintuitive theory, since it is modal realist and imagines that all possible worlds exist—like in certain science-fiction movies where they are parallel but never meet. But this argument allows him to frugally account for several fundamental aspects of reality and thought: causality, the existence of propositions and significations, the notion of "property" and "intrinsic property" of a thing, etc. In the end, the argument's price—namely, its counterintuitive aspect—seems reasonable for such a rich metaphysical theory.

I do not want to advocate for "Lewisism" here. His example simply shows that in spite of the absence of empirical differences between metaphysics ("empirical" in the sense that different conceptions would result in different predictions, which would allow them to be empirically tested and for us to keep the one whose predictions are truer and more interesting), there exist criteria by which we can compare them: parsimony, fecundity, generality, how much weight we give to our intuitions as well as how much we agree with the best scientific theories that are available at the time. The question is thus to order these different values, which leads us back to a debate between arguments supporting different epistemic values—but this time applied to metaphysics. And just like in mathematics, the choice between metaphysical frameworks—and thus between metaphysical presuppositions in light of which certain why-questions appear as self-evidences and limits to "why?"—is not a pure convention.

It may be that, as in mathematics, the questions will remain open and that only criteria bound to specific metaphysical aims will prevail—namely, which metaphysical theories will be most useful for us for whatever it is we would like to do; for example, to account for our usual conceptual scheme, or to propose a framework for the empirical sciences, or to propose a theory on which an ethics can be based, etc. In this case, self-evidence as a limit to "why?", as it was thematized and illustrated by the examples in this chapter, is not an absolute fact. Different metaphysical options—on the nature of causality, on the reference of words like "me," "essence," etc.—will involve different bounds of meaning. Self-evidence is a limit to "why?", but self-evidence is no longer an epistemic absolute.

To Sum Up

"Why am I me?" seems to have no response because the fact is self-evident; this question apparently limits the scope of "why?"—along with questions concerning linguistic conventions, or the reason why something has the nature that it does. Nevertheless, these limits to "why?" are relative to whatever metaphysical framework is at play. By shifting this, answers become possible, even if they are most likely not very interesting. It is thus a question of deciding between different metaphysical frameworks, which in principle do not allow for empirical tests. They are evaluated according to diverse epistemic values (parsimony, fecundity, unity, etc.), whose own hierarchy will be the object of further epistemological and metaphysical questioning.

Conclusion

Why "Why"?

BEFORE CLOSING THIS BOOK, WE CANNOT ESCAPE ASKING, "Why do we, and can we, ask why?"

Several distinct questions lurk within that dual question. First, while I have insisted on the differences between the different forms of "why?" and the multiplicity of "because" genres, we have reason to wonder about their unity. We have repeatedly seen that the different meanings of "why?" are joined together despite their differences. As such, we will need to explicitly examine how this is possible—namely, why it is not by chance that we have the same word for these distinct questions.

Next, what is it that makes people ask "why?" so commonly? Here again, I insisted on the role that "why?" plays in science and in our experience: without explanations or justifications, the world and our lived experience would be chaotic. But is this the only reason why we ask "why"? And how come we ask the question even when it is beyond its limits, which leads us to construct metaphysical idols to respond?

Last, how is it possible that we can *legitimately* ask why? How is it that answers are available? For a long time, philosophers have speculated about this last question. Leibniz's expression that "everything has a sufficient reason" is emblematic in this regard. But does this "Principle of Sufficient Reason" respond to our question here? Is it a fact? Or is it, rather, the ground of any possibility for identifying facts? And in this sense, is it a fact of another order (and which?) or a metaphysical decision?

Reason, *Reason, and Reasons*

By dint of distinguishing meanings, of showing that "why?" can mean a cause (or another sort of scientific explanation) or a reason for a belief, or a goal, we expose ourselves to the objection of what might be called homonymy: there are different usages of the word; and ultimately, the "grammatical" confusions and mistakes we have been discussing (following such great thinkers as Nietzsche, Spinoza, and Wittgenstein) unluckily come from the fact that the French and English languages (as well as many other languages) have the same word to say all these different things. Philosophers like Gottlob Frege think that the arbitrary form of ordinary language induces metaphysical problems that could be avoided by resorting to more formal language. As Frege notices (after Kant), for example, language uses the same word "to be" to say two things that have nothing to do with each other: the fact that a thing is in such and such a way, whether it exists or not ("Jolly Jumper *is* a horse"); and the fact that a thing exists ("Here there *is* a horse"). On the other hand, a formal language would use different signs to say these two things.[1] Could the same idea be worthwhile regarding our "why?", which is said in three different ways?

Even if I appreciate skeptical and minimalist conclusions, I will not go so far as endorsing this argument about homonymy. The different meanings of "why?" are not as distinct from each other as those of the word "pen," for example (meaning either a writing instrument or an enclosure for animals). Questions such as "how?" and "what for?"—which are often used as synonyms for "why?"—illustrate this further. "How?" asks for an explanation about the mechanism behind something; "what for?" asks for the goal; "why?" is very general and does not have an equivalent when one is asking for a reason-for-belief. However, "how?" and "what for?" cannot be switched, as they mean different things. It is therefore not a matter of a simple plurality of words, of distinct meanings of "why?" that can be disambiguated.

Let's then review what we have thus far. In the philosophical tradition, the Aristotelian theory of causes showed how these meanings that I have distinguished can be joined: Aristotle's intention was not to explain several different concepts, but rather the different meanings of one same word (what he called "cause," *aitia*). Next, the rather subtle case of the explanation of the parts and behaviors of living beings presented us with a situation where why as a "cause" might have legitimately transitioned into why as a "goal." Through natural selection, causes behave as goals—or in any case can be understood in this way—giving rise to analogies of machines and rational agents. Yet if "cause" and "goal" had nothing to do with each other, this logic of the cause of the living would not even be thinkable.

We must thus keep two things together: (a) "why?" can signify very distinct questions (and we have seen how confusions and metaphysical idols such as destiny, providence, the myth of the *Symposium*, and even conspiracy theories are born from these mistakes in the registers of "why?"); (b) the diverse meanings of "why?" are not independent but are ultimately joined with each other (according to the rules laid out in chapters 4–7).

To me, this unity seems to be grounded in the very general concept of "Reason." In the most general sense, a Reason is that which accounts for why something exists, is there, takes place, or becomes. This thing could be a *phenomenon* (where asking "why?" often involves seeking a *cause* or at least an *explanation*); it could be a *belief*, a proposition (where asking "why?" would demand a *justification*, a reason-for-belief); last, it could be an *action*, a behavior (where asking "why?" means inquiring after a reason-for, a *goal* or an *intention*).

According to this argument, "reason" has two meanings. The first is this general concept—of which cause (or explanation, more generally), justification, and goal are the three major subcategories. A Reason is the ground for some things, beliefs, or actions; and "to be the reason of" ultimately means "to ground."[2] In the second, "reason" is itself one among two of these categories: justification as reason-for-belief, or goal as reason-for-action (which could itself be a cause within certain conceptions of causality, like that of Aristotle). The multiplicity of meanings of the question "why?" is thus ultimately reflected in this equivocation of the word *reason*: on the one hand, *cause* is opposed to *reason*—namely, to the reason-for-belief (chapter 1) and the reason-for-action (chapter 3); on the other hand, cause is a form of Reason (but taken this time in the most general sense of a response to a "why?" question—namely, that by virtue of which the object of the question arises). In this sense, Reason is what we call a *ground*: it grounds an act, a belief, a phenomenon or a matter of fact.

Regarding ground, the case of living beings (where there are no goals but where causes behave like goals [chapter 4]) and the case of the justification of certain beliefs (for which the cause of a phenomenon can both justify the belief in this phenomenon and cause the phenomenon itself [chapter 1]) showed us two ways in which different meanings of "Reason" as ground can merge together. The grammar of why is the set of rules that make a certain kind of why correspond to a certain kind of object about which we ask why, and according to which some kinds of merging can legitimately take place in certain precise cases. It thus forbids *confusions* between "why?" that in turn engender metaphysical idols—which can also appear when we are at the limits of "why?", where questions no longer have meaning regardless of how we interpret them; as well as when they have a certain legitimate meaning (for example, the cause of X) that is different than expected (for example, an intention or a goal that would unify many accidentally convergent causal series).

As we have seen several times now, the cognitive faculty we call "reason" very directly concerns this triplicity of reason. A rational agent gives reasons for their actions; a rational cognitive agent justifies their beliefs; a rational approach to the world—like that defined by science—strives to understand the reasons behind phenomena. Reason, as a faculty, has revealed itself to be crucial in philosophy since Plato (under the names *logos*, *ratio*, reason, *Vernunft*), even to a point where humans have been traditionally defined as rational animals: at the highest degree of generality, it is a faculty for grounds. By this, I mean that a rational being is likely to provide grounds for their beliefs, to act on some ground (a reason) that it somehow represents, and to seek out grounds for what happens. Nothing is too controversial here; Kant, for instance, saw reason as the "faculty of principles" (*Critique of Pure Reason*) and by "principles" he meant something close to the grounds of our judgments and our actions.

Reasons and Order of Reasons

These reasons or grounds are thus joined together according to various figures, certain of which I have analyzed. Classical metaphysics (which was elaborated during the seventeenth century by Descartes and his successors) was primarily interested in the way that series of reasons of diverse natures can link together in order to guarantee that knowledge is possible. Descartes wanted to establish what he called the *mathesis universalis*—the universal order of knowledge, in which mathematics would play a decisive role. He is indeed known in part for having algebratized geometry with his introduction of what is now called analytic geometry, which supports our basic knowledge of physics.[3] To this day, students still learn it in high school, working with Cartesian graphs and coordinates.

By definition, the system of knowledge (the *mathesis*) is ordered. To conceive it, we must understand how statements and propositions cohere with each other, and in particular how they make sense of each other. This is what Descartes called "the order of reasons," according to which a truth must necessarily be preceded by another truth that is the reason for it. Thus, in this system of knowledge, *metaphysics* (by which I prove that I can access truth in general) precedes *physics* (in which the basic truths about nature are stated with certainty, based on their reasons), with the physics of simple motion preceding the physics of movements that are more complex.

Of course, the *ratio cognoscendi*—the reason which makes it so that a proposition is justified, as we saw in chapter 1—is at the centerpiece of this order of reasons. It differs from the *ratio essendi* (the reason for an extant thing, or its cause). Even if the *cogito ergo sum* (the first truth that I can know, since it founds itself in some way) establishes knowledge in such an order, my existence is obviously not the cause of everything I know. On the contrary, it is caused by many things (my parents, states of the world, etc.). We thus see that the order of reasons according to the *ratio cognoscendi* is not the order of the reasons according to the *ratio essendi*—even if the two can coincide in a given proposition, like that of "this man tossed his cigarette butt" who is simultaneously the cause (*ratio essendi*) of the fire at the Massif des Maures, and (should I happen to see him in the woods) the reason (*ratio cognoscendi*) for my knowledge of this.

The idea of a *mathesis universalis* belongs to seventeenth-century philosophy. Many of its thinkers imagined that there could be an entire system of knowledge written entirely in one same mathematical language and established in one same metaphysics, itself including a theology (namely, in the terms of Descartes's "Fourth Meditation," a firm knowledge of the existence of a guarantor of truth, which is a nondeceiving and truthful God). This would be strongly put into doubt in the following century—as much by the divorce of metaphysics from theology induced by Kantianism, as by the growing evidence of a multiplicity of forms of rationality in the natural sciences.[4] These forms were often irreducible to one same mathematics and one same body of laws, as we have seen in the case of biology. But such a retreat from the ideal of the *mathesis universalis* did not result in the requirement for an order of reasons being abandoned. On the contrary, it simply seems less total or general: in all disciplines, certain propositions justify others; and these same propositions require others in order to be justified. That is enough to define at least a local order of reasons.

If we put the reasons-for-action aside for a moment, how does this local order of reasons connect with causes and other reasons for facts? First, as we saw in the first chapter, the justification of a proposition concerning an event or a thing X is not necessarily the cause of this thing. But the story is slightly more complex than that. Let's again think about the initial statement that "the Massif des Maures is on fire." Why do I believe this? Because I saw smoke; this is certainly a good reason.

However, the reason behind the *truth* of the proposition that "the Massif des Maures fire is taking place" is not necessarily the reason why I *legitimately believe* that the Massif des Maures fire is taking place. This point is subtle because it relies on a consideration of what "*p* is true" means, and this is a central concern in philosophical debate. But for a moment, let's accept that for any proposition *p*, if I say "*p* is true," I am saying *p*, and reciprocally.[5] To say that "it is true that the Massif des Maures fire is taking place" thus goes back to saying that the Massif des Maures fire is taking place. Thus, the reason for the *truth* of this proposition is the reason for the *proposition itself*; in other words, it is the reason for the Massif des Maures fire. Hence, it is the *cause* of the Massif des Maures fire.

"Why?" thus turns out to be an even more formidable question because in reality the distinction between the cause of a thing and the belief in a proposition about that thing must subdivide in order to distinguish the reason for the *belief* (which can be more or less good, in proportion to the strength of the probable connecting link as described in chapter 1) and the reason for the *truth* of the proposition in which we believe—a reason which can potentially be a cause, like in my example, but which can also be a mathematical reason, as seen in chapter 2.

For our post-Cartesian rationalists, the notion of cause thus turned out to be crucial in the grammar of why: if I know the cause of X, this means that in addition to having an answer to "why X?" I also have an answer to "why should I believe X?"—since I have an answer to "why do I have a *good* reason to believe X?", where the reason in question is that concerning the truth of the proposition claiming X. This is highlighted further by how Descartes and particularly Spinoza made ample use of the expression "*Causa, sive ratio*" (Descartes) or "*ratio, sive causa*" (Spinoza): "cause, or reason," "a cause, namely a reason."[6] The knowledge of a cause is indeed a reason for the knowledge of an effect (as we have already seen), and it is even a particularly good reason for this knowledge.

"*Causa, sive ratio*"—an often-cited expression, in particular by Spinozists from all eras—can thus be understood as such: a cause of X is *ipso facto* a reason for which the proposition describing X is a true proposition.

If this is the case and if there is an order of knowledgeable reasons (*ratio cognoscendi*), there must be an order of causal reasons (*ratio essendi*) that corresponds to it. This equivalence is postulated in a fundamental claim from Spinoza's *Ethics*: "The order and connection of ideas is the same as the order and connection of causes" (Book II, Proposition 7). In other words, causes necessitate their effects in the same way and in the same order that ideas necessitate their consequences—and are the reason for other ideas, in other words. Therefore, true knowledge, in its order, reflects the order of things. This argument is a metaphysical basis for the *mathesis universalis* project that I mentioned earlier, which was crucial for classical rationalists and whose ultimate reason is the duality of meanings of "reason" (reason for propositions / cause of facts) and thus of the principle of reason. For a Spinozist, I can always ask "why?" about any subject since the world is causally ordered in the same way that our universe of knowledge is systematically ordered, because of the necessity that each proposition must have a reason.[7]

Why Always Ask Why?

As its name indicates, Kant's *Critique of Pure Reason* is dedicated to "Reason," in a triple sense: how does reason deal with the reasons for things and the reasons for its actions, what are the domains of its power, and what are the limits of its power? Its second part, which he calls "Transcendental Dialectic," studies the way in which reason inevitably deludes itself by precisely wanting to push itself to the limits of its power to know.[8] Although we will avoid going into the text's subtleties, I will mention that, according to him, reason always aims toward seeking "the condition for a conditioned," which is similar to the relationship between a ground and that for which it is the ground. In doing so, our reason creates for its own use what I call idols, and what he baptizes "Ideas," which are distinguished from each other according to the type of conditioned-condition relationships that are at play. The totality of events (Idea of the World); the synthesis of the totality of sensations, imaginations, and thoughts (Idea of the Soul); and the totality of thinkable determinations (Idea of God) are these three Ideas. Each specifies a domain of questions that do not have an answer, which are like the limits to any search for a reason: theology and questions about the existence of God; cosmology and questions about the limits of the universe in space and time; psychology and questions (which are far different from those of modern psychology) about the indivisibility and immortality of the soul.[9]

I am giving here a few morsels of Kantian philosophy because they clearly illustrate the heart of my question: Reason, as the faculty that provides reasons, is both a *limited power* and the inexorable *tendency* to transgress these limits. Kant thus shows us what question needs to be asked now: What is the reason behind this transgression? Why do we ask "why?" even in cases where there is no why? This could be the first way of understanding "why 'why?'" Kant himself evoked a "natural need for metaphysics" that belongs only to humans; and when he talks about metaphysics in this sense, he is referring to our impetus toward these Ideas to which in principle nothing in experience can correspond—such as the World as a whole or God.

Independent of the Kantian framework, we have now seen several examples where we were frustrated by a certain type of "because"—situations where there were causal series with no arrangement between them, or where there was a cluster of seemingly random causes and reasons. We saw how several rather natural ways of understanding causality make us prone to a certain dissatisfaction with the explanations of phenomena—especially those by scientists, who seem to lose themselves in infinite ramifications of causes that are more or less tenuous and contingent. Several dramatic shifts in thinking then revealed themselves to be possible, as if prewritten in the very grammar of the question "why?", and toward which particular psychological and sociological conditions could push us with more or less intensity. For example, we examined how the expectation of a symbolic proportionality between causes and effects could easily activate a form of conspiracy-oriented reflex when confronted with situations where minor causes lead to events that shake the world order (chapter 7).

The always possible confusion between cause and goal, between "why?" and "what for?", indeed lays the foundation for many mental dispositions: first, the animism stage (that is, when children perceive objects as being alive and capable of action, as demonstrated by Piaget and his followers); next, the world of intentional biases, which is studied by social psychologists in its various forms (such as conspiracy theories and the creationist resistance to Darwinian science[10] [chapters 4 and 7]); and last, certain variations stemming from Freud which, for lack of finding a reason-for-action instead of a causal series, discern unconscious intentions (chapter 8).

Throughout this book, I have inventoried various examples of such confusions and slippery meanings, from which the individual mythologies and the great historical social devices by which subjects relate to themselves and to others form avatars that are unique in each instance. If I wanted to lay out the lessons we have gathered along our journey, I would center them around what I have repeatedly called the *gap* between the "because"s that provide our best-informed explanations and the expectations of a different response—expectations that are often manifested in dissatisfactions like those we have just mentioned.

Regarding this gap, we sometimes call the latter group *meaning*, which stands apart from the series of causes and explanations. Of course, the "reason for" or intention often provides a meaning, makes sense of something: like *goal*, *meaning* (or *sense*) is indeed a term that precisely connotes a directionality. But what should we think of this gap in the end? How should we understand my initial question about the tree falling in front of me ("Why not me?") when a scientific analysis could provide a minute causal investigation of the reasons and causes for this tree falling on our unlucky tourist?

During our inquiry, I shed light on two examples of this gap between sets of causal series that explain phenomena and the expectation of a meaning that goes beyond the contingency of these causal series.

The contrast between "Why did Napoleon lose at Waterloo?" and "What started World War I?" (chapters 5 and 6) showed us this gap for the first time—this distance between the contingent and the inexorable.

Losing at Waterloo was contingent because if just a few small details had been adjusted (for example, if the map of Mont-Saint-Jean had been corrected, or if Grouchy had received clearer orders) the defeat would have been transformed into a victory. On the other hand, World War I was inexorable because even if the triggering events had been changed it would still have occurred in all likelihood. We then saw that numerous metaphysical idols are formed to bring together contingent events (Waterloo) and necessary events (World War I), among which the notion of destiny is foremost (chapters 7 and 8).

The confusion between efficient causes and final causes, which was denounced so vehemently by Spinoza, thus appears as another example of this gap between contingent causal series and a meaning that goes beyond them. Here, this meaning comes not from fate but from purpose and intention. We would prefer it if all the causes that bring about a given event were acting under an order or through an intention. In the Appendix from which I already quoted at length, this is precisely what Spinoza says when he uses the example of a stone falling on a man's head—an example that incidentally corresponds to my own experience with the Dutch tourist and his crushed car. But here again, we must distinguish two types of cases, depending on whether or not causal series can *legitimately* be related to something other than causes (which distances us from the kind of monistic determinism that Spinoza upholds). The purely physical world does not lend itself to this; but thanks to the omnipresence of natural selection, the living world allows researchers to express themselves in finalistic terms of machines and agents. In this second case, we can allow ourselves to cross the gap between natural random causes and our expectation of a meaning or purpose that might transcend them.

"Why why?", in the sense of "Why do we always want a supplementary and final 'why?'" does not have an unequivocal answer. Psychology, the sociology of religions, and anthropology may have answers to provide here. But philosophy can only show the gap between certain types of "because" and certain expectations; and can then distinguish situations where it is legitimate to cross this gap from those where this is not the case.

Why "Why"?

The Principle of Reasons and Its Reasons: Why There Are Answers to "Why?"

I already explained that we keep asking why because causality is the cement of the world, because without "why?" we could hardly gather together the events around us into a form that is coherent. Things, ideas, and actions are all held together through reasons, and reason is the faculty of reasons (or, in other words, the faculty for grounds): "why?" thus appears, in short, as the fundamental question of the rational agent.

It is thus understandable that this question occupies such an important role in our cognitive economy; and more simply, in our everyday life and all of our concerns. It is less easy to know why the world responds to it. Because it is clear that if the human species constantly asks why, it is also because there is most often an answer to the question. Otherwise, our ancestors would have stopped doing so a long time ago. Major philosophers in the Western tradition have therefore not hesitated to ask why things are in such a way that there exist answers to why-questions.

Leibniz is a perfect example in this regard with his "Principle of Sufficient Reason," about which Schopenhauer was so surprised that no one had expressed it earlier since it seemed so trivial.[11] Such a principle clearly explains why we can answer the question "why?"—it is even its own content. But a philosopher will want a justification of this principle, and things then get trickier.

Despite the fact that he never wrote a real treatise (like Spinoza, Kant, Hegel, etc.) and that his work exists only in occasional writings, articles, letters, and responses to books, Leibniz had a very systematic conception of his principle of reason—which for us has the value of tying together several aspects of "why?", as I explained in chapter 1. Now, let's imagine Leibniz explaining a winning penalty kick to the great French soccer player Kylian Mbappé. The trajectory of the ball can be expressed through differential equations that describe its movement instant by instant depending on the initial kick and the forces acting on the ball (gravity, air resistance). These are the causes of the entry of the ball into the upper corner of the goal. But the very trajectory of the ball can also be understood as that which minimizes the potential energy of the system (this is starting to sound like high school physics, I know). We thus have an explanation that resembles a final cause, since the system behaves as if it were aiming toward an optimum (minimizing potential energy). This is what Leibniz calls "a perfect harmony between . . . the system of efficient causes and that of final causes" in his *Principles of Nature and Grace*, one of the last summaries of the system that he never truly laid out in writing. But it does not stop there: why are the laws of physics what they are in the end? Because, according to Leibniz, God chose this world—in which France wins its match thanks to this penalty kick—rather than another one. And why is that? Because He wanted the world with as much "reality" as possible, and that is necessarily this world. Why? Because God is by definition a good being, and thus chooses the best: He chooses a world governed by laws that ultimately maximize the amount of reality—what Leibniz calls "the best of all possible worlds."

This notion—"amount of reality"—is obscure. But remember that many of the things we consider negative are just the lack of something: a cold place just lacks warmth, a lunatic lacks rationality, a broken car lacks a certain piece in a certain place . . . Negative properties are in general defined by the lack of something positively defined, and, for Leibniz, as for Spinoza or other rationalist thinkers, "real" means this positivity;[12] hence what is negative physically, intellectually, or morally is a lack of reality. The best of all possible worlds, according to Leibniz, is the one embracing as much reality as it is possible; but not all things can be maximally real within it, since two maximally real individuals may be contradictory, hence impossible to coexist. Therefore, such a best of all possible worlds results from a general trade-off. A world with more reality was not possible, but we cannot see it, since understanding those trade-offs would require an infinite knowledge of the universe (that God is supposed to have).

God's reasons-for-action thus determine in a sometimes opaque way the real world, which is itself such that all phenomena are both explainable by causes that follow laws and by final causes that are another aspect of these laws. We all know about Voltaire's mockery of this optimism in *Candide*; but in reality, Leibniz is following a very specific logic. There is indeed nothing within the world that allows us to say that it is less good or better than other possible worlds; from the moment we think that God has his own reasons, and that God is God (and therefore wanting the best as he is a perfect being), Leibniz scores a point against Voltaire. But he is of course assuming that God acts according to reasons—in other words, that every choice must have its own reasons and that God is also a rational agent himself. Ultimately, we do not escape the presupposition that it is better to be rational than irrational.

I will not, however, conclude on this Leibnizian answer. Hume and then Kant can be credited for indicating an implicit assumption of Leibniz and his predecessors, an assumption that threatens their whole reasoning: Leibniz treats causes and reasons as things that we can, in principle, know a priori—that is, without experiencing or looking at how the world is. His principle of reason is a logical claim that applies to all possible worlds. Granted, the principle of reason concerning beliefs and justifications is certainly acceptable a priori: every statement derives from other statements that ground it. But as Hume and Kant point out, the principle of reason concerning things (i.e., causality) is not immediately true because the relationship of cause and effect is not of the same order as that of principle and its logical consequences holding between two statements. Indeed, a consequence is *included* in the principle (or, like we say in logic, the *antecedent*) and I can deduce things from it. For example, from "all sailors eat spinach," I can conclude that "Popeye the Sailor eats spinach" since "Popeye" is included in "sailors." Yet an effect is *not logically contained* within its cause—in the sense that it would be possible for me to know the effect if I had a perfect knowledge of the concept of the cause. (For God, Leibniz would answer, the effect is indeed included in the concept of the cause; but deriving the effect from the cause is a problem that is mathematically too complex for our cognitive capacities, which are—when measured against God's intellect—like the finite when compared with the infinite.) If I know Mbappé perfectly, as well as the ball he is about to kick and the field, I cannot deduce the trajectory of the ball. For this, argued Kant, I must know the Newtonian laws of movement; and these are not "in" the concept of the ball (nor in the concept of Mbappé, nor the rest).[13]

Generally speaking, if we follow Hume and especially Kant, the principle of reason concerning causes is thus not a logical principle. For Kant, it is true not by virtue of the nature of things and the rules of logics, but by virtue of the fact that it makes experience possible and conceivable for us. This is what philosophers, starting with Kant, call a "transcendental" justification of the principle: without it, no knowledge is possible; yet we know things and have an experience of the world; thus, this principle is true. The question "Why 'why?'"—in the sense of "Why are 'because's accessible to us?"—thus leads us to this: depending on whether the principle of reason is thought of as being purely logical or not, very different justifications will be given.

It should be clear by now that I am not planning on resolving a cardinal metaphysical question here, one on which major philosophical systems diverge. I wanted to just give an idea of the issues at play, as well as the distinctions according to which the metaphysical arguments concerning this question are separated from each other.

If we now follow Kant on this minimal argument that, unlike the principle of identity, the principle of reason is not a purely logical truth, we must also think that the principle of reason is not a simple fact. That World War I began because Franz Ferdinand was assassinated is a fact. Yet everything in the world (World War I included) having a reason is not, contrary to appearances, the generalization of the fact that a host of known events have reasons. For Kant, without this principle, it is not likely that facts could even be established or known, since they would not be able to join the great network of things in the world—hence it is not itself a fact.

Yet, about this principle of reason which is not a fact and which is justified by Kant on transcendental grounds, we should add that there exist very un-Kantian justifications: a modern follower of David Hume would argue for a sort of pragmatic justification (along the lines of "everything has a reason because this mania for looking for reasons gets results!"); those philosophers who considered themselves to be pragmatists like William James and John Dewey would probably think likewise. In line with Susan Haack's characterization of the brands of pragmatism (which we saw in chapter 1), I would argue that these brands, and especially her "vulgar pragmatism," offer this kind of view of the principle of reason. Not all are pragmatists. But all pragmatists, who in general commit to the deflationary positions we have seen here regarding language and metaphysics, would agree with a Humean on the justification of the principle of reason.

More specifically, Humeans represent a major tradition of thought in modern metaphysics (for instance, David Lewis and W. V. O. Quine are Humeans to a certain extent). For the Humean, as David Lewis famously wrote, "all there is to the world is a vast mosaic of local matters of particular fact, just one little thing and another."[14] Contemporary metaphysics is even sometimes presented as a long discussion between Humeans, for whom what exists is only a mosaic of events, unrelated by anything like causes, forces, powers, necessities; and Aristotelians, for whom exist powers, causes, which underlie this mosaic of events. The Humeans therefore stand on the side of deflationism, skeptical of anything that seems to go beyond the range of the "here and now," whereas the Aristotelians are more inflationist since their ontology accepts much more than the mere events. Thinking on the principle of reason clearly represents a divide between these two metaphysical camps, and by rejecting skepticism on the unity of "ground" as well as admitting structural explanations (chapter 2) or etiological functions and functional norms (chapter 4), the present book intends to take a balanced position between the two families of views.

But surveying the accounts of the principle of reason doesn't stop there. I also imagine that Nietzsche would suspect here a collateral effect from our grammar—which always sees relationships between subjects and predicates ("the table is green"), thereby encouraging us to locate acting subjects everywhere and thus causes (agents) and effects (actions). In order to describe rain, we say "It's raining" as if we absolutely needed a subject ("it") that supports this event. Ultimately, according to Nietzsche, our belief in causality and reasons stems from these illusions of grammar, which he condemned in the passage quoted at length in chapter 1. His example shows us that certain analyses of the principle of reason offer far more deconstructions than actual justifications.

And So?

And so why "why?" In the previous chapter, I argued that the different available metaphysics are dissimilar from competing scientific theories in that the latter have access to empirical facts which allow one to decide between them (up to a certain point[15]). Instead, they look more like various axiomatized versions of mathematics, with each being as true as the next without empirical consequences; and where deciding between them depends on a plurality of possible epistemic values, according to which one evaluates their epistemic costs and benefits.

It would be the same with the principle of reason—and in general, with what makes it so that we can ask why and respond to it. There are no facts to explain this, whether they be cosmological or psychological. Several metaphysical explanations thus clash. Each stems from a set of philosophical theses on the nature of logic, causality, and on what constitutes the true justification of knowledge; and each therefore entails distinct epistemic benefits and costs. For example, adopting the Nietzschean version involves not only breaking with what is sometimes called common sense but also with the ease of expression offered by natural language. No one has yet managed to describe the world without causality—to say rain without saying "it's raining"—while keeping the richness of expression found in the natural language in which all novels and poems are written. On the other hand, subscribing to Kantian justification allows us to account for many things pertaining to science, but also involves a certain number of arguments that many would not accept (about the nature of mathematics, for example, but this is for another time). Pragmatism, however, is quite minimalist and has the potential of making anxious philosophers uneasy; after all, for some people, "we do X because it has always worked" does not constitute a sufficient justification for whatever may be in question.

Why "Why"?

In the end, and I apologize if you saw this coming, "Why 'why?'" has no unequivocal answer. There are distinct metaphysical arguments, all of which are represented by decisions based on privileging one value over another (simplicity, fecundity, the relationship to common intuition or to scientific theories, conformity to the usage of language, etc.)—in the sense of epistemic values pertaining to metaphysics, which cannot be assessed based on their degree of empirical acuity. We could defend one or another of these arguments, but that would be the subject of another book.

In a Retrospective Way

Starting with a conceptual and linguistic analysis of the question "why?" and its three cardinal meanings (cause, justification, and goal), this book has taken us into the territories of the philosophy of science and action, and then (meta)metaphysics. We mapped out the meanings of the question "why?", demonstrated the heterogeneity of these three cardinal meanings, analyzed how these significations can sometimes merge with each other and explained those cases where this is legitimate (as we saw with functional analysis in biology)—as well as those where this was illegitimate. In this, I demonstrated how narrativity plays a major role in these shifts in meaning.

And just as for Kant the normalized usage of our understanding allows for an illicit but spontaneous usage to emerge where reason believes that it knows the objects of those Ideas which are in principle not objects of knowledge, the question "why?" brings forth metaphysical idols that exist to soothe our dissatisfaction with a certain type of answer—one whose legitimacy seems insufficient in our eyes. This is particularly the case where there is a series of disjointed causes (or an element of randomness in other words), where there is no reason as intention behind the event or action. In other words, like any form of grammar, the grammar of why allows for exceptions (for example, situations where causes can be viewed as purposes); but above all, it defines rational and irrational ways of answering this question.

Throughout this journey, we have regularly encountered two philosophical figures from whom we have tried to maintain a careful distance. The first is the skeptic. One of the arguments of this book, which was recalled at the beginning of this conclusion, is the unitary character of "why?", which expresses the triple concept of reason or ground. I thus reject the idea that the conjunction of cause, justification, and goal in this one small word is a simple homonymy, a random fluke in language. The skeptic on the contrary would say that there is not a deeper unity to be found, that in other possible and better constructed languages we would simply have three different interrogative pronouns, and that all our reflections on causes, justifications, and goals are irrelevant. On the other hand, a dogmatist would say that the three meanings merge together, and that all causes always come together to work toward a goal, an intention, or an ultimate plan—like God's reason-for-action, which according to Leibniz proves to be the other face of the causes behind phenomena as well as the reason for our knowledge concerning these phenomena.

Thus, those familiar with the history of philosophy recognize in the stance adopted throughout this book the same position for which Kant argued: namely, a middle ground between the dogmatism represented by the metaphysics of his time (e.g., that of Leibniz, in which all knowledge can be grounded in the things themselves and whose knowledge is warranted by a truthful God) and skepticism (represented by Hume, and according to which our concepts are mostly reflections of our contingent psychological constitution). This is not to say that I wrote a Kantian book—since in the end I do not endorse Kantian theses—but what I have elaborated clearly stems from a Kantian inspiration.

The figure of the skeptic also appeared in the chapter about Romeo and Juliet as a deflationist. The deflationist skeptic would argue that there was nothing more behind the story of the two lovers than the set of causes that science can provide, and that the rest was purely just a pleasant subjective illusion. In a general way, this book considered the gap between the order of causes (which are often contingent) and the expectation of a reason that would satisfy us by reinforcing these causes with a sort of necessity or intention (destiny, unconscious desire, etc.). My argument here consisted in distinguishing between (a) the cases where there is effectively nothing besides these scattered causes—typically the case with conspiracy theories—and (b) cases such as World War I where the contingency is truly accompanied by an inexorability at the level of coarse-grained events.

A deflationist, the skeptic systematically thinks that there is nothing else besides causes. By distinguishing between these two cases (a) and (b), my goal was to show this skeptic that under certain conditions we can imagine something other than the aggregate of sometimes intersecting causes and reasons. I thus discussed along these lines individual and collective natures, very tight structuring causes, as well as—with respect to scientific reasoning—structural explanations that include the principle of the best, which Leibniz argued for and which he thought represented the acme of the principle of reason. But the deflationist skeptic was also represented in the figure of the neurophilosopher arguing that there are only causes (which are all ultimately physical), which means that the terms about mental states do not refer to anything robust. I countered this, and more generally the skepticism about reasons-for-action, with my argument concerning the efficiency of reasons-for-action—also citing explanatory reasons that are structural explanations (chapter 2).

For a long time, this skeptic was metaphysically opposed to the idea of a divine understanding acting as a guarantor of truth. With Leibniz, for example, a usual target of the skeptic, each individual materializes an "individual notion" that only exists within this divine understanding and which contains the reason for all of the events that occur inside their particular world.[16] If we step away from this classic metaphysical framework, justifying what exceeds the aggregate of sometimes randomly intersecting causes becomes problematic.

This was ultimately already Kant's concern: in his perspective where God is no longer a theoretically valid concept, he was looking for something in between our dogmatic metaphysician and Hume-like skeptic, for which nothing exists except for sometimes regular sequences of events. We also saw in chapter 2 how the use—however massive scientifically—of principles of optimality to encompass these causes was much more delicate for us than for Leibniz, who could always support the mention of these optima with the a priori truth according to which God always does what is best. "Why can we ask why in a world without God?" could have thus been a possible title of this book.

The divine guarantor allowed Leibniz to respond to the abyssal question "Why is there something instead of nothing?" To him, the principle of reason as unconditionally valid across all possible worlds almost compels us to answer; and this answer is the fact that God always chooses what is best. It could be that we no longer have a response to this vertiginous question; or rather, that there are only scientific answers like the standard model of physics, which supposedly best explains the birth of the universe. But to whoever is not satisfied by such a causal explanation and wants to know "what for?" in addition to "why?", we are not able to provide an answer in the way that religion or classical metaphysics does with its divine plans.

Another form of the skeptic met throughout these pages is centered around the notion of convention. The skeptic argues that the conjunction of three reasons in the word "why?" is a pure linguistic convention. They thus think that the idea of "limits" to the question "why?" which are defined by "self-evidence" ultimately relies on conventions—whether in the sense of language conventions governing what is questionable or not; or more profoundly, in the sense that all why-questions can receive an answer, which must be stated either in terms of facts, or in terms of linguistic conventions when there are no accessible facts. "Why am I me?" would thus not be a self-evidence without why, but instead a linguistic convention concerning the meaning of the word "me"—for which there could be causes drawn from the history of our language.

Here again, I recognize the strength of the skeptical argument about conventions. The two last chapters showed how the fact that certain questions are limits to "why?" is not absolute but instead sends us back to certain frameworks—and ultimately to certain metaphysical presuppositions that are privileged over others. Being the traditional opponent of the skeptic, the dogmatist would thus argue that certain questions are absolute instances of self-evidence and therefore of the limits of "why?", which means that there is ultimately only one true metaphysical framework in the end. We proved the dogmatist wrong, but this does not mean that the game goes to the skeptic.

In these pages, the discussion of "reason" as the answer to "why" elaborated a "grammar of why" that does not commit to the idea of a pure conventionality of such grammar. It had to debate conventionalist, skeptic, or pragmatist views of "ground" that would ultimately deny the unity of "reason" as ground; but at the same time, it acknowledged the limits of "reasons," the absence of final grounds, and thus the limits of reason as a faculty—a lesson that ultimately is also deeply Kantian. But I also had to accept that the pragmatist as well as the skeptic have sound arguments when it comes to these limits; and especially when it comes to the lack of a metaphysical foundation for any precise depiction of the territory of "why." Metaphysics is also in charge of deciding what is self-evident (i.e., which facts are self-evident, as well as in what "self-evidence" consists); thus, alternative metaphysics would draw distinct limits to "why" and then, on the margins, distinct territories of "why."

Ultimately, rather than receiving definitive answers, the questions "When ask 'why'?" and "Why 'why'?" would trigger a rational discussion about what should constitute a proper answer. Metaphysical frameworks are not conventions—which, because they are arbitrary, are in principle equal to each other. They require reasons and we have still not found the decisive ones. And this is why metaphysics will continue to be, in Kant's words, an *arena*.

Acknowledgments

THIS BOOK, IN ITS FRENCH AND THEN IN ITS ENGLISH version, benefited from many inputs from colleagues and friends. It is impossible to cite all of them. But for their patient reading of the text, their precious suggestions as well as their stimulating critiques, I warmly thank Eric Bapteste, Sylvain Bosselet, Christophe Bouton, Pascal Engel, and Annick Lesne. I am incredibly grateful to Alexandre Lacroix, editor of the book series "Les Grands Mots" at Autrement/Flammarion, who initially wanted this book, and inspired some essential aspects of its structure. I thank Sophie Berlin, who welcomed this book in her series at Flammarion, and Erica Wetter, who kindly offered to include its expanded translation in her series at Stanford University Press. I appreciate the honor I have been awarded by this simple fact. I also thank Paul A. Kottmann, series editor, for having given this book such an insightful foreword.

Last but not least, I am immensely grateful to a great friend and a great musician, Adam Hocker, who succeeded in making my prose in English probably more accessible and direct than the original. . . . I can appreciate how uneasy the exercise was. . . .

Once again, I praise the memories of Gérard Lebrun and Jean Gayon, who have been constant sources of inspiration during my career as a philosopher, as well as models of what a philosophical existence can be.

Finally, I thank my old friend Olivier Filippi, an amazing artist, whose most recent serigraphs and canvases inspired the cover design of this book (his work can be explored at http://o.filippi.free.fr/).

Notes

Introduction

1. In Auguste Comte's positivism, humanity crosses three successive cognitive ages: a mythical or religious age, a metaphysical age where people seek the essence of things, and a positive age where the positive sciences describe laws that govern phenomena. See Auguste Comte, *Cours de philosophie positive* (Paris: Vrin, 1980); translated by Frederick Ferré, *Introduction to Positive Philosophy* (Indianapolis: Hackett, 1988).

2. Today, this "second analogy" recalls what is sometimes called determinism (by Claude Bernard among others). For Kant, the Second Analogy was essential because it alone allowed for us to distinguish between a subjective time (the succession of my perceptions: I can indifferently look at a person by beginning with the face or the head) and an objective time (an airplane taking off cannot be seen in reverse). The existence of the "rule" that the principle stipulates indeed forbids all objective successions except for one.

3. In Schopenhauer's first writing before his masterwork *The World as Will and Representation*, namely his dissertation *On the Fourfold Root of the Principle of Sufficient Reason* (1813).

4. I am using "belief" in the minimal sense that is used in analytical philosophy: "to believe *p*" means "considering proposition *p* to be true." Discussions about the opposition between belief and knowledge are thus irrelevant as they consider belief in the sense of "nonjustified belief"—here, belief is a very general term that in no way involves the question of justifying what one believes to be true.

5. Of course, I am not pretending to describe the true history of science here, which is much more complex and elaborate, but rather to simply propose a useful

schematization for this book's goals. On Galileo, see Alexandre Koyré's books: *From the Closed World to the Infinite Universe* (Baltimore: Johns Hopkins University Press, 1957), and *Galileo Studies* (Atlantic Highlands, NJ: Humanities Press, [1939] 1978); see also Maurice Clavelin, *Natural Philosophy of Galileo: Essays on the Origins and Formation of Classical Mechanics* (Cambridge, MA: MIT Press, 1974), or the chapters that Karl Feyerabend devotes to him in *Against Method,* 4th ed. (New York: Verso, 2010).

6. A major objection could be made here right from the start. In short, it deals with what we call pragmatics—or the conditions of understanding for a statement that falls within the context of interlocution. We traditionally distinguish semantics—namely, the dimension according to which statements have a meaning—from pragmatics. Semantically speaking, the meaning of "I already ate" is that I ate before the current moment. But pragmatically speaking, if the statement is preceded by the question "Do you want to have lunch?", it could mean "I don't want to have lunch." Pragmatics enriches the meaning of a claim.

The border between pragmatics and semantics seems relatively simple. However, some thinkers show that it is not so simple: they can thus support the idea that semantics by itself is an abstraction, that true meaning is always pragmatic. According to this radical argument, the examples of senseless sentences that I just listed are no longer so. We can find a context of interlocution in which "green numbers yearn for calm" means something (for example, it could be a question of political ecology, the absence of ideological conflicts, etc.).

In this book, I am on principle discarding this radical argument concerning pragmatics, although I will say a word about it in the last chapters.

7. The question of knowing, whether it is ultimately a question of two types of nonmeaning or just one, is discussed in the philosophy of language. Wittgenstein argues that it is, in short, the same thing, which involves radical consequences regarding what we understand by "meaning," but they go well beyond the scope of this book.

8. Paul Veyne, *Writing History: Essay on Epistemology* (Manchester: Manchester University Press, 1984).

9. In very diverse ways, the great Hellenist Jean-Pierre Vernant (*Les origines de la pensée grecque*, 1965) and the philosopher of science Karl Popper (*Conjectures and Refutations*, 1963) exposed such an opposition-succession. Whatever the historical truth of this story, it says something correct about the difference between two types of discourse and legitimation.

10. In his *Abstract of the Treatise on Human Nature* (1740) Hume writes that resemblance, contiguity, and causation "are really to us the cement of the universe,

and all the operations of the mind must, in a great measure, depend on them." The phrase is now mostly cited when philosophers investigate causality, as in J. L. Mackie, *The Cement of the Universe: A Study of Causation* (Oxford: Oxford University Press, [1974] 1980).

11. Claude Lévi-Strauss, *Introduction to the Work of Marcel Mauss*, trans. Felicity Baker (London: Routledge, [1950], 1987).

12. Patrick J. Leman and Marco Cinnirella, "Beliefs in Conspiracy Theories and the Need for Cognitive Closure," *Frontiers in Psychology* 4 (2013): 378.

13. The analytic and dialectic compose two parts of the three Kantian critiques, with each dealing with a different faculty (knowledge in general, action, aesthetic or biological judgment). The present book is not a Kantian treatise, but it subscribes to this division between analytic and dialectic—except that we will be working with an analysis of what I call grammar instead of an analytic; and that this study of the confusions generated by the scrambling of grammatical categories will be less systematic in regard to the Kantian dialectic.

14. Charles Tilly, *Why?* (Princeton: Princeton University Press, 2006).

15. Bradford Skow, *Reasons Why* (New York: Oxford University Press, 2016).

16. Judea Pearl and Dana McKenzie, *The Book of Why* (New York: Basic Books, 2018).

17. Judea Pearl, *Causality: Models, Reasoning, and Inference,* 2nd ed. (Cambridge: Cambridge University Press, [2000] 2009).

18. Christopher Hitchcock, "Causality: Models, Reasoning and Inference," *Philosophical Review* 110, no. 4 (2001): 639; James Woodward, *Making Things Happen: A Theory of Causal Explanation* (New York: Oxford University Press, 2003).

Chapter 1 : Why Is Oscar Pistorius Guilty of Murder?

1. Remember that Leibniz formulates it in the following way in his *Monadology* (§32): the principle "of sufficient reason, in virtue of which we hold that there can be no fact real or existing, no statement true, unless there be a sufficient reason, why it should be so and not otherwise"; notice that the principle considers equally the "reality" of "facts" and the truth of "statements."

2. We call this doubt concerning the truly necessary character of this connection between cause and effect, which was raised by David Hume in his 1739 *Treatise of Human Nature*, the "problem of induction." We will return to it later and so I will put these difficulties aside for now.

3. In Wilfrid Sellars, *Empiricism and the Philosophy of Mind* (Cambridge, MA: Harvard University Press, 1997).

4. On the reasons and limits of this surprising usage of rationality among biologists, see Philippe Huneman and Johannes Martens, "The Behavioural Ecology of Irrational Behaviours," *History and Philosophy of Life Sciences* 39 (2017). The foundation of this bizarre practice will be explained later in chapter 4.

5. In the book's conclusion, I will come back to "reason" as a crucial human faculty.

6. The argument according to which knowledge is a justified true belief has been cast into doubt by what is known as the Gettier problem. In 1963, in his "Is Justified True Belief Knowledge?" (*Analysis* 23, no. 6: 121–23), Edmund Gettier laid out examples of situations where a justified true belief is not knowledge. But these subtleties that concern epistemologists are of little concern to our project here and so we will pass over them in silence, except to say that a major consequence of Gettier's examples is that one cannot "by chance" know something, even if one is believing a true proposition. This is central to my own argument: a good reason of a belief cannot essentially be pure chance.

7. Philosophers working on chance often distinguish three conceptions of probability: subjective (degrees of belief), objective (frequencies, or a metaphysical equivalent of the naïve idea of tendency that they would call propensities), and epistemic (namely, the confirmation ratio between a fact and a hypothesis). The matter is very complex, because a kind of subjective interpretation—based on Bayes theorem regarding conditional probabilities—also handles the epistemic relationships between stated facts and the confirmation of hypotheses. These subtleties are not relevant for our purposes here. See Donald Gillies, *Philosophical Theories of Probability (*London: Routledge, 2000); D. H. Mellor, *The Matter of Chance* (Cambridge: Cambridge University Press, 1971); Toby Handfield, *A Philosophical Guide to Chance* (New York: Cambridge University Press, 2012).

8. One may call "degree of belief" of a rational agent a measure of the strength of the reasons through which this belief is justified. Frank Ramsey, in the early twentieth century, used to say that the degree of a belief can be measured by the amount of money one is disposed to bet on the truth of this belief. It might be a good way to represent the fact that a reason to believe cannot be evaluated independent of the pragmatic context in which it is formulated.

9. For a philosophical analysis of the notion of reasonable doubt, see Marion Vorms and Ulrike Hahn, "In the Space of Reasonable Doubt," *Synthese* 198, S15 (2019): 3609–33.

10. The criterion "beyond a reasonable doubt" belongs to common-law judicial systems—namely, those of the United States and the United Kingdom among others. In France, the judicial system includes the idea of "intimate conviction,"

which is not exactly the same thing; but this minimal difference does not interest us here. In any case, we see that this analysis is valid beyond the confines of the rights governed by common law.

11. Susan Haack extensively characterizes what "pragmatism" should mean and its prospects, and importantly distinguishes several brands of pragmatism, the classical one of C. S. Peirce, William James, and John Dewey, which still commits to an idea of truth independent from our practical interests, and "vulgar pragmatism," for example represented by Stephen Stich and Richard Rorty, which denies this independence and accepts some relativism. "The philosophical tendencies known as "pragmatism" are formidably diverse; and it would be foolish to deny that there are elements in some pragmatist writers that might seem to suggest what I have called the "vulgar pragmatisms" of Rorty and Stich. For example, in James's urging that philosophers pay more attention to concrete truths and curb their obsession with abstract Truth, one might hear something akin to Rorty's impatience with anything supposedly grounding what is presently defensible. But this would be to forget that James maintains that the notion of concrete truth depends on the notion of abstract Truth, and could not stand alone." Susan Haack, *Evidence and Inquiry: Towards Reconstruction in Epistemology* (Oxford: Blackwell, 1993), 202.

12. A recent and exhaustive defense of evidentialism is given by Pascal Engel in *Les vices du savoir: Essai d'éthique intellectuelle* [The vices of knowledge: An essay on intellectual ethics] (Paris: Agone, 2019).

13. Heather Douglas, "Inductive Risk and Values in Science," *Philosophy of Science* 67, no. 4 (2000): 559–79.

14. Sharon Kingsland, *Modeling Nature* (Chicago: University of Chicago Press, 2002).

15. Richard Levins, "The Strategy of Model Building in Population Biology," *American Scientist* 54 (1966): 421–31.

16. The fact that epistemic values are unavoidable in principle is not contested by anyone, but the question of nonepistemic (or "contextual") values, and their role in principle and in practice in scientific activity, is hotly debated. Even though many philosophers of science would accept that they play a role in science in practice, not all of them would accept their necessity in principle. In philosophy of science, Helen Longino—*Science as Social Knowledge: Values and Objectivity in Scientific Inquiry* (Princeton: Princeton University Press, 1990)—provided one of the first systematic accounts of the role played by values in science, arguing for their inevitability and against an ideal of value-free science because science as such is a social process and not just an individual having to decide whether a prop-

osition is true or not, and the arguments given here are close to Longino's views. The first critique of the naïve idea that science is only concerned by matters of fact and should never make value judgments is by Richard Rudner, "The Scientist Qua Scientist Makes Value Judgments," *Philosophy of Science* 20, no. 1 (1953): 1–6. See also Philip Kitcher, *Science, Truth, and Democracy* (New York: Oxford University Press, 2001), who argues that science as a social process needs to be "well ordered," and this involves necessarily contextual values. Importantly, because science does not consider all truths but only "significant truths" (who would care about the total number of leaves in Australia on March 12, 2022, even if there is a true proposition about that?), we need value criteria to decide what is significant.

17. Any similarity with the more familiar story of the Higgs boson is not wholly fortuitous.

18. Cognitive scientists have recently explored the specificity of legal causal reasoning; see, for example, David Lagnado and Tobias Gerstenberg, "Causation in Legal and Moral Reasoning," in *The Oxford Handbook of Causal Reasoning*, ed. M. Waldmann, 565–602 (New York: Oxford University Press, 2017).

19. It is not by chance that one of the most important books for philosophers who are interested in causality is a book about law: H. L. A. Hart and Tony Honoré, *Causation in the Law*, 2nd ed. (Oxford: Oxford University Press, [1959] 1985).

20. Joshua Knobe, "Intentional Action and Side Effects in Ordinary Language," *Analysis* 63 (2003): 190–94.

21. On this question one can now read David Lagnado, *Explaining the Evidence: How the Mind Investigates the World* (Cambridge: Cambridge University Press, 2021).

22. This is essentially the example given by Gottlob Frege in his *Foundations of Arithmetic (1884)*—a key text for understanding the difference between the psychological and the logical (or philosophical, in our case). Algebra explains the role of prime numbers. The notion of the "smallest common multiple" allows us to understand how all numbers can be seen as the product of prime numbers, which are themselves indecomposable (from which stems their importance in arithmetic).

23. Bertrand Russell, "On the Notion of Cause," *Proceedings of the Aristotelian Society* 13 (1913): 1–26.

24. For an analysis of the various kinds of dialogue routines that allow us to give reasons, in conversational contexts oriented toward specific interests, in the society of specific people (colleagues/friends/inquirers/partner, etc.), see the major book by sociologist Charles Tilly, *Why?*, that I considered in the introduction.

Chapter 2: Why Do Things Fall When We Let Them Go?

1. Science during the times of Galileo and Newton was called "natural philosophy"; philosophy used to encompass what we call natural science together with logics, metaphysics, and ethics. The distinction between science and philosophy as we understand it, and the exclusion of "natural philosophy" outside the academic domain of philosophy, arguably emerged in the nineteenth century.

2. This chapter should not give the impression that *all* scientific questions are why-questions. "How many living species are there on Earth?", "Is Pluto a planet?", "Does the Higgs boson exist?" are clearly legitimate scientific questions but are not why-questions.

3. John H. Lawton, "Are There General Laws in Ecology?" *Oikos* 84, no. 2 (1999): 177–92. This questioning of laws in ecology attracted a great deal of debate. It seems a bit outdated now, especially because some very powerful mathematical theories (such as the neutral theory in ecology by Hubbell that I mentioned, as well as the attempts to integrate it with previous ecological theories) shifted the terms of the debate.

4. I won't rely here on the important book Michael Strevens wrote about "depth": *Depth: An Account of Scientific Explanation* (New York: Oxford University Press, 2009). I use the word in a nontechnical sense, intending to suggest an intuitive understanding of the difference between these two general statements.

5. Another major Austrian-born philosopher of science, Karl Popper, also had a deductivist view of science. According to him, the scientific method is hypothetico-deductive. But Popper mainly focuses on the validation of theories and what makes them scientific, while Hempel questions the nature of scientific explanation. Thus, here I only deal with Hempel. Popper is historically important, perhaps more so than Hempel for practicing scientists (think of his well-known criterion of falsifiability), but this can be due to the lack of audience (among scientists) of more recent views in philosophy of science.

6. John von Neumann and Oskar Morgenstern, *Theory of Games and Economic Behavior*, Sixtieth Anniversary Edition (Princeton: Princeton University Press, [1944] 2007).

7. We saw ecologist Richard Levins arguing in his influential 1966 paper ("Strategy of Model Building in Population Biology") that models should aim at three distinct epistemic goals—realism, description, and prediction—but because these goals can't be reached together, certain trade-offs must be made among the three (e.g., sacrificing precision for more generality and realism) instead of relying on a norm of truth. However, for Levins truth would be propositions that can be derived from several distinct models (which make distinct trade-offs between

epistemic goals). A more radical pragmatist or instrumentalist, in the vein of von Neumann's quote, would not accept this latter claim. Regarding why truth should be the norm of our beliefs even if we can't know the truth, see Pascal Engel, *The Norm of Truth: An Introduction to the Philosophy of Logic* (Toronto: University of Toronto Press, 2001). In any case, the attention to epistemic goals of models and their variety may account for the native sympathy of many philosophers of science for pragmatism, which contrasts with the focus on the question of truth as addressed by epistemologists, in terms of the norms for believing or not believing in a proposition *p*.

8. For several philosophers, including Robert Brandon in *Concepts and Methods in Evolutionary Biology* (Cambridge: Cambridge University Press, 1996), the principle of natural selection is itself an a priori law and boils down to the law of large numbers: with a population that is large enough, the frequencies of the reproducing alleles or genotypes will match the chances of reproduction of these alleles or genotypes. Also, Robert Brandon and Daniel McShea, in *Biology's First Law: The Tendency for Diversity and Complexity to Increase in Evolutionary Systems* (Chicago: University of Chicago Press, 2010), see the "principle of drift" as a major a priori law of any system—such as biological systems—in which there is inheritance and variation of properties; according to this principle, the diversity in the system will naturally tend to increase. From this viewpoint, another way of arranging *explanantia* (facts and laws) would be possible, but it still provides us with a Hempelian interpretation of models as explanations.

9. Homozygous and heterozygous name two possible combinations of alleles on the same locus: XX and xx are homozygous, Xx is heterozygous. One usually writes X for the dominant allele and x for the recessive one; dominant and recessive, in turn, characterize the relation between an allele and a phenotype. X is dominant when either the XX genotype or the Xx genotype individuals have a given phenotype (for instance, as in Mendel's famous experiments and papers, the green peas); x is recessive when only the xx genotype individuals feature the other phenotype (for instance, the yellow pea). Most of the pathologies are carried by a recessive allele (therefore, one needs two alleles to express the disease; which intuitively means that natural selection will be less likely to wipe out these alleles, since many of their carriers won't have the disease).

10. The contemporary philosophical literature on causation is huge. For an influential view of causation as holding together variables, see Woodward, *Making Things Happen*. Jonathan Bennett in *Events and Their Names* (Indianapolis: Hackett, 1988) defends the idea that causation links events and should be understood through a semantic of events' names.

11. Granted there exists accounts of quantum physics that preserve determinism, often inspired by David Bohm's account and including hidden variables, but this will be left aside here.

12. Stuart Glennan, *The New Mechanical Philosophy* (New York: Oxford University Press, 2017), gives a systematic presentation of this influential view and develops many aspects or responses to common objections. Carl Craver and Lindsey Darden, *In Search for Mechanisms* (Chicago: University of Chicago Press, 2013), provide a groundbreaking investigation of scientific methods through the prism of this new mechanism. Such a view was indeed mostly elaborated by Glennan on the one hand, and Craver, Darden, and Peter Machamer on the other.

13. For a historical account of this finding and a few others, for which they deserved a Nobel Prize in 1965, see Michel Morange, *The Black Box of Biology: A History of the Molecular Revolution*, trans. M. Cobb (Cambridge, MA: Harvard University Press, 2020).

14. In Glennan, *The New Mechanical Philosophy*.

15. Neo-mechanicists don't agree on that, and this constitutes one of the major issues discussed by those who adopted this view. Craver won't follow Glennan here, because he holds an "ontic" conception of explanation; namely, what explains something is something else in the world—e.g., the specific DNA molecules involved in the lactose operon. For Glennan, the explanation is given by the model, not the thing itself (it's a more "epistemic" conception).

16. Ned Hall was one of the first to formulate the distinction between the two families of viewpoints on causation—"Two Concepts of Causation," in *Causation and Counterfactuals*, ed. John Collins, Ned Hall, and Laurie Paul, 225–76 (Cambridge, MA: MIT Press, 2004). While he named the first one "production," as I do here, he labeled the second "dependence." I will elaborate on it below.

17. One is not compelled to accept Lewis's modal realism in order to appeal to the theory of possible worlds. It is always possible to do like other philosophers, such as Robert Stalnaker in *Ways a World Might Be: Metaphysical and Anti-Metaphysical Essays* (New York: Oxford University Press, 2003), and consider that possible worlds are just ideal variations on the actual world.

18. An enzyme that allows the transformation of the superfluous phenylalanine into tyrosine, another amino acid.

19. A diverse investigation into the counterfactual views of causation is given in John Collins, Ned Hall, and Laurie Paul, eds., *Causation and Counterfactuals* (Cambridge, MA: MIT Press, 2004).

20. This contingent event of the massive extinction of reptilian dinosaurs because of an asteroid strike is at the center of Steven Jay Gould's major essay,

Wonderful Life: The Burgess Shale and the Nature of Mystery (Princeton: Princeton University Press, 1989).

21. Some developments about this difficult question of comparing possible worlds are given in Michael J. Loux, ed., *The Possible and the Actual: Readings in the Metaphysics of Modality* (Ithaca: Cornell University Press, 1979).

22. Judea Pearl, *Causality: Models, Reasoning, and Inference*, 2nd ed. (Cambridge: Cambridge University Press, [2000] 2009).

23. This is equally crucial for the manipulationist view of causation, since any intervention of a variable has to be guaranteed against side effects that would impinge on many other variables in an uncontrolled way; Woodward's major opus devotes many pages to this problem of isolating interventions.

24. More precisely: counterfactuals are about possible worlds that differ from ours by facts, hence events or laws of nature. Mathematical theorems are, in turn, derived from the axioms of mathematics. A counterfactual statement about such theorems would be something along the following lines: "If two points are not sufficient to define one straight line, then the Pythagorean theorem would be wrong." But the antecedent in this sentence is not a counterfact, it is the opposite of a logical truth, and it is impossible to conceive of it, as it is impossible to conceive of a contradiction. There are indeed no possible worlds in which this antecedent holds, hence one can't wonder about what would happen regarding rectangle triangles in such worlds. Such a counterfactual is therefore problematic even though some philosophers accept it (calling it "counterpossible").

25. In a series of papers since the 2000s Paolo Mancosu has revived the idea that there are explanations within mathematics—e.g., "Mathematical Explanation: Problems and Prospects," *Topoi* 20, no. 1 (2001): 97–117; they are not causal, but they are not only the proof that some theorem is true. They show the reason why the theorem is true, whereas many proofs prove a given theorem without showing why it holds; for instance, because they rely on a very different domain than the topic of the theorem (e.g., proving a theorem in number theory with topology or geometry). But whatever one decides on these matters, it does not modify my argument here.

26. Here the reader may think that the rationality of these agents is the cause of the positions of the vendors or, more generally, of the Nash equilibrium. This is handled directly in the next chapter, but for now, we can say that the assumption that agents are rational is a condition for explaining human actions in general. It is so general that it can't be counted as a cause or a reason—otherwise, this would be like counting the principle of causality itself—namely, the principle that all events have a cause—as a cause of a given event, which is absurd.

27. Alan Baker, "Mathematical Explanation in Science," *British Journal for the Philosophy of Science* 60 (2009): 611–33; Robert Batterman, "On the Explanatory Role of Mathematics in Empirical Science," *British Journal for the Philosophy of Science* 61 (2010): 1–25; Marc Lange, *Because without Cause* (New York: Oxford University Press, 2016).

28. Alexander Reutlinger and Juha Saatsi, eds., *Explanation beyond Causation: Philosophical Perspectives on Non-causal Explanations* (New York: Oxford University Press, 2018).

29. In Philippe Huneman, "Outlines of a Theory of Structural Explanations," *Philosophical Studies* 175, no. 3 (2018): 665–702.

30. John Nash, "Equilibrium Points in n-Person Games," *Proceedings of the National Academy of Sciences* 36, no. 1 (1950): 48–49.

31. For example, David Ruelle, *Chaotic Evolution and Strange Attractors* (Cambridge: Cambridge University Press, 1989).

32. For an account of the current use of big data in science, which implies networks of more than thousands of nodes, see Sabina Leonelli, *Data-Centric Biology: A Philosophical Study* (Chicago: University of Chicago Press, 2016).

33. Kevin Bacon was a popular example in the early works about the science of networks in the 1990s; he featured in many movies with many other famous actors, hence the desire to represent the network of his interactions with movie stars in movies.

34. Philippe Huneman, "Topological Explanations and Robustness in Biological Sciences," *Synthese* 177, no. 2 (2010): 213–45.

35. Robert M. May, *Stability and Complexity in Model Ecosystems* (Princeton: Princeton University Press, 1974).

36. For instance, Stuart Pimm, *Food Webs* (Chicago: University of Chicago Press, 2002); Hans Olff et al., "Parallel Ecological Networks in Ecosystems," *Philosophical Transactions of the Royal Society of London B: Biological Sciences* 364 (2009): 1755–79.

37. For example, José Montoya, Stuart Pimm, and Richard Solé, "Ecological Networks and Their Fragility," *Nature* 442 (2006): 259–67.

38. Robert May, Simon Levin, and George Sugihara, "Complex Systems: Ecology for Bankers," *Nature* 451 (2008): 893–95.

39. G. W. Leibniz, *Discourse on Metaphysics*, in *Philosophical Essays* (Indianapolis: Hackett, 1989), 54.

40. Historians have indeed complexified the naive view of the Scientific Revolution as a turn toward efficient cause, inertia principles, experiments, and mathematics, due to a few individuals such as Galileo. See, for instance, the account

by Steven Shapin, *The Scientific Revolution* (Chicago: University of Chicago Press, 1996).

Chapter 3: Why Did Mickey Mouse Open the Fridge?

1. We can see the double meaning of the French word *fin* at play here: drinking the orange juice is the *fin* of the action (in the sense of "finish") but also the *fin* of the agent (in the sense of "goal").

2. We will come back to the structure of narration directly in chapter 6.

3. See Lagnado, *Explaining the Evidence*, about reasoning and evidence in court.

4. Notwithstanding the gap between these critical thinkers and views of the human mind based on Darwin's thought and called "evolutionary psychology," there is a noticeable convergence here. Psychologist Jonathan Haidt, in *The Righteous Mind: Why Good People Are Divided by Politics and Religion* (Cambridge, MA: MIT Press, 2012), argues that most of our justifications for actions are rationalizations, constructing a morally acceptable narrative instead of capturing the real motivations, while economist Daniel Kahneman in *Thinking, Fast and Slow* (Cambridge, MA: MIT Press, 2012) argues that most of our behavior is led by a system of quick automatic responses to events that does not rely on explicit reasons transparent to ourselves, even if we make up ad hoc justifications when asked to do so.

5. One has heard of Weber's most famous thesis, expressed in his *Protestant Ethics and the Spirit of Capitalism* (1905). There, he reconstitutes the ideal type of the first capitalist entrepreneur, and shows how his Protestant beliefs in the value and necessity of work, and God's commandment to fructify Earth, leads him to work and reinvest in his productive work instead of enjoying his wealth, and to value money as a sign of his commitment to the splendor of God's creation. No consensus was reached among historians about this idea supposing to explain why capitalism arose in Protestant rather than equally rich Catholic countries (Belgium and the Netherlands but not France or Spain), but it has been intensively debated.

6. The best way to get a sense of this particular approach to social sciences is to scan through the journal *Cliodynamics*, established in the 2000s.

7. About psychology see Robert Richards, *Darwin and the Emergence of Evolutionary Theories of Brain and Behavior* (Chicago: University of Chicago Press, 1996). Some economists intended to use the Darwinian framework to explain economic life as a process: Robert Nelson and Sydney Winter, *An Evolutionary Theory of Economic Change* (Cambridge, MA: Harvard University Press, 1982). As

for psychology, the program of explaining human cognition as a set of evolved modules shaped by natural selection has been elaborated in the 1980s under the name "evolutionary psychology" and is very influential now, but some of its realizations are very controversial.

8. Another way to formulate the distinction between human sciences and natural sciences consists in emphasizing, instead of "understanding," the dimension of narrativity proper to human sciences. Actually, history is a major source for human sciences, and history is to some extent narration. (As Arthur Danto, a major philosopher of history, used to say, "History tells stories"; quoted in Louis Mink, "History and Fiction as Modes of Comprehension," *New Literary History* 1, no. 3 [1970]: 541–58.) See chapter 6 on a development about narrativity.

In any case this distinction is not enough to single out human and social sciences. Evolutionary biology, for instance, as well as cosmology, includes a decisive aspect of narrativity, since they have to tell a story that happened once in the universe. On evolutionary biology see Robert J. Richards, "The Structure of Narrative Explanation in History and Science," in *History and Evolution*, ed. M. Nitecki and D. Nitecki (New York: State University of New York Press, 1992), 19–54; John Beatty and Isabel Carrera, "When What Had to Happen Was Not Bound to Happen: History, Chance, Narrative, Evolution," *Journal of the Philosophy of History* 5, no. 3 (2011): 471–95 (the connection with contingency is also explored here in chapters 6 and 7). Another account is recently provided by Thomas Reydon, "The Proper Role of History in Evolutionary Explanations," *Noûs* (2021): 1–26.

On a formal way to define historicity of systems notwithstanding their living or inert character, see Hugh Desmond, "Symmetry Breaking and the Emergence of Path-Dependence," *Synthese* 194 (2017): 4101–31.

9. Fred Dretske, *Explaining Behavior: Reasons in a World of Causes* (Cambridge, MA: MIT Press, 1992).

10. See, for instance, Jaegwon Kim, *Supervenience and Mind: Selected Philosophical Essays* (Cambridge: Cambridge University Press, 1993).

11. For Kant, in his two first *Critiques*, to be free is to be capable of commencing by oneself a novel causal series.

12. For a presentation of what is "behavioral economics," see Michelle Baddeley, *Behavioural Economics: A Very Short Introduction* (New York: Oxford University Press, 2017).

13. Alexander Rosenberg undertook a detailed examination of the pretensions of microeconomics to understand behavior in general and has shown that its applications cannot a priori be taken as universal and true—especially because human decisions and actions may not feature the properties of fine-graininess and

preciseness required to allow actual computations of preferences, as done by economists, to be efficiently executed. Rosenberg, *Microeconomic Laws: A Philosophical Analysis* (Pittsburgh: University of Pittsburgh Press, 1976).

14. Actually, another clause is involved in rationality: namely, the fact that the order of preferences between two items, when compared to a third one, does not change when they are taken together with another third item. This is not obviously satisfied: suppose you hesitate between chocolate at 3€, 4€, and 7€. You prefer the 3€ chocolate. But when faced with the same 3€ and 4€ chocolates and a new 14€ chocolate bar, you may very well prefer the 4€ chocolate instead of the 3€ because the two lower-priced chocolates now appear "cheap," and you like the 4€ slightly better. This clause therefore seems to be easily violated, and I'll talk later about redescribing preferences in relation to conserving rationality. But transitivity will become even more important in what follows.

15. It would also make theoretical economics clash with everyday discourse—in which we are often witnessing people behaving "irrationally"; and with current "behavioral economics," which precisely investigates how people fail at being rational (see below).

16. See, for instance, Gary Becker, *The Economic Approach to Human Behavior* (Chicago: University of Chicago Press, 1976).

17. Philosophy of action offers a wide literature on these notions and the distinctions between them. According to each conception, desires and goals, as well as intentions and practical reasons, are differently connected. However, for our present purposes these differences are not relevant; it suffices to say that these concepts behave in the same way in how they provide a response scheme to any why-question about actions in the form of a structured reason for these actions. Elizabeth Anscombe—*Intention* (Cambridge, MA: Harvard University Press, [1957] 2000)—who inherited Wittgenstein's critique of the substantiality of mental states (in which understanding, and signification, are not mental states), denies that an intention is a cause within the mind preceding an action. Rather, it is manifested in the action itself: seeing someone waving just before a cab stops is seeing her calling a cab, which manifests her intention of riding in a cab; and this includes the reasons for this action. Others—like Michael Bratman in *Intention, Plans and Practical Reason* (Cambridge, MA: Harvard University Press, 1987)—want to avoid this issue concerning the ontology of an intention by referring to the notion of "plan"; so that "making plans" and "executing plans" capture the subtle connection between reasons for action, action itself, and its outcome. (We are operating here under the assumption that the relevant analysis for the philosophy of action is not an act but a sequence of acts that constitute the

action—e.g., flying to Madrid, which includes buying tickets, packing, calling a cab, etc.).

In any case the theoretical dissensus on these issues concerns the ontology of the reasons for action rather than the overall grammar of the question "why?"; and thus the articulation among three types of reason. This is why this chapter is not a digest of the most recent views in philosophy of action, and still allows for whatever one's favorite ontology of intentions and desires may be.

18. In *Reasons Why?*, a book whose focus is more limited than this one, Bradford Skow concentrates on the first kind of reason (the cause and effect) to which he adds the relation of grounding (see below); reasons-for-action are not the object of his analysis.

19. This view is most precisely articulated in his *Critique of Practical Reason*. Among many commentaries, Thomas Hill—"Humanity as an End in Itself," *Ethics* 91, no. 1 (1980): 84–89—provides a defense of Kant, arguing that only a human being is an end in itself, which constitutes a moral standard that is very hard to support.

20. For academic philosophers, I am mixing wholly incompatible concepts: as is well known, Kantian ethics are in opposition to Aristotle's ethics (as well as most other ethics) because they are not presented as a theory of happiness, leaving the determination of happiness to each individual. (If biathlons make me happy, and if Mary's happiness comes from sailing, this can't pertain to ethics; these are just individual facts about our physiologico-psychological constitutions.) Instead, ethics is about being "worthy of being happy," and this can be formulated in a purely universal way.

I don't deny that this opposition between Kant and Aristotle constitutes one of the deepest divides in ethics and I don't want to bridge it here. I only want to suggest that both reasonings about reasons-for-action display the same structure of regress, based on the possibility of iterating the quest for a reason. Determining what stands at the term of this iteration is a metaethical question that is not relevant to my own thoughts here.

21. Piaget's empirically based idea that there are stages of cognitive development, and that children go through a period of "animism," has inspired much research; Jean Piaget, *The Child's Concept of the World* (London: Routledge, 1929). More precisely, for him a child basically goes from ascribing purposes to everything, and thus seeing everything as being alive, at 4–5 years old, to understanding that only plants and animals are alive, at 9–12 years old. The tricky question concerning the intentions of living beings is addressed in the next chapter.

22. Baruch Spinoza, *Ethics*, trans. Samuel Shirley (Indianapolis: Hackett, 1992), 57.

23. Spinoza, *Ethics*, 58.

24. Spinoza, *Ethics*, 58.

25. Spinoza, *Ethics*, 58.

26. Spinoza, *Ethics*, 60.

Chapter 4: Why Do Triceratops Have Horns?

1. On Descartes's conception of life and animals, see Daniel Garber, *Descartes Embodied: Reading Cartesian Philosophy through Cartesian Science* (Cambridge: Cambridge University Press, 2001); Dennis Des Chene, *Spirits and Clocks: Machine and Organisms in Descartes* (Ithaca: Cornell University Press, 2000); and on the relation between thought and language in humans and animals according to Descartes, see Catherine Wilson, "What Is the Importance of Descartes's Meditation Six?," *Philosophica* 76 (2005): 67–90.

2. In *Knowledge of Life* (New York: Fordham University Press, 2008), Georges Canguilhem develops the idea that each period in the life sciences favored a particular technique as a source for its analogies—often the one that was most flourishing at the time. Regarding the general analogy between machines and organisms, see Tim Lewens, *Artefacts and Organisms* (Cambridge: Cambridge University Press, 2004).

3. Descartes's philosophy revolves around the notion of the "order of reasons," as we will see later: each proposition should be proved on the basis of other already justified propositions. This sequence ends with a proposition that is obviously true—namely, "I think therefore I am," which is presented as the first truth in the *Discourse on Method* and then in the *Meditations*—because it is the only claim that can stand the test of radical doubt. On this basis, Descartes proves that there exists a God and that this God is truthful, which justifies our scientific enterprises—since our power of knowledge stands on solid ground, even though it can fail from time to time. Any science of animals is ensured that there is a God who created the animals: as such, they are well designed, and therefore their parts have functions.

4. In "The Pen and the Sword: Recovering the Disciplinary Identity of Physiology and Anatomy before 1800—II: Old Physiology—the Pen," *Studies in History and Philosophy of Biological and Biomedical Sciences* 34, no. 1 (2003): 51–76, Andrew Cunningham calls this inference of the functionality of parts from the rationality of a creative God the "design argument"; he contrasts it with the "argument from design"—which we will encounter later on, and which infers God from the presence of a design.

5. Tobias Cheung, in "From the Organism of a Body to the Body of an Organism: Occurrence and Meaning of the Word 'Organism' from the Seventeenth to the Nineteenth Centuries," *British Journal for the History of Science* 39, no. 3 (2006): 319–39, made a convincing case that a primary definition of "organism" is that organisms are arrangements of matter proper to living beings alone—in contrast with the structure of ordinary matter, which is arranged in a way likely to produce regular machine-like aims (and are thus called "mechanisms"). It's only after Leibniz and Stahl, who debated about organisms and mechanism in a correspondence published under the name "*Negotium otiosum*," that the term organism started to refer to certain kinds of things rather than a form of arrangement. See Francois Duchesneau and Justin E. H. Smith, eds., *The Leibniz-Stahl Controversy* (New Haven: Yale University Press, 2016) and their commentary therein. On Leibniz's view that living creatures are infinitely organized machines, see my comment in "Kant vs. Leibniz in the Second Antinomy: Organisms Are Not Infinitely Subtle Machines," *Kant Studien* 105, no. 2 (2014): 155–95.

6. Preformation and preexistence have been extensively studied. On the use of microscopes see Jacques Roger, *Les sciences de la vie dans la pensée française au XVIIIème siècle* (Paris: Colin, 1963); translated by Robert Ellrich as *The Life Sciences in Eighteenth-Century French Thought*, ed. Keith R. Benson (Stanford: Stanford University Press, 1998). The detailed study by Marc Ratcliff on the microscope, which explains at length Trembley's views, is also very rich: *The Quest for the Invisible: Microscopy in the Enlightenment* (Aldershot: Ashgate, 2009).

7. On the demise of preformationism, see Peter Bowler, "Preformation and Pre-existence in the Seventeenth Century: A Brief Analysis," *Journal of the History of Biology* 4, no. 2 (1971): 221–44; Michael H. Hoffheimer, "Maupertuis and the Eighteenth-Century Critique of Pre-existence," *Journal of the History of Biology* 15, no. 1 (1982): 119–44.

8. See my "Developmental Explanation," in *Encyclopedia of Systems Biology, ed.* W. Dubitzky, O. Wolkenhauer, K. Cho, and H. Yokota (Dordrecht: Springer, 2013), on the recurrence of preformation as an explanatory scheme.

9. This solidifies the connection between argument from design and design argument, as Cunningham, "The Pen and the Sword," distinguishes them.

10. The landmark text about physico-theological arguments is Hume's *Dialogues Concerning Natural Religion (1779).* I won't comment on his work here; since it is a dialogue, determining which claims are defended by Hume himself is not straightforward. The book can be read as an exercise in skepticism regarding physio-theology.

11. Bernardin de Saint-Pierre was a disciple of Rousseau. His novel *Paul et*

Virginie (1788) is a milestone in pastoral literature, and is often read by French students. In *Métaphysique et biologie: Kant et la constitution du concept d'organisme* (Paris: Kimé, 2008), forthcoming in translation (Routledge, 2023), and "The Unity of the Only Possible Argument: Theology and Philosophy," *Contemporary Kantian Philosophy* 4 (2019): 72–84, I addressed the topic of the contingency of ascriptions of external purposiveness more extensively because it is a major leitmotif throughout all of Kant's thought concerning the order of nature.

12. I analyzed in detail this pervasive argument connecting increasing complexity and design in "Redesigning the Argument from Design," *Paradigmi* 33, no. 2 (2015): 105–32.

13. In "Resistances to Psychoanalysis" (1925), in *The Standard Edition of the Complete Psychological Works of Sigmund Freud*, vol. 19 (London: Hogarth Press, 1994), 211–24.

14. This phrase is from Darwin's *Origin of Species* (1859).

15. *Heritability* should not be confused with *heredity*. It is a statistical measure, and it is proper to a trait of interest. Essentially, formulated in nontechnical terms, it measures the constancy of the distance between the trait value of the offspring and the mean value of the trait in the offspring population against the same distance in the previous generation. In my example, running speed is heritable if the offspring of those who run faster than the average also run faster than the average. But heritable does not mean that the offspring have the same race speed as their parents. Heritability is crucial in evolution because it measures the "response to selection"; namely, if a trait value is selected (for instance by fostering reproduction among those who feature this trait value), how quickly will the trait value in the population change? Heritability is therefore the measure of a statistical property, it is proper to a population and an environment, and it should not be conflated with the causal notion of innate vs. acquired. Importantly, even the traits with a very weak heritability can evolve, provided that the intensity of selection is strong enough.

16. In my example, foxes run at a constant speed. In reality, this is not the case: foxes will also evolve since the foxes that outrun other foxes catch more rabbits. This is a situation called an "arms race," where two species coevolve corresponding traits. It is more complicated than my example; but the arms race stops when, for both the foxes and the rabbits, running speed impedes other processes that are important for survival and reproduction. In addition, the selective pressure is higher on rabbits than on foxes—since, as Richard Dawkins famously said, foxes run for their meal while rabbits run for their lives; *The Selfish Gene* (Cambridge: Cambridge University Press, 1976).

17. John Beatty explained how the creators of the Modern Synthesis, following the first Darwinians, believed that genetic variation was abundant, generally homogeneous, and isotropic (instead of directional); "The Creativity of Natural Selection? Part II: The Synthesis and Since," *Journal of the History of Biology* 52, no. 4 (2019): 705–31. Random variation was empirically attested first in 1946 by experiments on *E. coli* that were led by Delbrück and Luria. This opposes so-called Lamarckism, in which variations are spontaneously directed toward what is adaptive, and therefore a series of offspring of an organism will become spontaneously more and more adapted after many generations. Francesca Merlin exposed the ways in which the modern discussion on mutations does not authorize a Lamarckian view, when the actual views of Lamarck are taken into account; "Evolutionary Chance Mutation: A Defense of the Modern Synthesis' Consensus View," *Philosophy, Theory, and Practice in Biology* 2, no. 3 (2010).

However, the claim that mutations are blind and random is too simplistic. For instance, the order in which mutations appear is relevant for evolution, since it conditions the possible genotypes from which selection will discriminate those that are the fittest. In *Mutations, Randomness and Evolution* (New York: Oxford University Press, 2021), Arlin Stolzfus developed a critique of the Modern Synthesis based on this nonrandomness of mutations; I expose the distinct dimensions of variation—homogeneousness, isotropy, randomness, directionality—and their possible impact on the Modern Synthesis in "Variation, Extension and Selection: A Synthesis of the Reasons for a New Evolutionary Synthesis," in *Challenging the Modern Synthesis: Development, Inheritance and Adaptation*, ed. P. Huneman and D. Walsh, 68–110 (New York: Oxford University Press, 2017).

18. Eva Jablonka and Marion Lamb first developed the idea that some Lamarckian processes are involved in evolution in *Epigenetic Inheritance and Evolution: The Lamarckian Dimension* (Oxford: Oxford University Press, 1995). They systematize these views, arguing that there are several independent channels of inheritance besides genes—whose variation can be adaptive—in Jablonka and Lamb, *Evolution in Four Dimensions* (Cambridge, MA: MIT Press, 2005).

19. Dan-E. Nilsson and Susanne Pelger, "A Pessimistic Estimate of the Time Required for an Eye to Evolve," *Proceedings: Biological Sciences* 256, no. 1345 (1994): 53–58.

20. David J. Depew, in "Conceptual Change and the Rhetoric of Evolutionary Theory: 'Force Talk' as a Case Study and Challenge for Science Pedagogy," in *The Philosophy of Biology: A Companion for Educators*, ed. Kostas Kampourakis (Dordrecht: Springer, 2013), examines the fates of these three words within the theory.

21. This view was first formulated in 2002, and then widely discussed. The au-

thors published a systematic paper explaining the major claims they make—Denis Walsh, André Ariew, and Mohan Matthen, "Four Pillars of Statisticalism," *Philosophy, Theory and Practice in Biology*, 9, no. 1 (2017)—which contains all relevant references to previous papers. In "Natural Selection: A Case for the Counterfactual Approach," *Erkenntnis* 76, no. 2 (2012): 171–94, and "Assessing Statistical Views of Natural Selection: Is There a Room for Non-local Causation?," *Studies in History and Philosophy of Biological and Biomedical Sciences* 44 (2013): 604–12, I defended an account in which causation means a counterfactual interdependence between the trait and its change in frequency. In a nutshell, when variation in the value of a trait counterfactually impacts the frequency of this trait value, then there is natural selection (and reciprocally). The connections with the statisticalist position and the many objections met by this view are therein addressed. Many positions exist between statisticalism and the original account of selection as a force acting upon populations like gravity acts on bodies in physics, formulated in Elliott Sober, *Nature of Selection: Evolutionary Focus in Philosophical Focus* (Princeton: Princeton University Press, 1984).

22. Sober, *Nature of Selection*, argues that natural selection explains the spreading of traits but not their arrival in a population, nor the fact that a given individual X has trait A. In "Pruning the Tree of Life," *British Journal for Philosophy Science* 46, no. 1 (1995): 59–80, Karen Neander responds by arguing that selection is able to impact upon the chances of new variants arriving in a population; thus, it contributes toward explaining the occurrence of new adaptations and not only their spreading.

23. Above all in Denis Walsh, *Organisms, Agency and Evolution* (New York: Oxford University Press, 2015).

24. The "mostly" here refers to the major claim of the Modern Synthesis: "Natural selection, acting on the heritable variation provided by the mutations and recombination of a Mendelian genetic constitution, is the main agency of biological evolution." Julian Huxley to Ernst Mayr, 3 September 1951, Papers of Ernst Mayr, HUGFP 14.15, Box 1, Harvard University Archives, Cambridge, MA. This defines what one could call "Orthodox Darwinism," namely in regard to two claims: the paramount power of natural selection in shaping evolution, and the Mendelian nature of inheritance. Alternative views of evolution, which come under various labels, reject one or both claims; see, for example, chapters in Philippe Huneman and Denis Walsh, eds., *Challenging the Modern Synthesis* (New York: Oxford University Press, 2017).

25. The disagreement started with the emergence of the Modern Synthesis itself: while Dobzhansky's definition of evolution as "allele frequency changes"

started to colonize textbooks, Mayr argued against it. For him, evolution primarily changes *organisms*; and it is because of the interactions between organisms that selection occurs. Allele frequency change is mere bookkeeping. Dobzhansky himself, who favors views where selection may possibly act upon organisms as well as groups, would not have seen his sentence as more than a characterization of evolution.

The status of the Modern Synthesis is itself hotly debated by historians, given that no consensus has been reached about whether it is a paradigm, a theoretical object, a convention, or an institutional tool intended to foster some unification between distinct disciplines. For an overview of this question, see Jean Gayon (who devoted much time to address this issue) and Philippe Huneman, "The Modern Synthesis: Theoretical or Institutional Event?," *Journal of the History of Biology* 52 (2019): 519–35.

26. Larry Wright, "Functions," *Philosophical Review* 85 (1973): 70–86,

27. Karen Neander, "Functions as Selected Effects: The Conceptual Analyst's Defense," *Philosophy of Science* 58 (1991): 168–84; Ruth Millikan, *Language, Thought, and Other Biological Categories: New Foundations for Realism* (Cambridge, MA: MIT Press, 1984).

28. Dretske, *Explaining Behavior*; Millikan, *Language, Thought, and Other Biological Categories*; Daniel Dennett, *Darwin's Dangerous Idea* (New York: Simons & Schuster, 1995).

29. There are a few other attempts to think of norms in terms of the "causal role view" of functions; see, for instance, Valerie Gray-Hardcastle, "On the Normativity of Functions," in *Functions*, ed. A. Ariew and R. Perlman (New York: Oxford University Press, 2002). I exposed the state of the function debate in "Introduction," in *Functions: Selection and Mechanisms*, ed. P. Huneman, 1–18 (Dordrecht: Springer, 2013).

30. Pluralism is often considered an option; etiological theory is promising but faces many obstacles that would push philosophers into attenuating it. In particular, the exact determination of the content of a function (e.g., is the function of claws to seize prey or to kill prey?) raises issues and may call for a weakening of the realism of the concept, as I argued in "Weak Realism in the Etiological Theory of Functions," in Huneman, *Functions*, 105–13.

31. Ernst Mayr, "Cause and Effect in Biology," *Science* 134 (1961): 1501–6.

32. Kevin N. Laland, Kim Sterelny, John Odling-Smee, William Hoppitt, and Tobias Uller, "Cause and Effect in Biology Revisited: Is Mayr's Proximate-Ultimate Dichotomy Still Useful?," *Science* 334, no. 6062 (December 2011): 1512–16.

33. I examined whether the separation between ultimate and proximate is

robust in "Variation, Extension and Selection: A Synthesis of the Reasons for a New Evolutionary Synthesis," in Huneman and Walsh, *Challenging the Modern Synthesis*, 68–110. This difference assumes that development differs from inheritance (which is a population-based notion characterizing the transmission of traits), whereas it is now commonly acknowledged that there are forms of non-genetic inheritance that are affected by development; see Étienne Danchin et al., "Beyond DNA: Integrating Inclusive Inheritance into an Extended Theory of Evolution," *Nature Reviews: Genetics* 12 (2011): 475–86. I claim that in many cases this latter difference (as well as Mayr's distinction) is still a correct approximation of what happens.

34. These are the three conditions that population geneticist Richard Lewontin proposed for evolution by natural selection in the landmark paper "Units of Selection," *Annual Review Ecology Systematics* 1 (1970): 1–18. Their fulfillment does not guarantee that natural selection will take place; because if the population is too small, stochastic effects that are called "random genetic drift" will trump natural selection; Sewall Wright, "The Roles of Mutation, Inbreeding, Cross-breeding and Selection in Evolution," *Proceedings: Sixth Annual Congress Genetics* 1 (1932): 356–66. Peter Godfrey-Smith, in *Darwinian Populations and Evolution* (New York: Oxford University Press, 2007), has shown that they can't be as universal as is claimed, and their application raises issues of borderline cases. In any case, Lewontin's very general formulation differs from Darwin to the extent that it does not primarily appeal to competition—Darwin's "struggle for life"—as a condition for natural selection; competition is a cause—generally the most frequent one—of differences in fitness, which in turn are the ground of natural selection, but logically speaking, fitness differences and not competition are required for the modern concept of natural selection.

35. François Jacob, *Le jeu des possibles* [The game of possibilities] (Paris, 1980). Gould expanded on this in many papers and books; for example, *The Panda's Thumb* (London: Penguin, 1980).

36. Acknowledging that such dysfunctions or dispositions to malfunction are part of the adaptive design of humans is the basis of the subdiscipline called "evolutionary medicine," initiated by Randoph Nesse; see Nesse and George Williams, *Why We Get Sick* (New York: Vintage Books, 1996).

37. On the emergence of "behavioral ecology," which succeeded the field formerly called "ethology," and how it introduced formal mathematical optimization models and game theory, see Jean-Baptiste Grodwohl, "Animal Behavior, Population Biology and the Modern Synthesis," *Journal of the History of Biology* 52, no. 4 (2019): 597–633.

38. David Lack, *The Natural Regulation of Animal Numbers* (Oxford: Oxford University Press, 1954).

39. For example, as David Marr demonstrated in his landmark book entitled *Vision: A Computational Investigation into the Human Representation and Processing of Visual Information* (Cambridge, MA: MIT Press, 2010), the act of seeing envelops extremely complex computations, allowing us to place objects in space based on our two retina images, which are done almost instantaneously and unconsciously.

40. Samir Okasha, *Agents and Goals in Evolution* (New York: Oxford University Press, 2018).

41. John Maynard-Smith, *Evolution and the Theory of Games* (Cambridge: Cambridge University Press, 1982).

42. This correspondence is not absolutely exact; my colleagues and I inquired to what extent the major concepts in biological evolution match the corresponding concepts in economics (e.g., market, competition, altruism, investment, strategy, etc.), ultimately showing the limited validity of this correspondence; Jean Baptiste André, Mikael Cozic, Silvia De Monte, Jean Gayon, Philippe Huneman, Johannes Martens, and Bernard Walliser, *From Evolutionary Biology to Economics and Back: Parallels and Crossings between Economics and Evolution* (Dordrecht: Springer, 2022).

43. In Susan Hurley, "Making Sense of Animals," in *Rational Animals?*, ed. S. Hurley and M. Nudds (New York: Oxford University Press, 2006).

44. Hurley writes: "We can make patchy sense of animal action at the animal level and correctly attribute reasons for acting to animals, even if these reasons are bound to certain contexts. The animal level emerges as an archipelago from the sea of causes" ("Making Sense of Animals," 113). The human rationality appears as the most context-unbound stage of this archipelago. Recently, Peter Godfrey-Smith inquired about the cognitive world of cephalopods, who are known to be very intelligent (whatever this word may mean) and yet are very distant from us phylogenetically; his inquiry, based on a substantial empirical science, shows that "minds" can be very different from our own minds but still exist; *Other Minds* (New York: Farrar, Straus and Giroux, 2018).

45. William Hamilton, "The Evolution of Altruistic Behavior," *American Naturalist* 97 (1963): 354–56. For a philosophical exploration of this notion and the issues raised by kin selection in contemporary biology, see Jonathan Birch, *Philosophy of Social Evolution* (New York: Oxford University Press, 2017).

46. See Alan Grafen, "A First Formal Link between the Price Equation and an Optimization Program," *Journal of Theoretical Biology* 217 (2002): 75–91. For a

nontechnical presentation, see Alan Grafen, "The Formal Darwinism Project in Outline," *Biology and Philosophy* 29, no. 2 (2014): 155–74.

47. For comments on Fisher's notoriously difficult proof of the theorem, see among others Jean Gayon, *Darwinism's Struggle for Survival: Heredity and the Hypothesis of Natural Selection* (Cambridge: Cambridge University Press, 1998).

48. Mimicry is a good example: for an insect, mimicking another, nonedible species of insect is advantageous. However, when a whole population adopts the mimicking behaviors, predators are more likely to eat one by chance and discover that they are indeed edible notwithstanding the mimicry. Hence its advantage decreases and it is no longer selected. This is called frequency-dependent selection.

49. On this controversy about the validity, meaning, and importance of the theorem, see among others Anthony Edwards, "The Fundamental Theorem of Natural Selection," *Biological Review: Cambridge Philosophical Society* 69, no. 4 (1994): 443–74; Steven Frank and Montgomery Slatkin, "Fisher's Fundamental Theorem of Natural Selection," *Trends in Ecology and Evolution* 7 (1992): 92–95.

50. There are many criticisms of Grafen's view. Jonathan Birch, in "Natural Selection and the Maximization of Fitness," *Biological Reviews* 91, no. 3 (2015): 712–27, and Okasha, in *Agents and Goals*, concur in saying that it should be seen as an empirical statement instead of an a priori principle; and that biologists should find population structures in which the isomorphism holds instead of postulating it and then identifying situations where it does not. See also, for applications of it, my comments in "Formal Darwinism and Organisms in Evolutionary Biology: Answering Some Challenges," *Biology and Philosophy* 29 (2014): 271–79; "A Pluralist Framework to Address Challenges to the Modern Synthesis in Evolutionary Theory," *Biological Theory* 9, no. 2 (2014): 163–77; "Inclusive Fitness Teleology and Darwinian Explanatory Pluralism: A Theoretical Sketch and an Application to Current Controversies," in *Biosemiotics and Evolution: The Natural Foundations of Meaning and Symbolism*, ed. E. Pagni and R. Theisen Simanke, 137–60 (Dordrecht: Springer, 2021).

51. In a recent paper, Hugh Desmond and I argued that the whole discussion conflates two separate issues: whether agency is indispensable for explanation (meaning that it is more than an analogy of heuristic use since we could not explain the living without it), and whether it is an ontic concept (namely, whether agents exist in the biological world). These are two different things—exactly like in mathematics where someone could simultaneously argue that mathematics are indispensable for science and that numbers don't actually exist. We therefore argue in favor of a Kantian solution, in which agency is indispensable for explanation—but not ontic, exactly like Kant's concept of "natural purpose"; Hugh Desmond and Philippe Huneman, "The Ontology of Organismic Agency: A Kantian Ap-

proach," in *Natural Born Monads: On the Metaphysics of Organisms and Human Individuals,* ed. A. Altobrandi and P. Biasetti , 33–64 (Berlin: De Gruyter, 2020).

52. For an overview of the research on the origins of life until 2000, see Iris Fry, *The Emergence of Life on Earth* (New Brunswick, NJ: Rutgers University Press, 2000). For an account of theories of prebiotic life recently using synthetic biology, see Christophe Malaterre, "Can Synthetic Biology Shed Light on the Origin of Life?," *Biological Theory* 4, no. 4 (2009): 357–67.

53. On Artificial Life as a project, see Christopher Langton, ed., *Artificial Life: An Overview* (Cambridge, MA: MIT Press, 1995), who coined the term in the 1990s. Philosopher Mark Bedau has extensively reflected upon the meaning of Artificial Life in "Artificial Life," in *The Blackwell Guide to the Philosophy of Computing and Information*, ed. L. Floridi, 505–12 (London: Blackwell, 2003), and also worked on the chemical artificial life program called "protocells"—Steen Rasmussen et al., *Protocells: Bridging Nonliving and Living Matter* (Cambridge, MA: MIT Press, 2008).

54. *The Logic of Life: A History of Heredity*, trans. Betty E. Spillmann (Princeton: Princeton University Press, 1973).

55. Edouard Machery, "Why I Stopped Worrying about the Definition of Life . . . and Why You Should as Well," *Synthese* 185 (2012): 145–64.

56. Christophe Malaterre, with Jean-François Chartier, recently used data-mining methods on corpora of scientific papers to show that "life" is rather used in this way than as a categorical concept; "Beyond Categorical Definitions of Life: A Data-Driven Approach to Assessing Lifeness," *Synthese* 198, no. 5 (2019): 4543–72. But in the past many biologists and philosophers believed that finding a "definition of life" is absurd; what is possible is to agree on characteristics of living things, a few of them being enough to consider something from a biological viewpoint (motion, respiration, metabolism, inheritance, reproduction, disease were historically among them). One of the most famous supporters of this idea was the physiologist Claude Bernard in his *Leçons sur les phénomènes de la vie communs aux végétaux et aux animaux* (Paris: Baillière, 1879); translated by Hebbel E. Hoff, Roger Guillemin, and Lucienne Guillemin, *Lectures on the Phenomena of Life Common to Animals and Plants* (Springfield: Charles C. Thomas, 1974). An overview of positions about the nature of life can be found in Mark Bedau and Carol Cleland, eds., *The Nature of Life: Classical and Contemporary Perspectives from Philosophy and Science* (Cambridge: Cambridge University Press, 2010).

57. As indicated above, all molecular biology is pervaded by information concepts (e.g., genes are supposed to carry information). A first philosophical question deals with the proper nature of this information. Should it be understood as

what we call Shannon information—which is mostly quantitative, since Shannon designed mathematical tools to decide how much information is contained in a sentence—or as semantic information? In any case, we should wonder about the content of information. Almost no biologist now thinks it concerns traits since one gene is never wholly about a trait (which runs contrary to the popular idea of genes, since many things together ultimately determine a trait related to a gene). In turn, other philosophers criticize the idea that information is an accurate concept, since it is only ascribed to genes and therefore excludes other processes from being important evolutionary factors. Paul Griffiths, Arnaud Pocheville, and colleagues proposed a concept of information based on the idea of causal specificity that is both formalizable and applicable to any kind of inheritance mechanism, and not only genes; "Measuring Causal Specificity," *Philosophy of Science* 82, no. 4 (2015): 529–55.

58. For a philosophical examination of the families of theories of the origin of life, see Fry, *The Emergence of Life*.

59. For Mark Bedau—"The Nature of Life," in *The Philosophy of Artificial Life*, ed. Margaret A. Boden, 332–57 (New York: Oxford University Press, 1996)—life is "supple adaptation," something close to what an evolutionary-minded biologist would think. But in this case financial markets or the internet are alive, as he acknowledges. He later defended a view of life as an articulation of metabolism, compartment, and program; "A Functional Account of Degrees of Minimal Chemical Life," *Synthese* 185, no. 1 (2012): 73–88.

60. Note that this latter fact was the major objection from evolutionary biologists to the famous Gaia hypothesis imagined by James Lovelock. Earth does not evolve in a Darwinian way, since it has no variants. See Sébastien Dutreuil, "James Lovelock and the Gaia Hypothesis: 'A New Look at Life on Earth' . . . for the Life and the Earth Sciences," in *Dreamers, Romantics and Visionaries in the Life Sciences*, ed. M. Dietrich and O. Harman, 272–87 (Chicago: University of Chicago Press, 2018).

61. Scott Turner supports this idea; see "Individuality in a Social Insect Assemblage," in *From Groups to Individuals: Evolution and Emerging Individuality*, ed. P. Huneman and F. Bouchard, 291–45 (Cambridge, MA: MIT Press, 2013).

Chapter 5: Why Did World War I Happen?

1. See Philippe Ariès, *L'homme devant la mort* (Paris: Seuil, 1977), translated by Helen Weaver, *The Hour of Our Death* (New York: Vintage Books, 1981), or for a shorter time period, in late Antiquity, Peter Brown, *The Ransom of the Soul: Afterlife and Wealth in Early Western Christianity* (Cambridge: Cambridge University

Press, 2015). This sequence itself is a unique fact, in the sense that it took place once in the history of humanity—unlike, for instance, the role of death in the development of human psychism.

2. In his famous essay on the method of history, *Comment on écrit l'histoire?—Writing History: Essay on Epistemology,* trans. Mina Moore-Rinvolucri (Middletown, CT: Wesleyan University Press, 1984)—the historian Paul Veyne argues that history ultimately entangles three causes: determinism, plans, and chance.

3. "Facts" and "events" are two ontologically different categories. A fact is what is meant by a proposition; for example, the fact corresponding to "Tuesday, September 12, it rains" is the rain on September 12. Rain in Paris, Tuesday, September 12, is an event, which is tied to this fact. But the fact "It rains *in Paris*, Tuesday, September 12" is different from the former fact, even though it corresponds to the same event. See for instance Bennett, *Events and Their Names.*

4. Hierarchizing events according to their degree of something is a classical strategy. Some use the notions of thick and thin events; for instance, Jonathan Bennett writes: "A certain qualitatively thick event, which is a push and a dislodgment, occupies a spatiotemporal zone which is also occupied by a thinner event which is just a push, and another thinner event which is just a dislodgment. These are qualitative or non-zonal parts of the thicker event, just as the property of pushing is part of the richer property dislodging by pushing"; see "What Events Are," in *The Blackwell Guide to Metaphysics*, ed. Richard M. Gale (London: Blackwell, 2002), 43. Fine-grained events in my sense are not exactly thin events, since they are not fine-grained by virtue of how they are composed, but by virtue of the degree of description required (and here it is very weak).

5. This account is developed in Husserl's *Ideas for a Pure Phenomenology and a Phenomenological Philosophy* (1913), giving rise to a method of imaginary variations intended to capture essences that is called "eidetic variations."

6. Michael Strevens, in *Bigger than Chaos* (Cambridge, MA: MIT Press, 2003), presented a sophisticated account of the requisites any system likely to be modeled through probability calculus should fulfill.

7. There is indeed something clearly conventional in putting trucks and gardens together, while it seems not so arbitrary to put all that is made of gold in one same class: however, it's not easy to explain what criteria would be needed in order to belong to such a class. Most of the "natural kinds" debate in current philosophy addresses this question. For a good exploration of the metaphysical issue of natural kinds, see Muhammad Ali Khalidi, *Natural Categories and Human Kinds: Classification in the Natural and Social Sciences* (Cambridge: Cambridge University Press, 2013); and Catherine Kendig, ed., *Natural Kinds and Classification in Scien-*

tific Practice (London: Routledge, 2016). For two recent accounts of natural kinds, see Matthew H. Slater, "Natural Kindness," *British Journal for the Philosophy of Science* 66, no. 2 (2015): 375–411; and Anouk Barberousse, Françoise Longy, Francesca Merlin, and Stéphanie Ruphy, "Natural Kinds: A New Synthesis," *Theoria: Revista de Teoría, Historia y Fundamentos de la Ciencia* 35, no. 3 (2020): 365–87.

Chapter 6: Why Did Napoleon Lose at Waterloo?

1. Antoine-Augustin Cournot, *Exposition de la théorie des chances et des probabilités* (Paris: Hachette, 1843); translated by Oscar Sheynin, *Exposition of the Theory of Chances and Probabilities* (Scholars Press, 2019).

2. In the next chapter, I will elaborate on what this structure exactly is.

3. With regard to any set, "fractal" means the property of being invariant whatever the scale chosen for examining this set—be it a shape, or a sequence of numbers. In nonlinear dynamics, the property of "fractality" plays an important role; counterintuitively, although designed for this purpose, fractal sets have a noninteger dimension. The notion was first proposed and explored by the mathematician Benoit Mandelbrot in the 1980s.

4. Once again, these views lead to more mathematical formulations, which involve technical frameworks such as "measure theory." But designing such formalism is not the point of this book.

5. There are many presentations of these notions (sensitivity to initial conditions; complex systems; or, as I will introduce later, attractors, basins of attraction, and phase spaces). Besides the now classic opus by Nobel Prize physicist Ilya Prigogine and philosopher Isabelle Stengers—*Order Out of Chaos: Man's New Dialogue with Nature* (London: Heinemann, 1984)—David Ruelle's *Chance and Chaos* (Princeton: Princeton University Press, 1991) is an excellent presentation that is written by a pioneer in complexity science. The ideas advanced here about determinism and predictability are developed in relation to the notion of emergence in my paper "Determinism, Predictability and Open-Ended Evolution: Lessons from Computational Emergence," *Synthese* 185, no. 2 (2012): 195–214.

6. Of course, actual systems are modeled along a plurality of parameters; the conditions described here would not be written as real numbers, but as intervals in a hyperspace of dimension n; and thus as a set of n small intervals. I use the linear case for the sake of simplicity and the ease of making figures. But such simplification does not affect the present argument.

7. Henri Poincaré, "Sur le problème des trois corps et les équations de la dynamique," *Acta Mathematica* 13 (1890): 1–270; available as "The Three-Body Problem and the Equations of Dynamics," trans. Bruce D. Popp (Cham: Springer

International, 2017). Historically, the formulation of the problem predates Poincaré, since d'Alembert and Clairaut already considered it in the eighteenth century. It now receives very sophisticated probabilistic solutions involving complex topological and statistical theories. It also gave rise to a more general "N bodies problem" discussed by mathematicians.

8. Those terms often do not respect additivity (i.e., operations on the variable x such that (f (x + y) = f (x) + f (y)) or more generally linearity (additivity, plus f (ax) = a f (x) for any real number a). For this reason, the set of theories dealing with unpredictable complex systems—sometimes called "chaos theory"; see James Gleick, *Chaos: Making a New Science* (New York: Viking Books, 1987)—received the general name "nonlinear dynamics."

9. I will not address in this book the question of what exactly is a narrative. It is sufficient, for my purposes, to equate it with "telling stories" and to acknowledge a diversity of levels of complexities in a narrative, from a teenager's diary or blog, to Proust or Tolstoy—and so to rely on our common notions about the differences between narratives, theories, poetry, and treatises. However, there is a huge literature on the question of the nature of narrativity and its limits, as well as its relation to history, and to ethics and the good life. Those questions are actually not so obvious. I can always assume that one can recognize, in general, instances of narrativity when one encounters them. Similarly, Hayden White, a major theoretician of history, thinks there is something universal in the form of narrativity. "Far from being a problem, then, narrative might well be considered a solution to a problem of general human concern, namely the problem of how to translate knowing into telling, the problem of fashioning human experience into a form assimilable to structures of meaning that are generally human rather than culture-specific. We may not be able fully to comprehend specific thought patterns of another culture, but we have relatively less difficulty understanding a story coming from another culture, however exotic that is." White, "The Value of Narrativity in the Representation of Reality," *Critical Inquiry* 7, no. 1 (1980): 5–27, at 6.

10. See, for example, Andrew J. Reagan et al., "The Emotional Arcs of Stories Are Dominated by Six Basic Shapes," *EPJ Data Science* 5, no. 31 (2016).

11. Robert Scholes, James Phelan, and Robert Kellogg, in a seminal treatise about narrative—*The Nature of Narrative*, 1966—characterize it in a minimal sense as follows: "By narrative we mean all those literary works which are distinguished by two characteristics: the presence of a story and a story-teller. A drama is a story without a story-teller; in it characters act out directly what Aristotle called an 'imitation' of such action as we find in life. A lyric, like a drama, is a direct

presentation, in which a single actor, the poet or his surrogate, sings, or muses, or speaks for us to hear or overhear. . . . For writing to be narrative no more and no less than a teller and a tale are required." Their book has impacted the whole field of the theory of narrativity, especially by enlarging it beyond a strict focalization on novels. From this period started a strong interest in narrativity within academia, including questions on what makes something into a narrative. For instance, literary criticist Gérard Genette wrote an influential piece, "Boundaries of Narrative," *New Literary History* 8, no. 1 (1976), where he aims to draw a boundary between discourse in general and narrative in particular. For an overview of these developments, see the revised and expanded version of *The Nature of Narrative* (New York: Oxford University Press, 2006).

12. Paul Ricoeur, *Time and Narrative*, vol. 1 (Chicago: University of Chicago Press, 1990).

13. Actually, the question of the relation between fiction and history has been a key issue in the study of narratives since the works of White, Louis Mink, and Arthur Danto in the 1970s. Mink writes: "The features which enable a story to flow and us to follow, then are the clues to the nature of historical understanding. An historical narrative does not demonstrate the necessity of events, but makes them intelligible by unfolding the story which connects their significance. History does not as such differ from fiction, therefore insofar as it essentially depends on and develops our skill and subtlety in following stories." Mink, "History and Fiction as Modes of Comprehension," *New Literary History*, 1, no. 3 (1970): 541–58, at 545.

14. Philosophy of narrativity often claims that narrativity is necessary for one to be able to make sense of one's experience, and even necessary for the capacity to live a "good life." Galen Strawson wrote a radical critique of these two ideas, which he labels the Descriptive and the Ethical theses about narrativity. He opposes them by explaining that some people, perhaps most of them, don't need the special diachronic coherence of experiences that the Descriptive thesis assumes; "Against Narrativity," *Ratio* 16 (2004): 428–52. I am yet closer to this Descriptive thesis, and to what Hanna Merotoja writes in answering Strawson: "While we should be attentive to the difference between experience and narrative, it can be meaningfully said that narrative interpretations of experiences have a constitutive role in our existence"; "Narrative and Human Existence: Ontology, Epistemology, and Ethics," *New Literary History* 45, no. 1 (2014): 89–109, at 105. Merotoja develops her account of narrativity in *The Ethics of Storytelling: Narrative Hermeneutics, History, and the Possible* (New York: Oxford University Press, 2018).

15. Among the rich literature devoted to narration, and the relationship between fictional narration and the writing of history, Ricoeur's *Time and Narrative*

is a milestone. It creates a dialogue between analytical philosophy of history, history written by historians, and structuralist analyses of the principles of narration. Hayden White also importantly reflected on the nature of narratives, especially in *The Content of the Form: Narrative Discourse and Historical Representation* (Baltimore: Johns Hopkins University Press, 1987). Among other important advances in the philosophical meditation on narrativity, Arthur Danto connected it to his philosophy of history in *Narration and Knowledge: Including the Integral Text of Analytical Philosophy of History* (New York: Columbia University Press, 1985). Paul Roth investigated the kind of knowledge provided by narrations in "Narrative Explanations: The Case of History," *History and Theory* 27, no. 1 (1988): 1–13.

16. The original 1916 paper by Freud is "Some Character-Types Met With in Psycho-Analytic Work," in *The Standard Edition of the Complete Psychological Works of Sigmund Freud*, vol. 14 (1914–1916), *On the History of the Psycho-Analytic Movement, Papers on Metapsychology and Other Works*, 309–333, and his original phrase for this mental issue was "Those Wrecked by Success."

17. There have been interesting controversies about the "exportability" of psychoanalysis to non-Western cultures. Jacques Lacan, for instance, provocatively said that the Japanese have no Unconscious. I will not enter into these disputes; however, in my opinion, the answer must take into account this deeply grounded link between psychoanalytic concepts, Greek myths, and the ideas of destiny based on them; and narrativity.

Chapter 7: Why Were There American Soldiers on the 15:17 Train from Amsterdam to Paris on August 21, 2015?

1. Among a huge literature, but mostly from psychology and social sciences rather than philosophy, I cite the recent book by philosopher Quassim Cassam, who considers conspiracy theories from the viewpoint of the epistemology of virtues and vice, in *Conspiracy Theories* (Cambridge: Polity Press, 2019). Another philosophy article—Brian L. Keeley, "Of Conspiracy Theories," *Journal of Philosophy* 96, no. 3 (1999): 109–26—identifies (slightly before 9/11) key epistemological issues raised by conspiracy theories.

2. Sociologist Luc Boltanski wrote an important book—*Enigmes et complots* (Paris: Gallimard, 2013); translated by Catherine Porter, *Mysteries and Conspiracies* (Cambridge: Polity, 2014)—about the simultaneity between the birth of the genre "detective story," conspiracy theories, and the emergence of sociology, a discipline that often can come across as aiming to demystify the "official narrative" about some event or state of affair.

3. In a paper with Marion Vorms, we focused on "conspiracy theories" about

science; "Is a Unified Account of Conspiracy Theories Possible?," *Argumenta* 3, no. 2 (2018): 49–72. We argued that in this case there is no principled difference between bizarre conspiracism and healthy critiques of scientific findings, that there is a plurality of "conspiracy theories," and finally that the term "conspiracy theory" is unsatisfying. In fact, if I were being perfectly rigorous, I would not use the term "conspiracy theory"; I use it here because it allows me to be quickly understood.

4. David Aaronovitch, *Voodoo Histories: The Role of the Conspiracy Theory in Shaping Modern History* (London: Vintage, 2010).

5. G. W. F. Hegel, *Phenomenology of the Spirit* (1807). Yet for Hegel the number of planets in the solar system—seven known at that time—was indeed rationally derivable.

6. With Joseph Berkovitz I tried to disentangle issues and accounts regarding the interpretation of probabilities in science at least, in "On Probabilities in Biology and Physics," *Erkenntnis* 80 (2015): 433–56.

7. There are many discussions about why exactly a coin has 1/2 chance to land on heads. One view is that given that there is no reason why it should land on tails rather than heads, the probabilities should be equal. This directly connects to a view of probabilities according to which a probability is a degree of belief; as a result, this indifference of reasons rationally justifies equal degrees of belief in two alternative options. Another hypothesis to explain the even probabilities (1/2, 1/2) of the pair (tails/heads) consists in looking at the physical setting of a coin toss and showing that its structure allows for an equal distribution of the two possible outcomes. Strevens's *Bigger than Chaos* follows this line of thought. My own demonstration is neutral regarding these questions.

8. I explained these two meanings of drift in "Inscrutability and the Opacity of Selection and Drift: Distinguishing Epistemic and Metaphysical Aspects," *Erkenntnis* 80 (2015): 491–518, and elaborated a detailed account of drift vs. selection. For an analysis of the meaning of drift, see Anya Plutynski, "Drift: A Historical and Conceptual Overview," *Biological Theory* 2, no. 2 (2007): 156–67. Some evolutionary biologists still reject the idea of drift because in their view it mixes up several different things; for example, John Gillespie, *Population Genetics* (Princeton: Princeton University Press, 2001).

9. I am of course leaving aside many aspects of chance and randomness. There exists a formal notion of randomness, taken from complexity theory, which applies to a string of characters and states that a string is random if there is no computer program shorter than this string that is likely to yield it. This idea comes from the mathematicians Kolmogoroff and Chaitin. And of course, once the notion of chance is assumed, there is probability calculus that allows one to compute

chances. But the mundane notion of chance is not exhausted by these formalizations since part of it concerns the relation to a purported intention, which is not considered in formal accounts. For a set of accounts of chance in evolutionary biology, see Grant Ramsey and Charles H. Pence, eds., *Chance in Evolution* (Chicago: University of Chicago Press, 2016).

10. Besides Strevens (*Bigger than Chaos*), Marshall Abrams—"Mechanistic Probability," *Synthese* 187, no. 2 (2012): 343–75—and Grant Ramsey—"Driftability," *Synthese* 190, no. 17 (2013): 3909–28—intend to account for the applicability of probability theory to a field of events and behaviors that are, at first glance, chancy.

11. "Cognitive biases" are not an object universally endorsed by psychologists and cognitivists. Some of them—for example, Marion Vorms, "Bayes et les biais: Le 'biais de confirmation' en question," *Revue de Métaphysique et de Morale* 4 (2021): 567–90—criticize the use of this notion since descriptions of belief systems and belief assessments can be made without it (for instance, by showing how the mind makes "Bayesian inferences"). This critique has its virtues: it brings some parsimony into a debate where, strikingly, researchers now invoke hundreds of various "cognitive biases" to explain all kinds of bizarre or interesting behaviors in their experiments—even when the evidential support for this inflation of biases remains weak.

Chapter 8: Why Does Romeo Love Juliet?

1. The reference book is E. O. Wilson, *Sociobiology: The New Synthesis* (Cambridge, MA: Harvard University Press, 1975)—even though most of Wilson's work had been major contributions to ecology.

2. Sexual strategy is a technical term in evolutionary psychology. See, for example, Martie G. Haselton, David M. Buss, Viktor Oubaid, and Alois Angleitner, "Sex, Lies, and Strategic Interference: The Psychology of Deception between the Sexes," *Personality and Social Psychology Bulletin* 31 (2005): 3–23. Strategy, as I explained it in chapter 4 about behavioral ecology, is not a conscious plan; it is regularly ascribed to animals and plants.

3. Gustave Flaubert, *Sentimental Education*, trans. Robert Baldick (London: Penguin Classics, 2004).

4. There have been numerous debates about what "social constructivism" means, as well as about the limits of its thesis. There exists a weak and uncontroversial meaning, according to which many social institutions (like marriage or prison) are socially constructed in the sense that social processes and conventions made them what they are—and that they can therefore change throughout history and across cultures. When sociologists of science talked about social con-

structivism after the 1980s, it sounded much more controversial. Some accused them of turning "gravity" into a social construct, which indeed seems odd since by definition gravity is independent of human activities. However, think of planets: Pluto was a planet when I was in elementary school and learned about the nine planets of the solar system. Now it's not a planet anymore. Yet it did not change; what has changed is our criteria for deciding what defines a planet. These criteria have been debated. They may not be purely social conventions, but they are dependent upon this particular society of astrophysicists. A social process of discussions led to this decision. Social constructivists argue that ideas like this one are not based on arbitrary conventions; but instead that "Pluto isn't a planet" can't be understood without referring to the social process where certain justifications about, for example, the minimum size required to be a planet, are accepted and others rejected. Are planets a social construction for this reason?

In any case, "to be a construct" does not mean plain arbitrariness: Pluto being a (non)planet comes with justifications, which one has to assess. Should we then see "social construction" as something that comes by degrees? Where "Pluto is not a planet" is less a social construct than the Royal Family of England, but more a social construct than "water boils at 100 degrees"? I leave this open. In any case, for now it's enough to see that a strong case can be made in favor of love (and not only marriage or family) being a social construct.

A key reference for learning about the fundamental claims of constructionism is Ian Hacking, *The Social Construction of What* (Chicago: University of Chicago Press, 1990). Bruno Latour is seen as a key figure of social constructivism; however, this approach has been strongly drawing upon phenomenology of the social world, such as the works of Alfred Schütz, a disciple of Husserl. A major work in this tradition that triggered social constructivism is Peter Berger and Thomas Luckmann, *The Social Construction of Reality: A Treatise in the Sociology of Knowledge* (New York: Anchor Books, 1967).

Chapter 9: Why Am I Me?

1. Evariste Galois was a mathematician (and a quite romantic character, because he died young in a duel to defend his fiancée's honor in the early nineteenth century), who proved a major theorem about roots of polynoms of any degree. It states that for any $n > 4$ and any polynom P of degree n, there is no general solution to $P(x) = 0$, as is the case with those general solutions for $ax^2+bx+c=0$ that one learns in high school. It is a fundamental theorem for algebra in general. Regarding Gödel's incompleteness theorem, see later in chapter 9 (and note 8 below).

2. Porphyry edited and published the work of his teacher, the major Neopla-

tonic philosopher Plotinus, who advocated an extreme version of Plato's transcendence of Ideas. Later, Porphyry authored a treatise on universals that is a seminal text for the question of the existence of references of general terms that pervades the history of metaphysics.

3. Here we meet the discussion of me as a poached egg by David Lewis; I am just alluding to it. My question on the limits of "why" does not need an elaborated theory of essences and counterfactuals.

4. The philosophical notion of "stereotype" has been put forth by Hilary Putnam in the context of his theory of reference, and his critique of the idea that the meaning of a word is a set of properties that are somehow in the mind of the speaker; "stereotypes" are bundles of properties that allow us to recognize things and name them; they are socially elaborated. See Putnam, *Mind, Language and Reality: Philosophical Papers* (Cambridge: Cambridge University Press, 1975).

5. In *Death: Perspectives from the Philosophy of Biology* (London: Palgrave, 2022), I extensively analyze the evolutionary theories that provide an answer to "why we die." The theory I just mentioned was presented by the Nobel Prize–winning immunologist Sir Peter Medawar; see his *The Uniqueness of the Individual* (London: Routledge, 1957). Another influential version was developed by George Williams, who showed that genes that are detrimental to organisms late in life might be selected against genes that extend lifespan when they also provide an advantage in terms of reproduction earlier on; Williams, "Pleiotropy, Natural Selection, and the Evolution of Senescence," *Evolution* 11, no. 4 (1957): 398–411. This is called Antagonistic pleiotropy; and I have explored the epistemology of the validation of these two hypotheses in detail.

6. Of course, I know that many, if not most, historians of science after Thomas Kuhn (*The Structure of Scientific Revolutions*, 1962) reject the idea that science advances along a progressive and continuous pathway that reaches better and better theories. For my purpose, it is enough to notice that—even though there might be no absolute progress in physics—the metaphysical views of Aristotle, Kant, and Quine can't be ordered in the same pseudo-progressive way that textbooks use when presenting physical theories.

7. The questions concerning the nature of real numbers represent a deep issue in mathematics and the philosophy thereof. Richard Dedekind famously proposed a view of how real numbers are constructed in *Was sind und sollen die Zahlen?* [What are numbers and what should they be?] (1909), a landmark text that sees real numbers as the limits of infinite series—which he calls "cuts." It is one among many competing views of this question, which is here left aside.

8. A useful and clear presentation of this history, including set theory and

Gödel's disturbing results, is provided by Morris Kline, *Mathematics: The Loss of Certainty* (New York: Oxford University Press, 1980).

9. Arithmetics is defined here by the Zermelo-Fraenkel axioms (after the two mathematicians who developed them); but there are alternative formulations of this set of axioms—especially the one provided by Bertrand Russell and Alfred North Whitehead in their seminal *Principia Mathematica* (1921), as well as an earlier one from the Italian mathematician Giuseppe Peano.

10. Of course, adding some axioms could allow the demonstration of the consistency of arithmetic; however, this new arithmetic would itself have to be proven consistent, which would require other axioms, and so on infinitely. Especially, one can take an undecidable proposition as such axiom: then this undecidable proposition will of course be true, but, according to the incompleteness theorem, in this new system of arithmetic, other undecidable propositions will necessarily arise.

11. An interesting conception of this relation between Newton's and Einstein's physics, the former being a particular case of the latter, is given by Thomas Nickles in "Two Concepts of Intertheoretic Reduction," *Journal of Philosophy* 70 (1973): 181–201. Nickles originally interprets this relation as one of the major kinds of reduction in science.

12. Craig Callender, *What Makes Time Special?* (New York: Oxford University Press, 2017), and Callender, ed., *Handbook of the Philosophy of Time* (Oxford: Oxford University Press, 2018), are good starting points for addressing this question. One can also see Sam Baron and Kristie Miller, *An Introduction to the Philosophy of Time* (Cambridge: Polity Press, 2018), for a solution that sees time as nonfundamental.

13. W. V. Quine, "Main Trends in Recent Philosophy: Two Dogmas of Empiricism," *Philosophical Review* 60, no. 1 (1951): 20–43.

14. As I mentioned in the introduction, I leave aside issues related to the relations between semantic and pragmatic, and especially the thesis that pragmatics doesn't ultimately differ from semantics, so that the meaning of sentences is always wholly determined by the context. Thus, in such a perspective, for any sentence there exists an interlocution context within which it means something for the speakers. In this all-pragmatics account, all the questions that appear to us as limits to "why?" can eventually receive an answer.

15. With respect to all caveats implied by this word in science: truths are falsifiable and provisory; scientists may commit to distinct epistemic goals, hence distinct criteria of truth; one can't confirm hypotheses but only falsify them, as Popper has shown; and so on. But metaphysics in principle can't hope for this

kind of truth (in the sense of corroborated and provisionally to be unanimously accepted statement—think climate change or evolution, for instance).

16. This discussion prolongs the examination of the role of epistemic values in science that I developed in chapter 2 on the basis of Levins's classic paper on the strategy of model building. A key element in all these discussions is the fact that, even though no empirical evidence can be invoked to settle the question, there are still arguments to justify the privileged role of one value over the others.

Conclusion: Why "Why"?

1. For Frege, as he explains in his classic 1892 paper "Ueber Begriff und Gegenstand"—translated as "On Concept and Object," in *Mind* 60, no. 238 (1951): 168–80—the concept "horse" in "Jolly Jumper is a horse" constitutes a function applied to something X, such that the value of this function is "true" when X is Jolly Jumper or Bucephalus, "false" when X is Socrates or Mount Fujiyama, or anything that is not a horse. The function "Horse (X)," as I write it, can be applied to anything, whether X exists or not. And the formal logics can use another sign to express that X exists (namely the existential quantifier).

2. The logic of "ground" has recently come to the fore among logicians and philosophers of logics, especially after seminal papers by Kit Fine, for example, "Some Puzzles of Ground," *Notre Dame Journal of Formal Logic* 51, no. 1 (2010): 97–118. For a formal treatment see Poggiolesi Francesca, "On Defining the Notion of Complete and Immediate Formal Grounding," *Synthese* 193, no. 10 (2016), and for a set of approaches see Fabrice Correia and Benjamin Schnieder, eds., *Metaphysical Grounding: Understanding the Structure of Reality* (Cambridge: Cambridge University Press, 2012). For a recent overview of the topic see Michael Raven, ed., *The Routledge Handbook of Metaphysical Grounding* (New York: Routledge, 2020). In this conclusion, I make explicit that the overall argument of this book could be seen as a contribution to the current renewed reflection on "ground" (and I say "renewed" because obviously ground was what philosophers like Leibniz were after), which addressed my question of the plurality of "reason" from another perspective, such as Selim Berker, "The Unity of Grounding," *Mind* 127, no. 507 (2018): 729–77.

3. Jean-Luc Marion authored an important commentary of the scientific methodology given by Descartes in his treatise *Regulae ad directionem ingenii*; see *Sur l'Ontologie Grise de Descartes: Science Cartésienne et Savoir Aristotélicien dans les Regulae* (Paris: Vrin, 1975); translated as *Descartes's Grey Ontology: Cartesian Science and Aristotelian Thought in the Regulae* (South Bend, IN: St. Augustine's Press, 2022). Among a prolix literature on Cartesian mathematics and science, one can

read the classical work by Jules Vuillemin, *Mathématiques et Métaphysique chez Descartes* (Paris: Presses Universitaires de France, 1960); or more recently Daniel Garber, *Descartes' Metaphysical Physics* (Chicago: University of Chicago Press, 1992).

4. I developed this idea in "Natural Sciences," in *The Cambridge History of Philosophy in the Nineteenth Century, 1790–1870*, ed. Allen W. Wood and Songsuk Susan Hahn, 201–38 (Cambridge: Cambridge University Press, 2011).

5. This thesis has been defended by Paul Horwich and is called deflationism. It implies that nothing more than *p* is asserted when someone says "*p* is true," which empties the concept of truth of any substantial content (hence the name). Deflationism is a major concern for epistemologists; see Paul Horwich, *Truth* (Oxford: Clarendon Press, 1998). However, most of my arguments don't need to rely on deflationism, therefore I will not discuss this claim directly here.

6. Spinoza uses this phrase pervasively in his *Ethics*, while Descartes uses it in replies to the "Second Objections to Descartes' *Meditations*."

7. Many scholarly works have been devoted to the idea of "*causa sive ratio*," and this proposition 2.7 by Spinoza. Among those works see Vincent Carraud, *Causa sive ratio: la raison de la cause, de Suarez à Leibniz* (Paris: PUF, 2006).

8. "Dialectics" for Kant means the logics of these illusions within which reason inevitably falls, because of its striving toward the "unconditioned." He uses the word in a very specific way, different from Plato's understanding of dialectics, which has to do with dialogue, and from Hegel's (and then Marx's) conception of dialectics as a process through which something or some meaning is negated, transformed, and reasserted. Commentators have emphasized the way Kant's idea has been understood and transformed by Hegel, and the roots of Kant's concept, but this does not concern us here.

9. Among a voluminous literature one can read Victoria Wike, *Kant's Antinomies of Reason: Their Origin and Their Resolution* (Lanham, MD: University Press of America, 1982), and Michelle Grier, *Kant's Doctrine of Transcendental Illusion* (Cambridge: Cambridge University Press, 2001), on the transcendental dialectic and these questions. Regarding psychology, notice that Kant here thinks about what he calls "rational psychology," a doctrine mostly devoted to these questions, which disappeared with the empirical psychology we know. Even though the question of the materiality of the mind, discussed by current philosophers of mind under the name "physicalism," sometimes evokes discussions of rational psychologists debating the immateriality of the soul that Kant thought to be meaningless

10. On this resistance see Tania Lombrozo, Andrew Shtulman, and Michael

Weisberg, "The Intelligent Design Controversy: Lessons from Psychology and Education," *Trends in Cognitive Sciences* 10, no. 2 (2006): 56–57.

11. In Schopenhauer's first writing before his masterwork *The World as Will and Representation*, namely his dissertation *On the Fourfold Root of the Principle of Sufficient Reason*.

12. Kant breaks with this major metaphysical assumption: one of his major precritical works, known to be an important milestone in his pathway toward the *Critiques* and the critical philosophy in general, is his *Essay to Introduce in Philosophy the Concept of Negative Magnitudes* (1764), where he argues that negativity is not a mere lack of reality. Consequences of this view are numerous, and among them stands, obviously, the impossibility of an optimistic justification of the existence of the worlds such as the one Leibniz favors.

13. This exteriority between the subject of the proposition (Mbappé) and what is asserted about it (the trajectory of the ball) defines what Kant calls a "synthetic judgement," as in the sentence "How are synthetic a priori judgments possible?", which is the fundamental question of his transcendental philosophy.

14. Lewis, *Philosophical Papers*, vol. II (Oxford: Oxford University Press, 1986), ix. The Humean is clearly deflationist, skeptical regarding all that seems to go beyond events happening then and now; while the Aristotelian is more inflationist, the ontology admitting much more than events. The present book stands between the two.

15. Philosophers of science since at least Quine and Duhem doubt that any experiment suffices in order to decide between rival theories; nonetheless, the case of rival theories in relation to experience is obviously distinct in philosophy since it is often hard to even imagine what the world would look like with different metaphysics.

16. See, for example, Leibniz's *Correspondence with Arnauld* and his *Discours de Métaphysique* (1677). On Leibniz's ideas of individuality and complete notions, see Hide Ishiguro, *Leibniz's Philosophy of Logic and Language* (Cambridge: Cambridge University Press, 1972); and among recent work see Justin Smith, *Divine Machines: Leibniz and the Sciences of Life* (Princeton: Princeton University Press, 2011).

Milton Keynes UK
Ingram Content Group UK Ltd.
UKHW010927040424
440508UK00007B/241/J